ME

ME

Chronic fatigue syndrome:
How to live with it

Dr Anne Macintyre

Thorsons

Thorsons
An Imprint of HarperCollins*Publishers*
77–85 Fulham Palace Road
Hammersmith, London W6 8JB

First published by Thorsons 1991
This edition revised and updated 1998

11

A catalogue record for this book
is available from the British Library

ISBN 0 7225 3539 2

Typeset by Harper Phototypesetters Limited,
Northampton, England

Printed and bound in Great Britain by
Clays Ltd, St. Ives Plc

Contents

Foreword

To have ME is to experience hell twice over, firstly through the devastation of the disease itself, and secondly through the lack of diagnosis, information and support that most sufferers are still having to endure.

In the early days of my illness I dragged myself to the local library and combed the medical reference books for some indication of the name and possible causes of this ghastly affliction. I found nothing. My doctor and the various specialists I saw were hardly more helpful. I was eventually told it was a 'virus' – a vague-sounding diagnosis if ever there was one – and that was it. I was given no advice excepting 'total rest', and was offered none of the support which I so desperately needed. On the contrary, I, like so many sufferers before me, was made to feel guilty for my illness, as if I had brought it upon myself. The horrific mental symptoms were put down to reactive depression: had I had an upset recently? An unhappy love affair perhaps? As a single parent, wasn't life a bit much for me? The fact that, until my illness, my life had never been happier or more fulfilled was overlooked. My real mistake, of course, was to have developed an illness which cannot be diagnosed by simple blood tests, which has a bewildering array of strange and sometimes vague symptoms, and for which there is no magic cure.

By the time I had completed the first round of doctors my isolation was almost complete. Not surprisingly, family and friends found it difficult to understand a disease which had no name, no visible symptoms, makes you come apart mentally, yet often leaves you looking perfectly well. Rather than test their loyalty beyond reasonable bounds, I pretended my illness wasn't happening. I covered up the gaping holes in my life with lies and evasions: while I slept all day my answering machine said I was out; when I stumbled over words or walked into thingsI joked about having had a late night; and my social life was reduced to almost nothing by constantly pleading a previous engagement.

I began to live the life of a recluse – a lonely, isolated and desperate recluse. Looking back, it was a living nightmare. Yet many sufferers have experienced far, far worse: alienation, denigration, loss of employment and the break-up of relationships.

It is my ambition and that of my colleagues in the ME Action Campaign that ME sufferers should never again have to endure their illness in such appalling isolation and ignorance. Although much progress has been made in the recognition of the disease, there is still a very long way to go. In particular, there is an urgent need to reach the many sufferers who, though desperate for information and support, still do not know where to turn.

This book should do much to help those people. It provides the widest and most detailed information on ME yet published. Anne Macintyre, who is both a doctor and a sufferer, has explained the disease in the light of the latest available research, and taken an impartial look at all the various therapies and treatments currently in use.

I hope this book will prevent sufferers from making the mistakes that I and so many other desperate people have made. I wasted much energy, not to mention money, on traipsing up and down Harley Street seeing numerous doctors, both orthodox and alternative, who swore they knew exactly what was wrong with me (their diagnoses nearly always differed), who pressed me into following their ineffective, bizarre, even dangerous remedies, and who, in the end, left me worse off both physically and financially.

None of the treatments and therapies discussed in this book will effect a miracle cure, for none exists, but all have been tried by ME sufferers and in some cases, though inevitably not all, provided improvement or relief. All of us who have battled with ME over any length of time know the importance of approaching the disease from many different angles simultaneously – diet, supplementation, and lifestyle – and of experimenting to find out what suits us as individuals. This book provides the information on which to build a programme to suit yourself and your unique set of difficulties and problems. Self-help, as most ME sufferers learn through long and hard experience, is the only way forward.

It is unfortunate that sufferers of such a debilitating disease should be thrown back on their own resources, and yet, since self-help is by far the best way of tackling the illness, it is no bad thing. We expect too much of medicine and science. Indeed, we are the victims as well as the beneficiaries of this scientific age. We find ourselves in a situation where, if routine tests cannot pick up an illness, it cannot exist. Textbooks are consulted as it they were written in stone. The medical profession feels bound to give answers even where there are none.

Yet leading scientists will always be the first to admit that what is known is always exceeded by what is unknown. It is sometimes forgotten that the intricacies of the immune system are only now beginning to be unravelled. And in the field of enteroviruses, which are heavily implicated in ME, virtually all work ceased after the development of the polio vaccine in

1954. Research does not continue in a smooth curve, but in fits and starts instigated by necessity.

Other diseases have had to battle for recognition – notably multiple sclerosis, an illness which also responds to self-help. An other diseases have been misunderstood – isolated cases of polio were often labelled neurotic or hysteric in origin. All became accepted in time.

But however slow acceptance may be in coming, there is the consolation that the majority of ME sufferers do eventually recover. This may offer small comfort to those in the thick of the illness who can see nothing but months of gloom ahead, and for those who have already endured years of unremitting symptoms, but the facts do point to eventual improvement for most.

I have had enormous ups and downs, but experimentation with many of the treatments and remedies described here has brought slow improvement and ever-quicker recovery from relapse. Furthermore, the more I have learnt about the illness, the more I have been able to come to grips with it.

I hope that, for all the sufferers who read this book, it brings a glimmer of light to the end of the tunnel.

CLARE FRANCIS

Preface to the 1998 Edition

During the six years that have passed since the previous edition of this book, there have been several noteworthy events.

Awareness of ME as a real illness has spread, so that the average man or woman in the street has heard of ME, or knows someone with it. In the medical profession, also, the level of awareness has risen steeply, although this celebration must be tempered by the fact that some doctors still believe it is an illness with no demonstrable physical abnormalities, and so must be psychological. Many doctors and researchers refer to it as chronic fatigue, and the sufferers as fatigue patients, thus sending the message that tiredness is the only problem. This is a pity, as these terms tend to trivialize the potential chronicity and severity of the illness which was so clearly described after the 1955 outbreaks, by Dr Melvin Ramsay.

A significant event has been the publication, in September 1994, by the National Task Force (in UK) on chronic fatigue syndrome (postviral fatigue syndrome/myalgic encephalo-myelitis) of a comprehensive Report about this group of conditions. This report detailed all the known facts, relevant research and the ongoing controversy about ME and CFS. It admitted that in some cases psychological and social factors are important in causing and/or maintaining the illness, and made realistic recommendations for future research.

The Task Force report was succeeded two years later by a report about chronic fatigue syndrome from the Royal Colleges of Medicine, Psychiatry and General Practice, in October 1996. This report, although acknowledging that CFS exists as an illness and causes substantial suffering and disability, was heavily biased towards psychological causes and management, and tended to dismiss research that show physical abnormalities.

However, I feel confident that research will show what causes the typical symptoms of rapid loss of energy of muscles and brain. The malfunction will probably turn out to be at the level of individual living cells. It is already clear that ME is mainly a disorder of the brain – with so many symptoms pointing to problems with the autonomic nervous system, abnormalities of intellectual function, sleep problems and emotional instability, what else could cause all these, other than something going on in the brain?

ME has suffered, like other diseases, from the old misconception that if we cannot see something wrong using available technology, it must be psychological! However, research in the last 10 years clearly suggests that some infection triggers the illness, also that the brain is affected. It is also becoming obvious that within the umbrella term 'chronic fatigue syndrome' there are subgroups of patients. This explains why research may sometimes give conflicting findings, and also why useful treatments, such as recently publicized graded aerobic exercise, do not work for all patients diagnosed with CFS.

Finally, a more personal event. Although I had an acute post-viral onset of ME in the 1980s, with all the typical features, in the past few years this has become replaced by fairly aggressive rheumatoid arthritis. This does not mean I have forgotten what ME is like, but there has been a change from one set of disabilities to quite different problems. No one can say if the two conditions co-exist, or whether ME can lead to an auto-immune disease like RA, due to the dysfunction of the immune system. The type of fatigue is quite different, I no longer get the 'post-exertional malaise' that is the hallmark of ME. However, the lessons I learned from adjusting to ME have been enormously helpful to me in coping with pain and crippling deformity in the hands. The whole experience has taught me that the difficulties and frustrations caused by ME and CFS happen in other disabling diseases. The difference of course is that if you have something such as RA, which is accepted without question by doctors and the Department of Social Security, you do not have to fight to prove you are ill.

Surely the time has come that people suffering from ME and CFS should receive the same acceptance, sympathy and help from doctors as is given to people with other disabling diseases!

I would like to thank several people who have given me a lot of help with this edition:

Ellen Goudsmit, for tracking down the names and references of numerous research papers.

Dr Vance Spence and Stephanie Woodcock for scientific information; David Axford for saving my sanity whenever the computer defeated me; and my closest friends Philip and Carole, for their encouragement and patience.

ANNE MACINTYRE 1998

Preface to the 1992 Edition

In the three years since I finished work for the first edition of this book, there have appeared many new medical papers about ME, more often called Chronic fatigue syndrome (CFS) in Britain now. There has been a lot of writing from physicians and psychiatrists, who hypothesize that the illness is due to depression, or overbreathing, or deconditioning from too much rest. On the other side, very valuable objective medical research is being done, early results of which are confirming that ME is an organic disease, with demonstrable pathology in muscle and brain. But still the arguments rage – is ME caused by untreated depression, with a virus as an opportunist? Or is it a persistent viral infection in genetically susceptible people, with depression as a major secondary effect?

With the increasing use of 'chronic fatigue' as a description of the illness, I believe that there is now confusion between:

1. Myalgic Encephalomyelitis, the condition described in many past outbreaks, carefully described by Dr Melvin Ramsay, probably caused by a relative of polio virus, and
2. Chronic Fatigue Syndrome, which encompasses many fatigue states (some of which may be depression in disguise),

some post-viral fatigue syndromes, some chronic over-breathing syndromes, and some myalgic encephalomyelitis.

Research projects are currently underway, whose final results will not appear in print before this book goes to press. By the time this book is published I hope that further important studies on the abnormalities in the brain, in particular the hypothalamus and its connections, will have been published.

I address the book mainly to sufferers from ME, but hope that it will be helpful to anyone with any post-viral fatigue state or any chronic fatigue syndromes. If the information on research is difficult to understand, I apologize; I have found the task of compiling it, and translating 'medicalese' into plain English, a great strain on my brain, and a good test of cognitive non-function!

I would like to thank all those who have supplied useful information, and acknowledge the help from IFMEA (International Federation of ME Associations).

ANNE MACINTYRE
MARCH 1992

Preface to the 1988 Edition

There may be 100,000 people in Britain today, who are suffering from a strange illness which nobody yet understands. This illness can have a devastating effect on one's life.

My own story is a typical example: Five years ago I was able to work full-time in a busy hospital department, and to spend my free time gardening, decorating my home, socializing, and generally living a full life. I went to Scotland every year, and was able to achieve a whole day's hill walking, maybe 18 miles. Like most people, I got colds in winter, and sometimes felt worn out after a busy day.

Four years ago, during a spell of very hard work while in India, I had a severe throat infection, but had to carry on working. After I returned home I remained unwell and tired for many weeks. Over the following three years I had periods of severe exhaustion alternating with short spells of nearly normal energy. My doctor could find nothing wrong, and did lots of tests, the results of which were all normal.

I had bouts of unexplained depression and feelings of utter 'awfulness' when I felt more ill than at any previous time in my life. I had to cut down my work to part-time, and to rest when not working. In the past I had found that a long walk in the countryside, or a swim, would lift me out of 'the blues'. But now any exercise was having a disastrous effect, and I had more benefit from spending the weekend just sitting in a chair. I knew that something was wrong, but no one could identify it. I feared that I was very neurotic, or maybe losing my mind.

Then a flu-like illness in August 1987, which featured fever and terrible muscle pains, seemed to plunge me into a worse state. Over the following three months I became unable to walk 50 yards without collapsing, my brain turned into cotton wool, I was unable to read or bear the sound of music; weird symptoms plagued me, including waking in the night with palpitations and loud noises in my head, my vision was often blurred, and I smelled things that were not there. But the overriding problem was the extreme exhaustion brought on by the simplest task, even brushing my hair, or chopping some vegetables.

But I am luckier than many sufferers. I found out in October 1987 from a physician that I had Myalgic Encephalomyelitis, and that it had probably started four years before, the bout in August being a severe relapse. I now knew where I stood, and was able to reorganize my life to try to cope with it. My condition improved a little, now that I could stop worrying about what was wrong. I still have to be very careful not to do too much, not to work in the garden or to try and walk far, even on a lovely day. I have not sold my mountain boots, though: I hope to use them again one day!

This disease has been described all over the world, principally in developed countries. In Britain it was known as Royal Free Disease (following an outbreak in the London hospital of that name in 1955) and also as Iceland Disease (where there was an outbreak in 1948–9). A rough estimate of the incidence at present is about 1 in 1,000 people. This makes it as prevalent as Parkinson's disease, and more common than Multiple

Sclerosis. In countries where it does not appear to exist, this is because it is not yet recognized by the medical profession, and sufferers are given other labels. In Britain, Canada, Australia and New Zealand, the illness is known as Myalgic Encepha-lomyelitis; in the United States as chronic fatigue syndrome. In this book I shall refer to it as ME or CFS.

I decided to write this book to provide useful information for people who think they may have ME and want to find out; for those who have been told they are suffering from it, but that there is no treatment; for friends and relations of sufferers; and for any doctors who still do not believe that ME is a genuine disease.

Many sufferers cannot obtain any diagnosis from their doctors, and even worse, some are labelled neurotic or hysterical after doing the rounds of various specialists. It is a sad fact of twentieth-century medicine that a diagnosis of disease depends more on laboratory tests and X-rays than on careful history-taking and examination. ME is a diagnosis based on the history of the patient's illness, and to date there is no single diagnostic test which gives a 100 per cent accurate answer.

The only branch of medicine that does not depend on tests or abnormal physical findings is psychiatry, and it is into this pigeon-hole that many ME patients are put. I wonder how many people are languishing in mental institutions who would be relieved to be told that they have a recognized organic disease, and whose health could improve from a regime that does not consist only of psychotropic drugs? This does not deny that very many people with ME do have mental symptoms as part of their disease, however.

Getting a diagnosis is one thing, and what a relief it is to know what is wrong with you. The next problem is: where do you get advice? Is there any cure? Is there anything that you can do for yourself to improve things? The answer to this last question is *yes*, and people with ME will cope a lot better if they stop expecting medical science to provide a cure, and instead set about organizing their own plan of action – or, rather, their plan of *in-action*; recovery from ME requires much less activity and more rest. One needs to learn to give *more* time simply to *being*, and *less* to *doing*.

If you who start to read this book have ME, then the chances are that you find it hard to concentrate for long. If you decide that you have read enough for today, please remember just two things:

1. you can certainly improve and have a good chance of some recovery
2. the more you rest now and stop trying to achieve anything, the less frustrated you will be by your limitations, and the better your chances of improving.

We live in a culture which worships achievement and all that goes with it. I can offer no proof nor scientific explanation that ME is a disease of the twentieth century and of 'developed' nations. But since the illness is made worse by both physical and mental effort, I wonder how prevalent it is in communities which practise meditation, prayer and tranquillity; such as in a Buddhist monastery?

There is no doubt that ME follows on from a viral infection in most sufferers, whether the infection is noticed or not. But surely there must be other factors involved? For why, in a family or group who all contract a virus, does only one person go on to develop ME? At the time of writing, there is no answer to this.

I see no reason for people who have this illness to wait until it has been fully explained before having some information and ideas about self-help.

This book brings together everything that is known so far about ME, and all known ways of coping with it. Some methods are based on my own experience, others I have gleaned from other sufferers. There is nothing offered in the way of self-management that is harmful, even though some methods have not yet been proven by controlled medical trials. One problem in testing treatments for ME is the up-and-down course of the illness, which makes any improvement difficult to evaluate. But we cannot wait for ever for permission to try and get better ourselves.

The Chinese have used acupuncture for thousands of years, because they observed that it worked. They have not been troubled by the fact that no one has discovered exactly *how* it works; therefore if something seems to be helpful for a person with ME it is sensible to pass on the information to others. What is beneficial to one sufferer may not help another. However, *rest* is universally essential. Each person should learn to listen to his or her own body and co-operate with it to help recovery.

I hope that this book will be helpful for sufferers with ME and those who care for them. I hope it can give encouragement to anyone who has been compelled by this illness to come to a halt in a busy life, and who may be baffled and depressed by the experience. I have written from the viewpoint of a sufferer, and also as a doctor.

In recent years there has been a lot of valuable research into ME; the threads of understanding are starting to be woven together to make a picture of the disease process. More research projects are being planned, and several treatments are going to be tested in the US. We can look forward to a time when the mystery of this devastating illness is solved, and hope that some definitive cure will become available.

ANNE MACINTYRE

SEPTEMBER 1988

Chapter 1

What is ME?

ME stands for *Myalgic Encephalomyelitis*.

It is a potentially chronic and disabling disorder of the brain and muscles, and causes profound exhaustion, pain and mental confusion.

It is a very unpleasant condition which is still poorly understood by the medical profession. *The main symptom is of profound fatigue* (mental and physical) made worse by exercise, with a variety of bizarre symptoms, in a person who may look well and in whom there are usually no abnormal signs on examination.

The effects of this disease can be devastating to someone who was previously active and led a full life. Not only are jobs lost and early retirement made necessary for many, but marriages may founder, relationships and friends be lost, and many hobbies and interests dropped. Even the most basic tasks of daily living may require such an impossible effort that the patient cannot survive without help. Some very severely affected people with ME may be unable to walk, speak or swallow, and so the condition has been referred to by some as 'a living death'. However, for most people the illness is not so severe.

Added to all this suffering is the fact that for decades, the disease was not recognized by the medical profession, apart from a few perceptive doctors, and patients were labelled as malingerers, neurotic or mad. Not surprisingly, a few who suffered from this condition have taken their own lives. They were not only very ill, but were denied the basic recognition of their illness and proper medical support.

Names of the Illness

Added to the controversy and lack of knowledge about what is causing all the symptoms, there is the muddle about what to call it. Dr David Bell, a child specialist in the US, called his book about it *The Disease of a Thousand Names*.[1] These are some of them:

Yuppie Flu – now hopefully obsolete, this was the name coined by the media because in the 1980s ME was mistakenly believed to hit middle-class high achievers

Chronic Epstein Barr Virus – in the US, not used now

CFIDS – Chronic Fatigue and Immune Dysfunction Syndrome, a US name

Icelandic Disease – from an outbreak in Iceland

Tapanui Flu – from an outbreak in New Zealand

Epidemic Neuromyesthenia

Royal Free Disease – from the 1955 London epidemic

Myalgic Encephalomyelitis – ME

Chronic Fatigue Syndrome – CFS

Post Viral Fatigue Syndrome

Here is a typical story of a woman with ME, first related to me in 1988:

Case Study – Jean's Story

Jean is a dentist, married with two teenage sons. She was 41 when she had a bout of diarrhoea following a meal out at an hotel...

'I didn't seem to recover from that, I felt very weak. I was very overworked, looking after sick and elderly grandparents. This was about five years ago. I'd had a hysterectomy a year previously, which was followed by various complications, and I'd had a very nasty bout of flu just before the hysterectomy.

'After the diarrhoeal illness, my energy levels went down and up, and I would get attacks of 'flu', low-grade fever, with tremendous exhaustion and weakness, lasting for several days.

'It was over a year before I was sent to hospital for tests. During this time my main symptoms were complete and utter exhaustion, severe aching muscle pains, inability to concentrate, inability to function normally – I was trying to run a job and a family. My ears became very irritated and sensitive to sound. I got very depressed, and iller and iller, and was more or less bedridden for about two years. I could just about get out to the shops and back, then collapsed in bed. I had to give up my job.

'I developed allergies to various foods which had not upset me previously. After becoming more and more ill for over a year following the diarrhoea illness, my GP referred me to an infectious diseases unit for tests. I had various blood tests, and the consultant thought I'd had a Coxsackie virus. He heard my story and told me I was ill with Myalgic Encephalomyelitis, and that he did not know how to make me better. I was too ill at the time to take much in, but at least, knowing I was ill, I could rest.

'The rest has been the main cure. For over two years I was so weak that all I could do was get out of bed and collect the things to prepare a meal and take them back to bed. I found cutting a carrot hard work. If I put coal on the fire that took so much energy I had to go back to bed again. I had great difficulty sleeping, because of the pain. I had two admissions to a psychiatric unit because of severe depression. Sometimes I was so tired that it was an effort to breathe. Once when I felt very ill, my temperature went very low for a few weeks.

'It was about a year after I got a diagnosis before I started to get better. My improvement has not been steady – the relapses always occur after physical effort. Once, when I was a bit better, I had to stand in queues at a hospital clinic with a grandmother whom I was accompanying, then foolishly had to push the car, which wouldn't start, to take her home. I thought, with the adrenaline of the moment, that I could do it! I came home, collapsed into bed, and could not get up for a month. My brain packed in, I couldn't function, and it took me months to get over it.

'Last year I began to get a bit better. My GP thought that a little physiotherapy would do me good because I was so weak. It was disastrous, even hydrotherapy, although I felt great for the first week, but after 10 days the aching and slight fever came back.

'When I was very ill I had dreadful ulcers in my mouth, and Fungilin lozenges helped enormously. It was thought to be a Candida [thrush] infection.

'I am now on a total "no exercise" campaign. As long as I lie down or sit, I can function mentally. Even at my worst, I tried to put clothes on every day, this kept the circulation going, and provided enough exercise to stop me seizing up.

'I found that complete bed rest when my temperature was up was beneficial, but only for a short time; when my temperature had settled I tried to get dressed every day.

'The first year of the illness I kept fighting it, so of course I just got worse. To begin with it was physical exhaustion. In the second year, I found the mental problems got worse. I couldn't finish a sentence I had started, and my brain switched off. It was so frustrating, I just wept. I felt completely useless, I was just a burden to everybody. I used to say to the boys, "put me out for the dustmen in a black plastic bag!"'

Jean has now been affected by ME for 14 years. However, apart from a relapse lasting several months following moving house last year, she is very much improved. She went back to work for two half-days per week and sustained that for a year, before various family pressures meant that she had to give that up in order to prioritize her energy for her family. The food allergies have improved, but she finds that sticking to a wholefood diet with plenty of salads and fish, not a lot of meat, and no bread, sugar or cakes, helps her.

Her husband and children are very supportive. 'He got me better through the emotional side of it. When you are very ill, you need lots of love and support. The members of my church have been very helpful, and I had several healing sessions.'

What Should We Call It?

Myalgic Encephalomyelitis is a name which describes the main symptoms:

Myalgia = muscle pain
Encephalitis = affecting the brain
Myelitis = affecting the spinal cord and nerves.

However, the term is not medically accurate for all cases, as 'itis' implies inflammation, and at present there is only scant evidence of inflammation of the brain or spinal cord, apart from a few cases in which there is an initial viral encephalitis (brain infection). A more accurate name, in fact, would be Myalgic Encephalopathy.

During the 1980s many doctors used the term Post-viral Fatigue Syndrome, as it usually follows an apparent viral infection. There are many post-viral fatigue states, including fatigue for weeks after influenza, post-glandular fever debility, and debility for months following hepatitis. Myalgic Encephalomyelitis differs from other post-viral syndromes in its severity, the type of muscle fatiguability, and chronicity.

An illness which has fatigue as its core symptom is now called chronic fatigue syndrome in the US, and increasingly elsewhere in the world (*see Chapter 3*). Many doctors argue that this name is preferable since it does not imply any viral cause, nor involvement of the brain or muscles.

However, ME is still the name commonly used by patients in the UK, the name now recognized by the general population.

Diagnosing ME

Myalgic Encephalomyelitis is recognized in a patient with these features:

1. gross, abnormal muscle fatigue, which occurs after a relatively small effort, and which may take days to recover from. This is quite unlike any fatigue the patient has ever experienced before.
2. a variety of neuropsychiatric ('encephalitic') symptoms, most prominent being cognitive loss – of memory,

concentration and comprehension – and disturbances of sensation

3. unpredictable variation in severity of symptoms from week to week, day to day, even hour to hour
4. a tendency to become chronic, that is, continuing over many months or years.

The diagnosis of ME should not be made unless the patient has the above features. Other post-viral fatigue states do not continue for years. Everyone feels tired when they have a bout of influenza, a cold, or any infection. Most people who get a severe dose of influenza will be under par for weeks, possibly months. Glandular fever and hepatitis are well known for the debility which persists for months. These conditions of prolonged recovery are accurately called 'post-viral fatigue states'.

Many doctors say they find ME hard to diagnose, or to distinguish from a state of chronic depression. Some may still label the patient as malingering or hysterical. However, for most GPs, it is a condition once seen, never forgotten. The post-exertional malaise after mild or moderate exertion is the most unique feature. Anthony Komaroff, a professor of medicine in Boston in the US, has studied the illness for 16 years. Describing the salient features of the illness, he has said:[2]

'In the great majority of patients, the fatigue begins suddenly with a flu-like infection onset, with fever, sore throat, cough and sometimes gastrointestinal symptoms. Typically, the patient tolerates physical exertion reasonably well and may even feel energized during and immediately after the exertion. However, 6–24 hours later the patients feel ill; the used muscle groups feel sore and weak, this occurs with a flare-up of fatigue, difficulty thinking, sore throat, sweating and feeling feverish; it is as if physical exercise provokes a response that affects the health of the whole body. We believe this involves an abnormal response of the immune system to exercise. In our experience, this post-exertional malaise is unusual in healthy people, and in those with other diseases that have some resemblance to CFS [ME].

The other thing that strikes many physicians about this illness is the possible involvement of the brain. Most patients complain of difficulty with concentration and memory, also tingling sensations, numbness, transient periods of limb weakness, photophobia [sensitivity to light] and hypersensitivity to sound.'

ME usually starts after an infection of some kind, with sore throat, sore glands in the neck, fever, often pain in the chest or neck, maybe vomiting and diarrhoea (gastric flu). There may be a period of apparent recovery, lasting a few weeks. This is followed by strange symptoms such as sudden collapse, vertigo, severe chest pain, abdominal symptoms or recurrence of flu symptoms.

At this stage, no one knows what is going on, and the patient may be put on antibiotics, sent to a cardiologist or other specialist, and given a few weeks off work. Complete rest for several weeks at this stage may lead to recovery.

But most people expect to be back to normal a few weeks after an infection. So the patient struggles back to work or school when the expected time-limit for recovery expires; then follow months of exhaustion, inability to perform life's daily tasks, a struggle to keep going, believing that mind-over-matter will win – and it doesn't. The patient's symptoms get worse, he or she may be depressed or even suicidal. The patient cannot believe that this pathetic creature whose muscles don't work, whose brain is like porridge, who cries from pain and exhaustion from doing nearly nothing – maybe trying to get up the stairs – can be the same fit and active individual he or she was before.

Most patients learn too late that battling on while in the early acute stage, and trying to get back to normal, is *the worst possible thing to do*. This is why it is so crucial that people know about the existence of ME, because if complete rest is allowed early on, before the illness becomes chronic, then there is a better chance of early recovery.

Unfortunately, most people expect a cure for nearly every ill nowadays. Old-fashioned principles of allowing the body to heal with rest, good food, fresh air and tranquillity have been forgotten; the majority of people only allow themselves one or two weeks to recover from a viral infection. If you had tuberculosis, or double pneumonia, or rheumatic fever, would you expect to be back working full-time after one or two weeks? Of course not.

What Causes ME?

In about two thirds of cases the illness is preceded by a viral infection of some kind. This apparent trigger gives us the name post-viral fatigue syndrome. Many patients, on questioning, also remember a period of exhaustion or stress during the months or weeks before the viral infection. The triggering infection may have seemed innocuous at the time. It is easy to remember an attack of influenza; but one of the commonest viruses now implicated in ME (in the UK) is the group called 'enteroviruses', which may give a day or two of mild summer flu with an upset stomach, or be symptomless and overlooked.

However, some sufferers cannot pinpoint the onset of their illness, and have gradually become more tired and ill over a period of time. And there are a few cases in which the triggering incident was a routine immunization.

In the past few years there has been increasing evidence to suggest that exposure to pesticide chemicals, in particular to organophosphates, is an event that is linked to developing ME in some agricultural workers (*see page 278*).[3]

Then there are predisposing factors which make an individual more vulnerable to developing ME. After all, if a group of students and their teachers at a school have, for example, a bout of summer gastro-enteritis (a fairly common event), what is it that singles out one or two people to continue to be ill for weeks, then develop the features of ME, when the majority make a full and uneventful recovery?

So at the present time, our knowledge of causes of ME can be summarized as follows:

Predisposing Factors

- Inherited (genetic).
- Altered immune response, due possibly to infections, such as glandular fever, or hepatitis, or gut parasites.
- Neurotoxins (such as organophosphates).
- Exhaustion and mental stress (athletic overtraining, work stress).

Triggers

- Viral infection, maybe severe, maybe trivial.
- Immunizations, for example hepatitis B in health professionals.
- A traumatic event (major surgery, car accident).

Perpetuating Factors

- Persistent viral infection, reactivated viral infection.
- Chronic bacterial or Rickettsial infection (such as Lyme disease).
- Repeated overactivity, inappropriate lifestyle, lack of rest.
- Emotional stress.
- Poor diet.
- Inappropriate rest and too little activity, which can lead to physical deconditioning, isolation, introversion and depression.
- Secondary psychological disturbance.
- Exposure to chemicals, environmental pollution.

History of the Illness

Most of the earlier observations about ME have been based on patients studied in epidemics. In fact ME occurs in both epidemic and endemic (isolated cases) form, and obviously a cluster of cases in one area will attract more attention than single, apparently unconnected cases scattered about. There is a history of recorded outbreaks going back to 1934, when an epidemic of what seemed at first to be poliomyelitis was reported in Los Angeles. This was the first of no less than 52 recorded outbreaks from various parts of the world, up to the present time.

A diagnosis of 'neurasthenia' was popularized by an American psychiatrist, George Beard, in 1869, for a condition with some resemblances to chronic fatigue syndrome today (*see page 87*).[4] The diagnosis became popular and fashionable, and probably some of the patients labelled neurasthenic had ME. But the diagnosis came to include so many non-specific symptoms that it fell out of favour. However, it exists in the *International Classification of Disease*, having now a narrower definition than Beard's original one.

Florence Nightingale became ill after returning from her heroic work in the Crimean war, and spent years housebound and too exhausted to speak to more than one visitor at a time. She certainly had something like ME; she also had a high risk career, being exposed to many infections while being constantly physically and emotionally stressed.

The Los Angeles Epidemic

The Los Angeles epidemic (1934) had features which initially resembled poliomyelitis.[5] At the Los Angeles County General Hospital, 198 staff became ill. The main features which differed from those of polio were:

- lack of severe muscle wasting, as would be expected in polio
- longer-lasting muscle pain and tenderness, and sensory symptoms
- memory lapses, loss of concentration, sleep disturbances, emotional instability, and inability to walk a short distance without fatigue.

Over 50 per cent of the staff were still unable to work six months after the peak of the epidemic.

The Royal Free Epidemic

The best-known outbreak of ME in Britain took place in 1955, when nearly 300 members of hospital staff at London's Royal Free Hospital developed what was obviously an infectious illness, over a period of four-and-a-half months.[6] Of the ill hospital staff, 255 had to be admitted to hospital, and yet only

12 of the patients who were already in the hospital during the epidemic developed the disease. It is probable that the existing patients were protected from developing the muscle and neurological symptoms of ME because they were resting in bed, whereas the hospital staff were busy and physically active when they became infected. In this way, ME behaves like polio in an epidemic.

The clinical features of this epidemic among Royal Free Hospital staff (doctors, nurses, ancillary workers and administrative personnel) were as follows:

- malaise, headache, sore throat, abdominal pain, nausea, enlarged glands – these were the initial symptoms, and they fluctuated for several days
- severe pain in the back, neck, limbs, or between ribs; dizziness or vertigo – these symptoms developed after a few days
- neurological signs and symptoms developed by the third or fourth week – 74 per cent of patients showed evidence of involvement of the central nervous system. Symptoms included double vision, difficulty swallowing, paralysis of the face, weakness of arms and legs, twitching or spasms of muscles, and bladder problems.
- spontaneous pains with muscle tenderness and weak limbs were common features.

There are some of these Royal Free Hospital staff who still suffer today from the illness, which was called *epidemic neuromyesthenia*. The infectious agent responsible was not isolated. A full account of the many outbreaks since 1934 has been written up by Dr Melvin Ramsay in his book *Postviral Fatigue Syndrome: the Saga of Royal Free Disease (see below)*.

THE POLIO CONNECTION

The clinical features of many outbreaks world-wide (for example Los Angeles 1934, Iceland 1948–9, Adelaide 1949–51, Coventry 1953, Durban 1955, which all corresponded with epidemics of poliomyelitis) had certain features in common:

- an obvious infection
- involvement of the central nervous system
- prolonged fluctuating course
- marked muscle fatiguability
- exhaustion.

A proportion of patients were left with many years of physical incapacity.

The Iceland Epidemic

The outbreak in Iceland in 1948–9 is very interesting, because in 1955 there was a poliomyelitis epidemic on the island, which did not produce cases in the districts where the epidemic neuromyesthenia had occurred in 1948. This implied that whatever virus was responsible for the ME provided immunity against polio.

Coxsackie Outbreak

In 1948 in New York, an outbreak of an illness very similar to polio occurred. Scientists, using what was then new technology, were able to isolate the virus responsible using tissue culture. To them it seemed to be a new virus. They called it *Coxsackie virus* after the name of the town where the outbreak happened, and they named the illness *atypical polio* because it was obviously some kind of polio, but without the paralysis. Since then, a large number of types of Coxsackie virus have been identified, but it is only in the last few years that scientists have discovered that Coxsackie viruses and polioviruses are very similar and of the same family. Another member of this family of *enteroviruses* is called echovirus, however the molecular makeup of polio, echo and Coxsackie viruses is so similar that they could equally well all be called polioviruses (*see page 38*).

What, for me, makes the argument for a close connection between ME and polio even more compelling is the study of post-polio syndrome in patients years after their attacks of polio. The clinical features of post-polio syndrome are identical to those of ME (*see Chapter 2*).

The Symptoms of ME

The symptoms of ME were first clearly described by Dr Melvin Ramsay, who was a physician at the Royal Free Hospital during the 1955 outbreak and who subsequently devoted his professional life to the study of the illness. In his classic book *Postviral Fatigue Syndrome; the Saga of Royal Free Disease* he says:

'Typically the illness follows an infection, usually a viral illness (which may be subclinical), in a previously fit and active person. The main symptom of ME is severe fatigue and malaise following exercise, with weakness and pain in the muscles after use, and frequently visible muscle twitching. This feature of muscle fatiguability is the dominant and most persistent feature of the disease, and in my opinion a diagnosis [of ME] should not be made without it. The exhaustion typically comes on 24 to 48 hours afterwards, not during the exercise. Fatigue can also result from intellectual exertion.

Then there are a variety of neurological (brain) symptoms: for example – impairment of temperature control and circulation with ashen-gray facial pallor and abnormal sweating; poor concentration and memory; sleep disturbances and emotional instability.

The two other typical features of ME are first the fluctuation of symptoms from day to day or within a day, together with remissions and flare-ups during a year; and secondly the tendency for the condition to persist for several years.

Other symptoms common in ME are: disturbances of sensation – oversensitivity to sound or light, tinnitus, abnormal pain, numbness or pins and needles; also blurred vision and problems with balance. There is usually a total intolerance to alcohol, and digestive disturbances and food allergies are common.'

Dr Ramsay's book remains, to my mind, the best description of the clinical features of ME, and also gives an excellent account of the various outbreaks of the illness recorded between 1934 and 1956. It is published by Gower Medical Publishing, London, and is available from the ME Association (address in Appendix A).

One of the difficulties that doctors experience when listening to a patient who may have ME, and trying to decide if this person fits the illness description or not, is that people suffering from ME can have a great number of different symptoms which appear to affect virtually every part of the body. Over the past five years during my many visits to local patient groups, I have frequently been asked 'is this part of ME?' by people who experience unusual or inexplicable symptoms. Since this illness affects brain function, and the brain and central nervous system control virtually all body functions and sensations, it is not surprising that ME can produce many different symptoms.

A QUESTIONNAIRE

In an informal questionnaire survey carried out in 1987 of people who gave a typical history of ME, and had the cardinal symptoms described by Dr Ramsay, this open question was asked: 'What symptoms have you had since the onset of illness?' The following responses were given, roughly in order of frequency:

made worse by exercise – 100 per cent

exhaustion and severe malaise – 85 per cent

muscle weakness after using muscle, lasting days

muscle pain (mainly back of shoulders, upper arms, and thighs)

blurring of vision

sensation of pins and needles or numbness

loss of concentration

headache

muscle twitching

difficulty in speech – using the wrong word or not being able to think of a word

poor circulation – cold hands and feet

abnormal sweating, with a sour smell

impairment of memory

breathing difficulty

extreme sensitivity to sound

noises in ears – called 'tinnitus'

sleep disturbance

palpitations, and/or racing heartbeat

difficulty standing for any time

vivid dreams or nightmares

joint pains

disorientation

depression
nausea
chest pains
emotional instability – crying easily, rapid mood change
constipation or diarrhoea
recurrent sore throats
enlarged or painful lymph glands
altered sense of taste and/or smell
balance problems
difficulty walking
panic attacks
poor temperature control
poor co-ordination – clumsiness
pallor when ill – quite common
poor bladder control
skin very sensitive to touch
spontaneous bruising, skin rashes
great thirst.

These symptoms were not present all of the time, but the features common to every person with ME are:

Exhaustion, and symptoms worse for exercise.

SECONDARY FEATURES
These affect a relatively small number of patients, and may sometimes confuse the diagnosis, but nevertheless they do occur in people with ME. It is important that doctors know about them, because a common misconception is that there are never any physical abnormalities:

viral myocarditis

vestibulitis – tinnitus, poor balance, sensory confusion – these are more common after encephalitis

auto-immune conditions may develop after some years, for example rheumatoid arthritis, lupus, thyroiditis, Sjogren's syndrome

spasms of hands and feet, leading to clawed deformities

convulsions, suggestive of temporal lobe epilepsy, and myoclonus (an electro-encephalo-gram [EEG] may show abnormalities)

severe progressive weakness of the limbs, maybe even paralysis

loss of ability to chew and/or to swallow

the voice may become very weak or fall to a whisper, then total loss of speech

prostatitis in men.

DURATION OF THE ILLNESS

Various studies have produced slightly different figures, but it seems that, from the date of onset of the illness, sufferers have a 30 per cent chance of still having the symptoms of ME five years later. Many chronically affected sufferers may not be as ill or disabled after five years as they were at the outset. Also, most will not have been continuously ill, but will have had remissions and relapses. A rough estimate of recovery is that about 20 per cent of people diagnosed ME or CFS will make a nearly complete recovery within two years. About 60 per cent will partially recover, and continue for many years with variable symptoms (relapses and remissions) and be able to function at about 70 per cent of their former level of activity. About 20 per cent will remain seriously disabled, but still have some periods of remission, and some of these may unfortunately steadily deteriorate, with no remissions, and become bed-bound.

However, recovery is an inexact word. What most patients mean by 'better' is to be able to live a nearly normal life for much of the time, but avoiding strenuous exercise. I know of very few people who had typical ME following a viral illness who have returned 100 per cent to their pre-illness fitness level, including playing strenuous sports.

One of the problems for GPs trying to diagnose ME is that many of the symptoms patients mention occur in other diseases and are non-specific. However, there are some *symptoms that are very typical of ME:*

- *exercise-induced fatigue* precipitated by physical or mental exertion which is trivial compared to pre-illness exercise tolerance. The post-exertional fatigue and malaise is delayed, and develops between 12 and 48 hours following the exertion, and may last for days.
- impairment of short-term memory and reduced concentration, together with other neurological and psychological disturbances, such as emotional lability, nominal dysphasia (losing names for things or people), sleep disturbance, tinnitus (ringing in the ears), and problems with balance
- sudden onset of pallor when feeling ill
- fluctuation of energy levels and symptoms from day to day or week to week, and all symptoms being made worse by physical or mental exertion
- a tendency for remissions and relapses
- a marked intolerance to alcohol, even in small amounts.

Particular Muscle Symptoms

• Muscle weakness develops after minimal effort, and may take days to recover from.
• Inability to stand – the legs shake and ache after standing for a short time, the patient has to sit down, on the ground if necessary.
• The sufferer cannot hold up the arms or cannot hang up washing, there is difficulty carrying bags or holding a telephone handset.
• Aching back or neck if sitting in unsupporting chair.
• Intermittent blurring of vision – due to fatigue of the eye-focusing muscles.
• Aching in face after chewing.
• Inability to write for long.
• General muscle tenderness, with some acutely sensitive local spots.
• Twitching in muscles, which may be visible to other people.

Note that the problems arise from *sustained* use of a muscle group; the muscle function may be normal to start with, for example in the morning, but pain and weakness develop in the muscles in use after a short time.

Slow walking is always easier than standing.

The muscles most commonly affected are the girdle muscles – the back of the shoulders, buttocks and thighs.

Brain Symptoms (Neurological and Psychological)

- Poor concentration – typically concentration cannot be sustained for long, whether you are listening to the radio, reading, studying, or having a conversation.
- Poor memory – forgetting name of someone you know well, forgetting what has just been said, not knowing where you are or why you are there (for example if driving, being totally disorientated and lost though in a familiar place).
- Nominal aphasia – being unable to find the word for something.
- Muddled or even slurred speech when tired.
- Loss of arithmetic skills – inability to count money or do simple addition.
- Hypersensitivity to sound – voices, the radio, even clocks ticking may become unbearable.
- Hypersensitivity to light (photophobia).
- Poor balance and feeling of unsteadiness, with loss of spatial awareness, such that you find yourself bumping into doorways.
- Altered skin sensation – painful to the touch or a creepy-crawly feeling or numbness, 'pins and needles' in arms or legs.
- Transient blurred or double vision.
- Increased sense of smell, or bizarre smells.
- Nightmares, sleep disturbance, deficiency in certain levels of sleep.

AUTONOMIC NERVOUS SYSTEM DISTURBANCE
(ALSO PART OF BRAIN DISTURBANCE)

- Sudden racing heart beat, or palpitations.
- Profuse sweating, even when cold.
- Pallor – often ashen grey – at onset of feeling ill.
- Poor temperature regulation – feeling suddenly cold in warm weather.
- Poor circulation to hands and feet – maybe only affecting one side.
- Alternating diarrhoea or constipation.
- Dizziness on standing.
- Feeling faint and sweaty between meals.
- Difficulty passing urine, or incontinence.

ACUTE NEUROLOGICAL EVENTS (THESE OCCUR IN
ONLY A FEW PATIENTS)

- from Professor Komaroff again – 'Primary seizures (7 per cent), acute profound ataxia (6 per cent), focal weakness (5 per cent), transient loss of vision (4 per cent). These were mostly during the first year of the illness.'[7]

Symptoms Suggesting Immune Overactivity or Low-grade Infection

- Persistent or recurrent sore throat. The throat looks purplish-red, but is not septic.
- Enlarged and/or tender lymph nodes, in the neck or armpits.
- Episodes of low-grade fever (less than 38.6°C by mouth), or feeling feverish.
- Painful aching joints which are not swollen.

Other Typical Features

- Sudden mood changes, untypical of the person.
- Development of new allergies – particularly to chemicals and some foods.
- Difficulty breathing – especially at night – the 'I wake up feeling I cannot get enough oxygen' symptom.
- Prostatic symptoms in men.

The Progression of ME

The natural progression of the illness is a slow improvement, if proper rest is allowed. Most ME sufferers relapse because they are active by nature, and as soon as they start to feel better they do too much, then become ill again.

MAIN CAUSES OF RELAPSE
- Physical exercise beyond the safe limit for the day.
- Mental overwork, intense concentration, studying for exams.
- Developing another infection.
- Emotional stress – divorce, bereavement, family illness.
- Hormonal changes – menstruation, after pregnancy.
- Traumatic stress – surgery, accidents.
- Exposure to chemicals – e.g. organophosphates, new paint, diesel fumes.
- Extreme change of climate.
- Winter – not only the cold, but the lack of daylight.
- Surgery, anaesthetics, dental treatment.

There are a small number of sufferers who do not seem to have any remissions and who gradually deteriorate, but these are relatively few. More often the illness fluctuates, with relapses and remissions occurring, sometimes quite unpredictably. This is one of the features of ME which makes it so hard to assess clinically, especially in any trial of treatment. The marked variations in symptoms and in the degree of illness felt by a patient also results in disbelief on the part of family, friends and the GP. People find it hard to accept that you have a genuine illness if they see you in a wheelchair one week, and walking the next. What they don't see is that you can still only walk a short way, and they don't observe your collapse when you get home!

Other Names – The Chronic Fatigue Syndrome

In many parts of the world, and originally in the US, the name chronic fatigue syndrome (CFS) is used for an illness very similar to ME. In the US the name Chronic Epstein Barr Virus disease (CEBV) was used at first. In the 1980s it was believed that the illness developed following 'infectious mononucleosis' (glandular fever), and therefore was a chronic infection of the glandular fever virus. However, this name was dropped when it became evident that the ongoing fatiguing illness was not a chronic Epstein Barr infection.

In order for this fatiguing condition to be recognizable, and also to improve the basis for clinical research, a working case definition was required – one which could be accepted worldwide. In the US a number of physicians got together in 1988 and drew up the criteria for a case definition of chronic fatigue syndrome. (Another name used in the US is Chronic Fatigue and Immune Dysfunction Syndrome – CFIDS.)

CRITERIA FOR CFS

The first criteria for CFS were published by the Centers for Disease Control (CDC) in the US in 1988.[8] (*See Chapter 3* for list of the first CFS criteria.)

In 1990 a group of British doctors met in Oxford to discuss the criteria for research into CFS. Their conclusions were published and are now known as the 'Oxford Criteria'[9] (*see Chapter 3*).

The work of the Centers for Disease Control was further refined and modified and republished in 1994, and has become loosely know as the Fukuda Criteria, from the first name on the list of authors.[10] These are now the standard diagnostic criteria for research, in use throughout the world.

Diagnostic Criteria for Chronic Fatigue Syndrome, CDC 1994

Major Criteria

1. Unexplained, persistent, or relapsing chronic fatigue that is of new or definite onset (not lifelong).
2. Fatigue is not due to ongoing exertion.
3. Fatigue is not substantially alleviated by rest.
4. The fatigue results in substantial reduction in occupational, educational, social or personal activities.

Minor Criteria

1. Self-reported impairment in short-term memory or concentration severe enough to cause substantial reduction in occupational, educational, social or personal activities.

2. Sore throat.
3. Tender cervical or axillary lymph nodes.
4. Muscle pain.
5. Multi-joint pain without joint swelling or redness.
6. Headaches of a new type, pattern or severity.
7. Unrefreshing sleep.
8. Post-exertional malaise lasting more than 24 hours.

For a diagnosis to be made, the case must fulfil all the major criteria, plus four or more of the minor criteria. Each minor criterion must have persisted or recurred during six or more consecutive months of illness and must not have predated the fatigue. In addition, other medical illnesses, including drug or substance abuse, must be excluded.

Is ME the Same as CFS?

Because the description of chronic fatigue syndrome covers a broader category of symptoms than the description of Myalgic Encephalomyelitis, it is becoming obvious to patients and to researchers that the names CFS and ME do not always describe the same group of patients. This has sometimes led to confusing and conflicting research findings. In addition, many patients with ME loathe the name 'chronic fatigue syndrome' because 'fatigue' is totally inadequate to describe the experience of ME, trivializing the severity of ME in some patients and not always reflecting what may be for some sufferers a different and much more disabling symptom.

The term chronic fatigue syndrome, used in the broader category as in the Oxford and Fukuda Criteria, has also caused a certain 'psychologization' of the illness, and a belief on the part of some doctors that ME and CFS are illnesses of mainly psychiatric origin. (*In Chapter 2 and where applicable, the two names are used interchangeably. However, for a more detailed explanation of why ME – a clearly described neurological illness – has become known as 'chronic fatigue' – an umbrella term – see Chapter 3.*)

INCIDENCE OF ME

Several different surveys have been carried out, in the UK, Australia and the US, to determine the incidence of ME.

In Australia[11] a study of a population of 114,000 found 42 cases of ME/CFS (1988 criteria). This gives a prevalence of 37.1 cases per 100,000. The incidence of Multiple Sclerosis is 36.5 per 100,000 in that area. The onset followed an acute 'viral' illness in 75 per cent of cases.

A survey of General Practices in the west of Scotland in 1991, using criteria that is employed to diagnose Post-viral Fatigue Syndrome, found an incidence of 1.3 per thousand.[12]

A telephone survey of a cross-section of inhabitants of San Francisco (1996) found an incidence of 2 per thousand with CFS-like symptoms.[13]

A community survey of a random population, in 1996, using the broader CFS criteria, found an incidence of 2.6 per cent, which seems very high.[14]

The figures obtained seem to vary according to what diagnostic criteria are used.

The Organic versus Psychological Controversy – Is ME a Disease, or All in the Mind?

In 1970, two psychiatrists at the Middlesex Hospital, London, produced two papers in the *British Medical Journal*: 'Royal Free Epidemic of 1955: a reconsideration', and 'Concept of Benign Myalgic Encephalomyelitis'.[15]

In these articles they considered that the Royal Free epidemic of 1955 had been an outbreak of mass hysteria, and that other outbreaks in the world also had features of hysteria. They admitted that those outbreaks which showed a resemblance to poliomyelitis probably weren't mass hysteria, but took no account of the clinical features of those affected. When they wrote these articles, neither of them had bothered to interview or examine any of the Royal Free staff who had been involved.

In spite of the fact that there were obvious flaws in their reasoning – such as the signs of infection and neurological involvement, which do not occur in hysteria – this psychiatric hypothesis given by McEvedy and Beard was taken up by the media, and has unfortunately been accepted without question by many of the medical profession ever since.

The damage done to people who suffer from this illness, both those of the Royal Free outbreak and others since, has been incalculable. Of course it is much more convenient to label the condition hysterical; there is then no need to research the illness, patients can be ordered to pull their socks up and go back to work, and those who have had no experience of the devastating symptoms can rejoice in being far too well-balanced to get 'that sort of complaint'.

Thanks to the tireless efforts of certain doctors who never doubted the reality of the disease, in the last few years evidence has emerged, through various research studies, of the real and organic nature of the illness. Special credit is due to Dr Melvin Ramsay, who as mentioned earlier was Consultant in Infectious Diseases at the Royal Free Hospital at the time of the 1955 outbreak and went on to devote a large part of his life to working for recognition of, and research into, ME. Dr Ramsay died in March 1990; he is greatly missed by the many people he has helped during his long battle to get ME recognized.

Not only some doctors, but also patients themselves have campaigned for better recognition and understanding. The ME Association, founded in 1976, and Action for ME, founded in 1987, have provided support and information to people with ME, and have worked to educate doctors, social services and politicians about the nature of the illness and its debilitating effects.

It is useful to remember that 30 years ago, patient with Multiple Sclerosis were labelled as neurotic or hysterical. Now MS is recognized, and yet its diagnosis is largely a clinical one. There is still no single specific diagnostic test for MS.

Modern medicine relies increasingly on laboratory tests and X-rays to make a diagnosis, and less and less on each patient's history. And yet the typical symptom complex of ME as described by Dr Ramsay in 1976 is quite recognizable. The problems arise when a GP has a patient who complains of being 'tired all the time'. Fatigue is a universal daily life experience, and has probably evolved as a safety mechanism to get us (and animals) to rest at the right times. An exhausted wild animal or early human would be at risk from predators or animals and lose out in the competition for food, if it or he carried on hunting when the muscles and body needed rest. So the sensation of great fatigue is sometimes appropriate and does not necessarily indicate illness. With ME, it is the nature of the fatigue, the post-exertional feeling of illness, plus the rapid onset of brain fatigue that differentiates it from the symptom of 'feeling tired all the time'. The majority of people with ME do not feel fatigued all the time, sometimes they feel they have normal energy, it's just that the energy runs out very quickly.

Fatigue, and depression, are common symptoms of other brain disorders such as Parkinson's disease, Alzheimer's disease and MS. The difference in medical perspective is that in these disorders there are objective signs of something wrong, and yet in ME/CFS, it is only in the last 10 years that evidence has gradually began to emerge (*see Chapter 2*).

Here is an extract from an article called 'Chronic fatigue, viruses and depression'[16] – note the use of the term chronic fatigue, which could mean tiredness or mean a severe case of ME:

'It is important to recognize that, in a society where ME is portrayed as a mysterious, rather glamorous, and disabling illness, people who have acquired this diagnosis may obtain attention and sympathy from friends and relatives, and perhaps also a justification for not fulfilling career ambitions or coping with the demands of everyday life. They may therefore lead less unhappy lives with their symptoms and their diagnosis than they could do otherwise.'

This personal view from one person (a professor of psychiatry) is not based on any scientific study of numbers of ill people, it is a vague opinion. You can find people in any area of life who have needs that could be satisfied by the taking on the role of invalid. But to print this biased opinion in a way that seems to apply to ME in particular, can only have far-reaching harmful effects on ill people who are struggling to cope.

One of the characteristics of people with ME/CFS is that they are highly motivated, frustrated by not being physically able to do things, and try by any means to get better. The loss of careers, breakdown of marriages, loss of ability to function in nearly every aspect of life – these devastating results of the illness cannot in any way cause people to 'lead less unhappy lives'.

Many people with ME/CFS get little or no sympathy or support from family or friends.

However, if this illness is portrayed as nothing more than being chronically tired, then such misconceptions will persist. Here is Professor Komaroff again:

'Fatigue is a common complaint of patients presenting at general medical practice. Most such patients probably are suffering from a primary psychiatric illness. A few may have a well-recognized organic cause of chronic fatigue, such as hidden malignancy, thyroid disease, anaemia or other illness. Probably only a few of many patients seeking medical care for chronic fatigue have ME/CFS.[17]'

To show how the ideas of McEvedy and Beard have influenced some doctors, here is the true account of a mother's difficulty when her daughter became ill. It also illustrates that children can develop ME:

'My daughter, aged 11, fell ill with a virus which was going round her school. She did not recover properly, and for months she kept on having swollen glands, vague sore throat, and a slight fever. After eight months she was keen to go to school, but some days she would fade out by mid-morning and have to come home. If she tried any sports or gym she collapsed. She was referred to a paediatrician, who did blood tests and found nothing wrong. We then took her to another children's doctor, privately; he said he could find nothing wrong, and that she should be encouraged to go to school (which she was keen to do). We took her to see a consultant rheumatologist, because she had these awful pains in her muscles and legs, and he told us that she just needed to exercise and get fit!

'Then I saw an article in the *Telegraph* which described her condition exactly. We were so relieved to find out what was wrong. I went back to see the private specialist and showed him the newspaper article, saying – 'look at this, our daughter has got Post-viral Fatigue Syndrome.' He just dismissed it, and said 'That is Royal Free Disease, that's been proven to be hysteria.'

'We were upset and angry. I knew she was ill and not putting it on. The trouble was that we needed a doctor to give a diagnosis so that she could rest from school if unwell, and be excused from having to do any sport.'

It was at this stage that this worried mother told me the story, and fortunately I was able to put her in touch with a doctor who had experience of ME, who recognized the illness with no difficulty. Happily the girl is now gradually improving, and a year after having the virus is able to go to school, provided she does no exercise at all.

But here were *three* specialists, all in one small city, who could not recognize that this child was ill, having relied on blood tests rather than the history and experience of the child and her family.

Chapter 2

What Causes ME and CFS?

The history of investigations into this group of illnesses reads rather like a detective story: along the way there have been many clues, but time after time some clues turn out to be 'red herrings'.

There are many theories about what causes ME/CFS, and the mechanisms at work in the body and brain – in medical terms these are called the 'patho-aetiology' of an illness – and science does seem to be getting closer to solving the mystery than it was 10 years ago. Here are some early quotations from three researchers, each of whom had seen and investigated many hundreds of patients:

1. 'Post-viral fatigue syndrome is a metabolic disorder, caused by persistent virus infection and associated with defective immunoregulation.' (Behan, 1985)[1]
2. 'The condition (ME) appears to be a rare complication, mainly in non-immune adults, of a widespread often asymptomatic childhood infection. The group of viruses most consistently associated with ME are the non-polio enteroviruses – including Coxsackie and echoviruses. When the host immune response is ineffective, viral

parasitism leads to mitochondrial damage with resultant energy deficits at cellular level.' (Dowsett, 1990)[2]

3. 'It is presumed that CFIDS (CFS) is a cytokine-mediated illness, virally induced, in genetically susceptible individuals.' (Goldstein, 1990)[3] [CFIDS = Chronic Fatigue and Immune Dysfunction Syndrome].

Epidemiology – Studies on the Incidence of Illness

Various figures on the incidence of Post-viral Fatigue Syndrome (PVFS), ME, and more recently CFS, from different countries including Australia, the UK and the US, have tended to show an average incidence of around 1 case per thousand in the general population. However, 1 in a thousand may be an underestimate, and is usually obtained from records of patients attending a doctor. If you screen the general population in the community, the figure rises, because not everyone with mild ME/CFS visits a doctor.

As mentioned in Chapter 1, a telephone survey of a cross-section of residents of San Francisco, people of all social and ethnic groups, screened 8,004 households, with 16,970 residents.[4] Of these, 0.2 per cent of adults were classified as having 'CFS-like' symptoms and history, that is – 2 per thousand. The prevalence was higher in Black and Native Americans than in Whites, and higher in low-income groups. If all those CFS-like people were to have examinations and investigations to exclude other causes for their symptoms, the prevalence would certainly end up lower than 0.2 per cent. The results of this survey in California clearly dismiss the belief that ME/CFS is an illness of the white middle classes!

Using the latest criteria for diagnosing CFS, which allows the inclusion of people who have depression or anxiety as well as fatigue (*see Chapter 1*), the figures rise dramatically. A community survey of 2,376 people in the UK[5] found a prevalence of 2.6 per cent who met the criteria for CFS – but if psychological disorders were excluded the prevalence fell to 0.5 per cent. That is still 5 per thousand, higher than estimates over the past 10 years and higher than the San Francisco investigation results.

Clearly, the number of cases of ME/CFS in any community depends on what questions are asked, what criteria are used for diagnosis, and also probably on whether there have been any local mini-outbreaks or clusters of cases.

The incidence of ME/CFS in children under 20 is probably lower than 1 per thousand, but there have not been any community studies of the epidemiology of ME/CFS in children, although a survey of schools where ME/CFS was recognized found an average incidence of 70 pupils per 100,000 (i.e. 0.7 per thousand).[6] This may be a high figure, and not representative of all schools.

Another interesting study by Professor Komaroff in the US also showed how debilitated patients with ME/CFS are: The health status of patient with CFS was compared to that of healthy people, also to people with other diseases – heart failure, high blood pressure, diabetes, heart attack, MS and major depression.[7] The CFS patients had significantly lower scores of function in all areas except mental health, than any other illness group. This study demonstrated that ME/CFS is a very debilitating illness.

The Role of Infection in ME/CFS

The viruses that trigger ME/CFS and may play an ongoing part in the illness have been investigated for two decades, and there are still no clear answers. The majority of patients say their illness started following a viral-type illness from which they did not recover. Looking at the documented outbreaks from 1934 through to the 1950s, it seems obvious that in these epidemics an infectious agent was responsible. However, a recent survey of patients visiting their GPs in the UK, following up people who consulted their doctor with a common virus such as influenza or a cold to see if they later reported symptoms consistent with CFS, did not find that getting a common upper respiratory infection was a risk factor for developing CFS.[8]

This, however, is not surprising, because the group of viruses that appear to trigger ME/CFS most often in the UK are enteroviruses such as Coxsackie B, and these more usually cause an illness with gastro-enteritis, sore throat and muscle pains rather than the common cold. They can also cause viral meningitis, which in some cases is the start of ME/CFS.

In summary, several viruses have come under suspicion:

- Enteroviruses – especially in the UK (*see below*). Earlier outbreaks were associated in time and place with poliomyelitis. Polio viruses are also enteroviruses.
- Epstein Barr virus (*see page 43*). This is a common cause of glandular fever (called infectious mononucleosis in the US).
- Human herpes virus 6 (HHV6) (*see page 44*).
- Human LymphoTropic Virus 2 (HLTV 2, related to the AIDS virus, now discounted as a cause of ME/CFS)
- Borna virus. This is known to be neurotropic and can cause disease in horses and ostriches. Some studies have found an

association with depression (Germany), however research has not shown any significant role for Borna virus in ME/CFS.

- Inoue-Melnick virus and Stealth virus (*see page 45*).
- Cytomegalovirus (*see page 48*).

THE CASE FOR ENTEROVIRUSES

In a small town on the Hudson River in New York State in the late 1940s, a new virus was isolated from children with a disease that resembled poliomyelitis. The virus was named Coxsackie after the town. It is now known that Coxsackie viruses are a member of a group called enteroviruses, which include polioviruses and live in the human intestine. Enteroviruses can affect many tissues, but have a particular affinity for the central nervous system and muscles.

In two outbreaks in Scotland in 1983, designated as Postviral Fatigue Syndrome (PVFS), antibodies to Coxsackie B virus were higher in patients than in the general population.

In patients with symptoms of ME in a west of Scotland general practice (1984), nearly half had high Coxsackie B antibody levels.[9] In this same practice, 55 per cent of those with Coxsackie infection were still ill after one year, nearly all having persisting high antibody levels.

The most comprehensive summary of the role of enterovirus infection in ME can be found in a paper by Dr E Dowsett entitled 'Myalgic encephalomyelitis – a persistent enteroviral infection?'

The human enterovirus family comprises over 90 types, including polioviruses, Coxsackie A and B, Echoviruses, hepatitis A and B, sub-groups of these, and others.

A recently developed technique for identifying viruses and sequencing their molecular make-up is called Polymerase

Chain Reaction, or PCR, and this has now demonstrated that polioviruses are so similar to Coxsackie and echoviruses that, were it not for an accident of naming, all enteroviruses could have been called polioviruses 1 to 90!

Now that a polio vaccine has reduced the incidence of paralytic polio, the other enteroviruses are becoming more important in causing human disease, and they have a great capacity to cause new outbreaks. Indeed, some strains of echovirus and Coxsackie virus have caused paralysis.

Examples of enteroviral illnesses are:

respiratory infections
gastro-enteritis
hepatitis
meningitis and encephalitis
poliomyelitis
Bornholm's disease – this mimics pleurisy and heart attack, with agonizing chest pains caused by viral inflammation of the intercostal muscles
myocarditis and pericarditis
hand, foot and mouth disease, and other skin conditions
conjunctivitis (infection of the lining of eyelids)
pancreatitis and juvenile onset diabetes
myalgic encephalomyelitis (some cases).

Enteroviruses are known to be myotropic and neurotropic – that is, they affect muscle and nerve particularly.

Enteroviruses are spread from the gut via sewage, rivers, estuaries, beaches and agriculture, to reinfect humans in drinking water and food. They are easily picked up on beach and water holidays; by hospital workers from bedpans and other equipment; by those who work with young children (who frequently harbour enteroviruses without signs of illness) and land and water workers. Most enteroviral infections do not cause any obvious illness – in other words, the infection is subclinical. Enteroviruses are not killed in 'treated' sewage before it enters the sea.

In several outbreaks of ME, patients were initially thought to have polio (for example Los Angeles 1934, Iceland 1948), and health authorities thought another polio epidemic had started, until it became clear that the illness, although resembling poliomyelitis, had some different features (*see page 38*). One aspect in which ME behaved like polio was that *those who were most physically active when they contracted the infection were most likely to develop muscle weakness.*

In a follow-up study of ME cases from a Glasgow college,[10] out of the 31 patients, 12 had been runners pre-illness, whereas only 2 of the 25 healthy controls were runners.

Evidence showing that enteroviruses were present in a proportion of ME patients resulted from the work of Professor James Mowbray and colleagues at St Mary's Medical School, London, in 1988.[11] It is difficult to detect virus in the stools because it is bound with antibody, so a method was devised which would detect enterovirus-group-protein in the blood. This protein, called VP1 polypeptide, is common to all members of the enterovirus family. VP1 was detected in the blood of 51 per cent of the tested ME patients.

However, the test is also positive in a number of healthy people, and reflects the amount of that particular enteroviral infection in an area at any time. Enteroviral infections are extremely common, and frequently asymptomatic. The VP1 test is no longer used to support a diagnosis of ME, as it is too non-specific.

AKUREYRI, ICELAND – 42 YEARS ON[12]

In Iceland in 1948, the outbreak of epidemic myalgic encephalomyelitis occurred among high school pupils in a small community called Akureyri. In 1990 Dr B M Hyde from Canada studied some of the patients still alive: 10 people aged between 58 and 84 were interviewed, examined and had blood tests performed. Only two out of the 10 had made a complete recovery after 42 years. They had all had features typical of myalgic encephalomyelitis when they were ill. Eight out of the 10 had a positive enterovirus VP1 test; the two who were negative were the two who had made a complete recovery. Those who had not made a complete recovery all had some degree of chronic disability, although they perceived themselves as having made a good recovery. They had all achieved satisfying lives or careers in spite of variable levels of disability. This outcome is fairly typical of what happens to people who develop ME: the majority recover enough to have some sort of life and maybe work, but nevertheless still have residual disabilities.

EFFECTS OF ENTEROVIRUSES IN THE BODY

Enteroviruses are known to infect muscle, including heart muscle, nerves and brain. They may also infect endocrine glands (such as the pancreas, leading to diabetes). Enterovirus RNA has been identified in muscle cells of ME patients.[13] Some strains may favour heart involvement, others the brain, and in a few patients with ME the heart conducting system or muscle may remain affected.

Enteroviral protein has been identified in the brain of a number of patients who died as a result of suicide.[14] Whether this indicates a persistent infection in the central nervous system has not been proven.

Nor is there as yet any proof that enterovirus persists in the muscle cells of ME patients. Using PCR, enteroviral RNA has been demonstrated in blood,[15] but not conclusively in muscle.[16] However, many patients who are diagnosed with ME or CFS have raised IgM titres to Coxsackie B during their first year of illness, sometimes longer, and a raised IgM antibody titre indicates an active infection.

Post Polio Syndrome – Another Possible Connection of ME with Polio

PostPolio Syndrome (PPS), although mentioned earlier this century in isolated reports, has only been generally recognized and seriously studied since the 1980s, through the campaigning of sufferers. It is defined as:

New muscle weakness and fatigue in skeletal or bulbar muscles, with no other cause, that develops 25 – 30 years after an acute attack of poliomyelitis.

Decades after recovering from varying degrees of paralysis, nearly 30 per cent of polio survivors are now developing fatigue, muscle weakness and atrophy, and in some cases difficulty in breathing. And not only new muscle symptoms, but frequently brain symptoms such as loss of concentration or memory, attention deficit, somnolence by day and disturbed sleep by night.

These patients are being studied by Professor R Bruno and his colleagues at the Department of Physical Rehabilitation, New Jersey Medical School. They have found that the centrally-mediated fatigue is due to damage by the poliovirus to the mid-brain, especially affecting the ascending reticular activating system, which is responsible for maintaining wakefulness and attention. Similar symptoms of drowsiness and cognitive disturbances affect people with ME/CFS, especially young people. Brain scans of PPS patients have found abnormalities in magnetic resonance imaging (MRI), with lesions in the white matter and other areas.[17]

Virological investigation has found fragments of enteroviral RNA in the cerebrospinal fluid (CSF) and spinal cords of some PPS patients.[18] In some these were of poliovirus, but in 3 out of 24 PPS patients the RNA fragments were identified as Coxsackie virus. This suggests that some cases of PPS might be caused by a later infection with the type of enterovirus which causes a milder disease than polio.

While none of the researchers believes that PPS is identical to ME/CFS, there are many similarities, and studies of PPS could lead to a better understanding of the pathology in the more severe type of ME, in which patients can develop severe weakness of one or more limbs, or paralysis, and also weakness of the bulbar muscles (swallowing, speech, breathing) severe enough to lead to tube-feeding and loss of voice.

A summary of the informative paper 'The post polio syndrome – advances in the pathogenesis and treatment' by Dr E Dowsett, can be read in the journal *Perspectives* (March 1996; 'Medical Matters', page ix).

THE EPSTEIN BARR VIRUS

Chronic fatigue syndrome was known as Chronic Epstein Barr Virus disease (CEBV) in the US in the 1980s. EB virus is best known for causing infectious mononucleosis, known as glandular fever in the UK, although this illness can be caused by other viruses, including Human Herpes Virus 6. Epstein Barr virus is a member of the herpes family, which comprises viruses that cause herpes simplex, chickenpox, smallpox and shingles.

Glandular fever is well known for the prolonged debility that persists for months after the acute infection.[19] Most people have been infected with the EB virus by the age of 30, usually with few symptoms; in only a few is the infection severe enough to cause glandular fever. If you look for evidence of past EB infection you will find it in about 95 per cent of adults, with or without ME/CFS.

However, other viruses can cause glandular fever, and people diagnosed with ME or CFS will often say 'my illness began with glandular fever, but blood tests for Epstein Barr virus were negative.'

If tests indicate an active current EB infection in someone with symptoms of ME/CFS, it is probably a reactivation of an old latent infection. The EB virus can hide in surface cells of the nose and throat, and in B lymphocytes for years. Depression of the immune system (maybe from another virus) allows it to flare up. We have no proof that the reactivated EB virus is responsible for symptoms of ME/CFS.

HUMAN HERPES VIRUS 6

Another herpes virus, HHV6, has been considered as a cause of ME/CFS. By the age of 12 months, about 60 per cent of children have antibody to HHV6, showing that it is very common and acquired early in life. A study from Boston[20] found 60 per cent of 154 CFS patients were positive for HHV6 early antigen IgM (an indication of current active infection), compared to 12 per cent of healthy controls. However, the authors note 'the evidence of active infection in CFS patients probably represents reactivation of a latent infection, secondary to immune dysfunction or another virus, and therefore may have no relationship to the symptoms of CFS.'

STEALTH VIRUS

This is the name given to a virus isolated from patients in an outbreak of infectious illness in the Mohave valley region of the western US in 1996.[21] This outbreak was notable because several hundred people were affected. The symptoms began with a flu-like gastrointestinal illness, but after the acute phase many affected people had varying neurological episodes, such as numbness, gait disturbance or memory loss. The symptoms resembled those seen in the Royal Free Hospital outbreak of 1995. The virus responsible was difficult to identify and is called 'stealth virus' by local researchers. It is most likely a member of the herpes virus family.

INOUE-MELNICK VIRUS

The Inoue-Melnick virus, called after the two doctors who identified it,[22] was first isolated in Japan in 1971 from the cerebrospinal fluid of patients with an unusual illness called subacute myelo-optic-neuropathy (SMON), which had some clinical similarities to ME/CFS:

- the diagnosis of SMON is clinical (no diagnostic test)
- most patients are young to middle-aged females
- neurological symptoms and fatigue are common
- relapses are common.

It has been postulated that IMV could be implicated in cases of ME where neurological features such as optic neuropathy and cranial nerve palsies (causing double vision and/or loss of vision) are common, as occurred in the Iceland and Royal Free outbreaks. It has not been possible to test this hypothesis because identification of IMV is technically very difficult. But blood serum from patients in the Royal Free outbreak was sent to Dr Inoue by Dr Melvin Ramsay and Dr Gordon Parrish, and the samples, which included those of three patients who had cranial nerve palsies, were found to have antibodies to type 2 IMV. Also, sera collected and tested from patients in the Iceland epidemic were antibody positive to type 1 IMV.

It is suggested that IMV belongs to the herpes virus family, but little is known about its relationship to other known herpes viruses. The stealth virus responsible for the outbreak in the Mohave valley could be a close relative of the IMV.

Until now, little research has been done on the Inoue-Melnick virus, partly because the men who named it have retired, and also because of the difficulties of laboratory diagnostic tests. With the recent development of PCR (*see page 50*), hopefully new researchers will be able to find out more about this virus, which could be implicated in some cases of ME/CFS, especially those with involvement of the brain and cranial nerves.

COULD ME/CFS BE A PERSISTENT VIRAL FATIGUE SYNDROME?

It now seems possible that in some cases, part of a virus is remaining inside cells, and is interfering with the cells' functions. This is a feature of persistent virus infections, which may be implicated in some poorly understood illnesses. Certain viruses are known for their ability to survive in the body and cause persistent infection.

Dr M Oldstone,[23] writing about persistent viral infections:

'Such viruses do not kill the cells, and do not elicit an effective immune response. These tactics enable the viruses to establish a long-term presence within cells, where they can have a subtle and persistent effect – by altering the specialized function of the cell, such as the production or secretion of a hormone. Such 'luxury functions' are not essential to the cell's survival, but may be vital to the health of the organism (e.g. a human). It is likely that immune, nervous and endocrine systems are primarily involved.'

ME/CFS in some cases could be a persistent virus infection. Other diseases, such as diabetes, Parkinson's disease and schizophrenia, may turn out to be caused by persistent virus infections as well.

Viruses and Allergy

It is known that histamine is produced in tissues infected by a virus, and many people seem to develop allergies following a viral illness. Multiple allergies are common in ME/CFS. Professor Komaroff writes, 'The patients' medical histories reveal one striking finding: a high frequency of atopic or allergic illness – up to 70 per cent.'[24]

OTHER MICRO-ORGANISMS THAT MAY BE INVOLVED

Lyme Disease

Lyme disease has symptoms similar to those of ME/CFS – fatigue, muscle aches, plus joint pains and a rash. It is caused by a member of the Rickettsia family called *Borrelia burgdorferi*. Rickettsia are not viruses but very small bacteria. These are transmitted by the bite of a tick that lives in low scrub or bracken in woodland areas. The importance of Lyme disease for people suspected of having ME/CFS is that it can be diagnosed by a blood antibody test, and it responds to treatment with tetracycline-type antibiotics such as doxycycline.

Q Fever

Q fever is another illness caused by a microbe related to Rickettsia called *Coxiella burnetii*, and is usually got from infected milk. However it is uncommon in the UK. It is a nasty though short-lived illness with high fever. In some cases it can lead to a chronic Q fever infection with symptoms similar to those of ME/CFS.[25] It is also treatable with doxycycline. It is most usually found in agricultural workers who come in contact with animals.

Cytomegalovirus

In a study on 18 patients with CFS who had very severe fatigue and also abnormal cardiac function (abnormal T-waves on ECG), immunological tests suggested a human cytomegalovirus infection.[26] They were all treated with intravenous ganciclovir (an antiviral agent that is expensive and very restricted in use) for 30 days. At follow-up 24 weeks later, 13 (72 per cent) patients had recovered to pre-illness health. The cardiac abnormalities were not those seen in normal people who are sedentary – in other words, could not be explained by unfitness.

Mycoplasma

An uncommon organism called *Mycoplasma incognita* has been found in about 50 per cent of 650 Gulf War veterans, in a study in the US.[27] Antibiotics were beneficial to most of those who received treatment. The significance of this is that Gulf War Syndrome (GWS) is clinically very similar to CFS and to the picture seen in chronic organophosphate (OP) poisoning, and it is possible though not yet investigated that mycoplasma could be involved in at least some cases of ME/CFS.

Other chronic infections that can be confused with ME/CFS and are treatable are *brucellosis* and *leptospirosis*. These can also be diagnosed by appropriate antibody tests.

AN INFECTIOUS ILLNESS?

People may worry that ME/CFS is itself infectious. The microbes that could cause ME/CFS are carried by a large percentage of the population, in the throat, nose or in the gut, without causing any ill-health. It does not appear that people with ME/CFS are any more likely to spread these common bugs about than the rest of the population. It is estimated that roughly one in four people with ME/CFS has a close relative or work colleague with the illness. In the case of more than one member of a family being affected, there may an inherited susceptibility. The infectiousness of ME and other chronic fatigue syndromes is not clearly understood.

FURTHER THOUGHTS ABOUT THE ROLE OF INFECTION

Identifying Bacteria and Viruses

In 1996 an article by Dr Bob Holmes appeared in the *New Scientist*, entitled 'Life Unlimited'.[28] It starts with the statement 'By changing the way they search for bacteria, researchers have discovered thousands of new species and the technique has turned up entirely new forms of life.' At the present time, identifying a bacterium depends on being able to grow it outside the body, and then to study it under the microscope. So the only species of bacteria we can associate with a disease process are those that can be grown and identified, and the numbers identified so far are quite limited. However, there are millions of species of micro-organisms around in the world that have not been identified, including viruses, bacteria and others that are neither, such as Rickettsiae, or the slow-growing 'prions' that are responsible for brain diseases such as Creuztfeld Jacob Disease, and others we have not yet classified.

However, a new technology called Polymerase Chain Reaction (PCR) is able to isolate a tiny fragment of genetic material and then determine the order and type of molecules of DNA and RNA (genetic prototypes) of an organism.

Just as tuberculosis only came to be understood as an infectious disease since the tubercle bacillus was first seen and identified, other illnesses whose causes were previously unknown have become linked to infective agents. A classic example in our time is the discovery that duodenal ulcers can be caused by a bug called *Helicobacter pylori*, which can be cleared by specific antibiotic treatment. Before this, duodenal ulcers were assumed to be caused by stress and by being the type of person who worries and may be a workaholic.

In the same way, TB used to be associated with being introspective and/or artistic – this psycho-jargon was thrown out after the infectious cause was found!

Could poorly understood illnesses such as irritable bowel syndrome and rheumatoid arthritis be caused by infectious agents that have not so far been identified? There are a significant number of people who had classic symptoms of ME/CFS and who have recovered after long-term antibiotic treatment such as with doxycycline. Could these people possibly have had an infection, such as a mycoplasma or rickettsia, or unknown bacteria? And yet many people with ME/CFS do not respond to antibiotics, or else develop after-effects such as bowel dysbiosis (*see Chapter 13*). It is possible in some cases that the apparent initiating virus could merely alter the immune response and allow another organism to take hold, one which causes long-term illness and which has not yet been discovered?

'Absence of evidence does not mean evidence of absence!'

Biochemical Evidence of a New Low-molecular-weight Enzyme in CFS

Dr R Sudaholnik from Philadelphia and his team have published several studies which show a dysregulation in an enzyme pathway that controls viral infection.[29] This the 2-5A synthetase/RNase L antiviral pathway.

The earlier studies demonstrated that the RNase L activity is 'upregulated', as though fighting some infection. The most recently published study has identified a new low-molecular-weight RNase L enzyme, not identified previously, which was present in every one of 10 patients with CFS (diagnosed using the CDC 1994 criteria), and present in none of the 10 age- and sex-matched healthy controls.

Moreover, while all patients tested positive for the new enzyme, some patients, the less severely affected, also tested positive for the normal RNase L enzyme. Extracts from the most severely disabled people with CFS had only the low-molecular-weight enzyme.

Sudaholnik's study was sponsored by the CFIDS Association of America. In a CFIDS press release, Sudaholnik said:

'These findings are from a limited number of patients. However larger studies are underway and have financial support from the National Institutes of Health (NIH). The newly discovered enzyme, which has a lower molecular weight than the normal enzyme in this viral pathway, may explain common observations in patients with CFS:

    a) an inability to control common viruses (like EB virus and HHV6)

    b) an inability to maintain cellular energy.

The 2-5A synthetase/RNase L antiviral pathway may control both processes. This new enzyme in CFS may not function as well as the normal RNase L found in healthy people. It may explain why CFS bodies have a hard time maintaining the energy necessary for cellular growth.'

Although this discovery could be said to be a diagnostic marker for CFS, studies of many hundreds more patients need to be carried out before this test could be confirmed.

Explaining his study to Congress in Washington in May 1997, Sudaholnik said:

'The research in my laboratory is directed to understanding of natural antiviral defense pathways in humans. This is called the 2-5A synthetase/RNase L pathway. When all components of it are functioning correctly, the human body can effectively control virus infections. Several components of the antiviral pathway are not functioning properly in people with CFS. Specifically the system is upregulated (overactive) in people with CFS. The name of the molecule that drives this pathway is 2-5A. What does it do?

2-5A is the molecule that activates RNase L, the enzyme that degrades viral RNA. If RNase L is defective, we have a problem overcoming virus infections. We have tested samples from more than 100 people with CFS from across the country. Something new is going on with CFS. RNase L was overactive, unlike anything we have seen before, and we have already studied RNase L activity in people with AIDS, MS, lupus, T-cell leukaemia.'

A Belgian newspaper carried an article entitled 'Cause of CFS is found ... now there is scientific proof for the very first time: chronic fatigue syndrome is not in the mind but a serious disease instead.'

Dr Kenny de Meirleir, a Belgian co-author of the study, said

'Many symptoms – extreme fatigue, muscle pain, recurrent infections – can now be explained. If something goes wrong with the synthesis of proteins, the recuperation following exercise will be much slower .... Why do these enzymes overreact in certain individuals and why do they affect the RNA? The cause could be viral or genetic. More research is needed.'

The Onset of ME/CFS in Some People Is Gradual

Although the majority, maybe 70 per cent or so, of people report an acute onset of ME/CFS usually following a triggering infection, but sometimes an immunization or accident, what is happening with those people whose illness comes on gradually with no obvious precipitating event?

It is likely that various things can alter the immune system function, and either allow a latent virus to be reactivated, or else allow a new virus that does not produce a clinical infection (no fever, sore throat, etc.) to become established.

Things That May Affect the Immune Response

- Viral infections – such as glandular fever, hepatitis
- Acute stress, for example sudden emotional shock, trauma, accident or assault, or prolonged unrelieved stress. Psychoneuro-immunology studies the close relationship between emotions, the brain and the immune system
- Immunizations, especially hepatitis B
- Dietary deficiencies

- Environmental poisons, particularly organophosphates, which in repeated low-dose exposure can cause a chronic OP exposure syndrome (*see page 278*)
- Bowel infestations such as amoebic dysentery or *Giardia lamblia*. If chronic, these can damage gut immunity and lead to altered gut function. Diagnosis of *G lamblia* is difficult, and may involve a biopsy of the small intestine, or giardia-antibody in stool.[30]

Most people with gradual onset can remember a period of unremitting stress around the time they are first aware of symptoms. Also, in some cases there may have been a trivial initiating event some years back which has not seemed relevant, and subsequent symptoms of slight fatigue, depression, repeated sore throats or muscle pains may be ignored for some time, until eventually the person realizes he or she is ill and has to stop work or seek medical help. Whatever the mechanisms in slow-onset ME/CFS, the end result is a condition with identical symptoms to those of acute-onset patients.

The Immune System in ME/CFS

IMMUNIZATIONS

While there has not yet been any published research about the link between immunizations and ME/CFS, there is plenty of anecdotal evidence. Many patients can date the onset of their illness to a routine immunization, and it is speculated that one of the contributing factors to Gulf War Syndrome (GWS) was the large number of compulsory immunizations given to these Armed Forces personnel shortly before they went to war. Their 'shots' included some that had never been tested on humans, such as vaccination against anthrax. Immunizations stimulate the immune system to produce antibodies, and a combination would undoubtedly give a large stimulus to the immune system at a time of great psychological and physical stress.

In the UK, an increasing number of health professionals, mainly nurses, are reporting ME/CFS following administration of hepatitis B immunization, which is obligatory for employment with most Health Trusts. Even people who have suffered a reaction to the first dose are being ordered to have a second dose, sometimes with serious results. Dr Charles Shepherd, Medical Director of the ME/CFS Association, has been collecting reports of such cases, and now has more than 80 case reports. If anyone reading this book has become ill following hepatitis B vaccine, you can write to Dr C Shepherd, c/o ME Association (address Appendix A) with details of your case.

IMMUNE DYSFUNCTION AND ME/CFS

The picture of immune dysfunction in ME/CFS is confused, because various studies have found a variety of abnormalities in different patient groups, sometimes with conflicting findings. So far there is no one test of immunological function that is consistently abnormal in 100 per cent cases. It can, however, be said that all the research results taken together do indicate that there is immune dysfunction in some cases of ME/CFS.

US researchers Komaroff and Buchwald, in a review of all laboratory findings in CFS, have commented on the inconsistency of immune abnormalities:[31]

'In some studies, even those who meet the case definition of CFS may have been suffering from different illnesses in which fatigue is the common denominator. Tests are obtained at various points in the clinical course, a circumstance that makes it difficult to determine if abnormalities are transient or fluctuate over time.'

The authors summarized all the findings from all published immunology research – those most consistently reported are:

- depressed numbers and function of Natural Killer cells
- low levels of circulating immune complexes
- low levels of several autoantibodies
- altered levels of immunoglobulins
- abnormalities in number and function of lymphocytes.

The authors of a study in 1996, looking at symptoms and immune abnormalities,[32] found a positive correlation between certain symptoms (not specified) and immune abnormalities in 472 out of 505 CFS patients. The authors, in their conclusion to this rather complicated research paper, said:

'...in increasing numbers of CFS patients we find clinical signs and other symptoms beside the classical criteria of CFS. Our data confirm the hypothesis that a reduced or unstable immune control, or delayed immune reaction to persisting viruses, or bacterial pathogens ... possibly triggered by common infections or other environmental factors, can lead to a chronic neuro-immune activation state and auto-immune disorders.'

In a recent paper from the US[33] about a study which had looked at markers of inflammation and immune activation, patients were subdivided according to viral or nonviral onset, or the presence of fever. 'Our findings that levels of several markers were correlated points to a subset of patients with immune activation ...' the authors noted, yet they also revealed that there was no difference between the subgroups of patients – those with markers pointing to immune activation were not confined to the patients with viral onset.

A study by Dr Tan and colleagues from Seattle[34] found auto-antibodies to insoluble cellular antigens (part of the nucleus in a living cell) in patients with CFS. The wording of the paper about this study is extremely technical, but the authors said, 'The high frequency of autoantibodies to insoluble cell antigens in CFS represents a unique feature which might help to distinguish CFS from other rheumatic auto-immune diseases' (*see page 58*).

The practical significance of Dr Tan's research is that it explains why many people with ME/CFS after several years of illness have auto-antibodies found in blood tests which are suggestive of conditions such as Lupus (a chronic auto-immune disease that can affect many systems of the body, and causes fatigue) but do not have all the clinical features of these diseases. This can sometimes cause confusion about the diagnosis.

THE ASSOCIATION BETWEEN RHEUMATOID ARTHRITIS AND ME/CFS

Following an episode of some infection, a significant number of people develop joint pains, sometimes with swelling, along with other symptoms of a post-infectious fatigue syndrome, such as diarrhoea, fatigue and muscle aching.[35] Many such patients end up with a diagnosis of ME or CFS, but some ME patients have abnormal auto-antibody tests to diseases such as Lupus or rheumatoid arthritis. In ME/CFS, joint pains that move and affect different joints at various times are not associated with changes on X-ray nor with structural damage to the joints. There are a number of infections which are known to cause a 'reactive arthritis', such as Lyme disease, brucellosis, glandular fever, Rubella (German measles), campylobacter (a gut infection), hepatitis, dysentery, cytomegalovirus, and certain *E coli* gut infections, as well as an uncommon bug called yersinia. All of these can be identified by blood antibody tests, and some of them respond to antibiotic treatment. There is work underway in a London hospital at present that is finding an association between certain common gut bacteria and rheumatic conditions such as ankylosing spondylitis and rheumatoid arthritis. So in the case of people who meet the criteria for ME/CFS and who also have flare-ups of joint pain and swelling, it is very feasible that there could be a low-grade unidentified infection going on somewhere, possibly based in the gut. It is obviously important for anyone suspected of having ME/CFS who has persistent joint inflammation to be referred to a rheumatologist to see if treatable rheumatic disease is developing (*see also page 195*).

It is probable that, in some cases, arthritis results from a sensitivity reaction to an infectious agent, and that this abnormal immune response continues after the infectious agent has been cleared from the body. Auto-immune antibodies (which attack body tissues, not bugs) are present in some patients with ME/CFS.

ME and Other Auto-immune Conditions

Another auto-immune condition that has an association with ME/CFS is called Sjogren's syndrome (SS). In this, there is drying up of the tear glands and salivary glands, with resulting dry eyes ('sicca symptoms') and potential damage to the eyes. In a study from Japan,[36] one third of CFS patients had symptoms of Sjogren's, but did not have exactly the same blood immune profile as people with primary SS. So this is a further pointer to the fact that some people with ME/CFS have immune dysfunctions.

Studies on Muscles

POSSIBLE INFECTION IN MUSCLE

A number of research studies since 1989 have found enterovirus in muscle tissue, also in blood. There is still a controversy over whether this is significant, and whether it means there is a persistent virus infection in some ME/CFS patients. One problem is that enterovirus, or parts of a virus, can be found in a significant number of healthy controls. At a recent scientific meeting, Dr John Gow has said: 'We now think there is no persistence of enterovirus in muscle. Ongoing studies have shown enterovirus in 65 per cent of CFS patients compared to 40 per cent of controls, but there is no difference between [the incidence in] CFS and [in] various neuromuscular disorders.'[37]

(*See also Cytomegalovirus, page 48.*)

STUDIES OF METABOLISM IN MUSCLE

Studies have found:

- abnormal lactate response to exercise in a subset (32 per cent) of CFS patients[38] (*see page 147*)
- abnormal function of the heart[39]
- problems in aerobic work capacity[40]
- abnormalities in oxidative metabolism.[41]

All of these are described in more detail in Chapter 7.

Abnormalities in Mitochondria

Muscle biopsies from ME/CFS in general show non-specific changes under the light microscope. However, on electron microscopy it is possible to examine the *mitochondria*, which are the 'power houses' of all living cells.

The cells in the body which have the highest requirement of energy are in muscles and brain, so if there are defects in metabolism and energy production, this is where you would expect to see mitochondrial abnormalities. Mitochondria are tubular structures within the cell nucleus. Inside mitochondria there are 'shelves' which have on them molecular complexes (ATP) where energy is created.

Energy can be made using oxygen (aerobic pathway) or without oxygen (anaerobic pathway).

In the *aerobic pathway*, glucose is converted to pyruvic acid, which goes into the normal energy pathway (ATP) and – using oxygen – releases energy, carbon dioxide and water. The molecule that sits in the mitochondria and takes part in this is Adenosine Tri Phosphate (ATP). In the energy cycle, ATP is converted to ADP then AMP, then reformed into ATP again.

In the *anaerobic pathway*, if there is insufficient oxygen for the energy required, glucose is converted to pyruvic acid, which then leads to lactic acid and carbon dioxide, releasing energy in the process. However, the energy production from the anaerobic pathway is much less efficient, and oxygen is needed afterwards to restore the chemical 'status quo'.

In Glasgow, Dr W Behan and her colleagues have been studying muscle from ME/CFS patients. In 1990 the first paper was published about mitochondria in ME.[42] Muscle biopsies from 130 patients were examined by electron microscopy, and abnormalities were seen in functions, energy storage mechanisms and the appearance of mitochondria. Inside the mitochondria which looked abnormal there was a proliferation of the inner 'shelves', giving a honeycomb appearance and suggesting that in these mitochondria there is a greater need for turnover of ATP molecules, which indicates a problem with energy production.

Dr Behan's team have recently completed another study of

muscle cells from ME/CFS patients, looking at the metabolism *outside* the body.[43] They made a laboratory culture of myoblasts (muscle cells), then compared metabolism in these cells with those of controls who were healthy but sedentary and therefore would have unfit muscles. They measured the ratio of lactate to pyruvate produced by the culture of muscle cells. The results showed that a proportion of CFS muscle had abnormal metabolism, similar to that seen in mitochondrial myopathies, but also that many of the CFS muscles had normal metabolism, similar to healthy controls. The abnormalities in the subgroup were clear-cut and at a different end of the scale to the others. 'This confirms that CFS is heterogenous, and there is a subgroup who have defects in muscle aerobic metabolism.'[44] The significance of this study is that other factors which might affect muscle weakness in an ME/CFS patient – such as lack of motivation, depression or deconditioning – could not be influencing muscle cells in the laboratory.

Nuclear Magnetic Resonance (NMR)

In 1985 researchers at Oxford[45] demonstrated *early excessive acidosis* (excess lactic acid in muscle tissue) in the exercised muscles of patients with post-viral fatigue syndrome (ME), using Nuclear Magnetic Resonance, which assesses biochemical changes in tissues. Muscles of patients were tested during exercise, and there was early excess abnormal production of lactic acid.

The conclusion drawn was that there was a defect in the balance between two kinds of energy production. In affected muscle of some people with ME/CFS there may be too much anaerobic metabolism in comparison to the aerobic route, producing lactic acid. This could account for the muscle pain and severe malaise after exercise.

Electron microscopy had already shown an increase in the size and number of Type II muscle fibres,[46] which are the muscle fibres that use the anaerobic pathway, releasing lactic acid.

Other studies have found low levels of *carnitine* in CFS.[47,48] Carnitine is essential for mitochondrial energy production. In one study, higher serum carnitine levels correlated with better functional capacity.

Abnormal Protein Synthesis in Muscle
Muscle biopsies from ME/CFS patients were examined for RNA, DNA, and protein content. There was a significant 17 per cent decrease in total RNA per cell, and further studies demonstrated a decrease in muscle protein synthesis in some patients with ME/CFS.[49]. A reduced ability for regeneration of muscle fibres could be associated with easy muscle fatigue and delayed recovery.

A Recent Hypothesis That Could Explain Fatigue in ME/CFS.
A physicist at Glasgow has been studying heart muscle in people with ME/CFS who also have angina-like chest pain. Dr Walter Watson performed Thallium scans on hearts of 10 patients who met the criteria for CFS and who suffered from chest pain and breathlessness on exertion.[50] Radio-labelled Thallium behaves like potassium ($K+$), and concentrates inside muscle cells after entering the body. In a healthy person the Thallium can be seen on a special scanner and shows up in the main muscle mass of the heart – the left ventricle.

Patients with 'Syndrome X' have abnormal heart Thallium scans. Syndrome X is defined as when a patient has angina-like chest pains, possibly changes in the ECG on exercise, but has *normal coronary arteries* shown on a coronary angiogram.

Syndrome X has been investigated by a Swedish cardiologist, Anders Waldenstrom,[51] who found that the heart muscle cells have abnormalities in their cell membranes, which allow potassium to escape from the cell. Such gaps in living cell membranes are called ionophores. If a muscle cell loses potassium it is unable to function properly, and a lot of energy is wasted in pumping potassium back into the cell by the sodium/potassium ($Na+/K+$) pumps on the cell membrane.

In Dr Watson's study, 7 out of the 10 patients had abnormal Thallium scans, the scanner showing reduced uptake of Thallium into the heart muscle. In a further study carried out by a different team (at Glasgow Royal Infirmary), 7 out of 8 CFS patients who had chest pains had abnormal Thallium scans, and they found reduced left-ventricular output on exercise. So it is postulated that CFS has a cell-membrane defect similar to that found in Syndrome X. The cell membrane defects – ionophores – would be the same in skeletal muscle, also probably in the nervous system.

If the cell membranes have holes in, and the $Na+/K+$ pumps have to work extra hard to restore the balance of sodium and potassium within and outside the cells, you would expect to find an increase in Resting Energy Expenditure (REE). It may surprise you to know that REE accounts for 60 per cent of total energy used by the body, and that 20 per cent of resting energy is used by the $Na+/K+$ pumps in maintaining levels of intracellular potassium.

Dr Watson carried out a further study on patients with CFS, by measuring total body potassium and measuring energy output using a calorimeter, and discovered that in CFS the Resting Energy Expenditure is raised, compared to the REE in healthy controls.

Total body potassium values were also found to be lower in CFS patients than in other people.[52] The authors of this paper from Australia suggest that abnormal potassium-handling by muscle in the context of low overall body potassium may contribute to fatigue in patients with CFS.

In another study, mice were infected with Coxsackie B virus, and their heart muscles examined with electron microscopy and found to have ionophores in cell membranes.[53]

So far, several things have been identified that may produce ionophores in cell membranes. These include parts of viruses such as Coxsackie B, a part of a poison called ciguatera (found in certain poisonous fish in tropical areas),[54] local anaesthetics, and possibly some poisons such as organophosphates. Acute stress may cause similar ionophores in the blood-brain barrier, and this could result in the passage of substances from the blood circulation into the brain, substances which should normally not enter the brain. An Israeli doctor has done some research on the blood-brain barrier,[55] looking at Israeli soldiers who had been very stressed during the Gulf War. He believes that the passage of pyridostigmine, which all Armed Forces took as a precaution against OPs in chemical weapons, across the blood-brain barrier, could have been a factor for some soldiers developing Gulf War Syndrome. GWS is clinically very similar to ME/CFS.

Electromyography (EMG) on Muscles
Dr Goran Jamal at Glasgow performed electromyography on 40 patients with PVFS (ME) in 1989, and abnormally high jitter values (measurements of muscle fibre irritability) were recorded in 70 per cent.[56]

In a further study, single-fibre EMG was carried out on 10 patients, and all the patients showed abnormal jitter values.[57]

'A muscle membrane disorder, probably arising from defective myogenic enzymes, is the likely mechanism for the fatigue and the EMG abnormalities. This muscle membrane defect may be due to the effects of a persistent viral infection. [*The muscle membrane defect would now be called ionophores: see above.*]'

Muscle biopsies were carried out on these 10 patients. All showed abnormal findings:

'Single widely scattered necrotic (dead) fibres were identified. Size and number of Type 2 muscle fibres were moderately increased in all patients. Electron microscopy showed increase of mitochondria at the periphery of muscle fibres in all, while in 4 patients occasional bizarre tubular inclusions were present'

– that is, abnormalities of microstructures were found in muscle cells, suggesting a problem with cell energy metabolism.

Four of these patients had nuclear magnetic resonance (NMR) studies carried out (see above); all had positive results.

Dr Jamal has also published a study which included EMGs on Gulf War veterans, in which abnormalities in peripheral nerves and the neuromuscular junction were found.[58]

GAIT ABNORMALITIES IN ME/CFS
Because of the muscle weakness commonly experienced in the 'girdle muscles' which maintain posture – muscles of the thighs, buttocks, upper back and shoulders – many people with ME/CFS walk with an abnormal gait, maybe with feet further apart than normal so that slow walking looks more like 'waddling'. This abnormal posture and gait may also result from poor balance control.

A study from the Department of Physical Medicine and Rehabilitation in New Jersey[59] assessed gait during variable walking speeds, and running speed in 11 people with CFS and 10 healthy but sedentary controls. They looked at 13 different kinematic variables, including stride length and time, stride frequency, flexion of hips, knees and ankles, and width of stance. They found a significant difference in the time taken to run 30 metres, the CFS group being slower, and in the CFS group they found the type of gait abnormalities expected with balance problems, where patients have trouble walking at slower speeds and have to take shorter and wider steps to increase stability.

FIBROMYALGIA AND ME/CFS

Fibromyalgia is a chronic condition characterized by muscle pain, tender trigger points, stiffness and sleep disturbances. It has therefore some clinical features in common with ME and with CFS. In a study of primary fibromyalgia, only 7 out of 33 patients diagnosed as primary fibromyalgia fulfilled criteria for CFS.[60] It is probable that some people diagnosed as having fibromyalgia may have ME/CFS. However, some cases of fibromyalgia respond to exercise therapy, to local injections into tender points and to low-dose amitriptyline (a tricyclic antidepressant), which improves the sleep disorder. The sleep disturbance is a disorder of alpha EEG rhythm (part of a brain wave recorded during a sleep electro-encephalogram). Fibromyalgia symptoms may be mediated by cytokines, as is true for CFS symptoms.

A recently published study into the effects of an aerobic exercise programme on people with FMS (fibromyalgia syndrome)[61] found initial benefits after several months in terms of pain, energy levels and sleep. However, at four-year follow-up the initial improvements had not been sustained, and this confirms the clinical observations that FMS can be difficult to treat and the majority of patients suffer long-term disability.

A Molecular Basis in ME/CFS –
Abnormal Chemicals Found in Urine

Work has been going on in Australia for several years, looking at the excretion of chemicals which could be abnormal products of metabolism in patients with ME/CFS.[62]

A summary of this work appears in the June 1996 issue of *Perspectives* (ME Association quarterly magazine). Twenty patients with CFS were studied, plus 45 controls. Participants had early-morning urine samples screened by gas chromatography-mass spectrometry for changes in metabolite secretion. Also, all subjects filled in a questionnaire about physical and psychological symptoms and had full clinical examination. The urinary metabolites differed significantly in the CFS subjects compared to the controls. The three most significant metabolites were:

1. Chronic Fatigue Syndrome Urinary Marker 1 (CFSUM 1), identified as aminohydroxy-N-methylpyrrolidine
2. B-alanine
3. an unidentified substance which was called CFSUM 2.

These main three substances that discriminated between CFS and healthy controls were then assessed to see if they had a relationship with symptom severity as reported in the questionnaires. It was found that CFSUM 1 and B-alanine correlated positively with disease severity, whereas CFSUM 2 had a negative correlation – or in other words, more CFSUM 2 meant less severe symptoms.

CFSUM 1 in higher concentrations was associated with increased reporting of 10 core CFS symptoms, particularly low-grade fever and swollen lymph glands. The researchers found that the chemical structure of CFSUM1 is similar to that of a neuroactive drug which inhibits one of the brain receptors and alters neurotransmitter activity and the HPA axis. They also found some similarities between CFSUM1 and an important solvent used in the pesticide and pharmaceutical industry. This particular solvent, N-methylpyrrolidone, has been independently reported as producing symptoms similar to CFS if there is accidental exposure.

The researchers propose that CFSUM1 could be a product of an infectious agent, or of dietary or environmental origin. Whatever its origin, from outside or within the body, it is clearly a significant metabolite of something in people with ME/CFS that is not found in the urine of healthy controls. In these studies, CFS people could be distinguished from non-CFS people by their urinary excretion profiles, and this points to an alteration in metabolism in CFS. The researchers consider that these data do not suggest a psychological cause for CFS, although psychological symptoms can occur secondary to the illness. It is therefore important that this pioneering work in Australia should be investigated further, and replicated at a different research centre.

Abnormalities of the Nervous System in ME/CFS

The nervous system comprises the brain (central nervous system) and the peripheral nerves. Many functions may be affected:

- movement, sensation, balance, speech and sleep
- functions controlled by the autonomic nervous system – these include heart rate, blood pressure, temperature, sweating, blood flow to skin and other organs, digestion and all gut functions, hormones, and sleep
- mental (mind) functions, thoughts, intellectual activity, emotions, behaviour.

TESTS THAT MAY SHOW OBJECTIVE ABNORMALITIES

Brain Scans

Various kinds of brain scans can provide objective signs of brain disturbance.

One type of scan looks at *structure*, such as CAT (Computerized Axial Tomography) scans, or MRI (Magnetic Resonance Imaging), which can detect areas of inflammation or patches of demyelination (as in MS, by a similar technique to MR scanning of muscles).

MRI scans in ME/CFS have shown abnormalities in some patients, mostly found on studies in the US. For example, in one study[63] two neurologists compared MRI scans of 52 CFS patients with 52 controls who had head injury or headache. In the CFS group, 27 per cent had abnormal MR findings. On follow-up, a few of these patients developed another disorder.

The data in this study indicated that some CFS patients have an organic disturbance in the brain, but that those who have abnormal white matter signals (which give the little white spots that show up on the MRI) should be monitored for other medical causes.

The small spots of increased intensity, if present, tend to be situated in different places in the brain in CFS patients than in those with other neurological illnesses, however researchers in the UK found no convincing data that would make MRI scans useful in diagnosing CFS.

In another US study by Dr Schwartz and colleagues,[64] MR abnormalities were present in 60 per cent of CFS patients, and 20 per cent of healthy controls. And on the same group, SPECT scans (*see below*) were abnormal in 81 per cent of patients. The presence or location of MR white spots did not correlate with SPECT abnormalities in the CFS patients, so the researchers concluded that MR abnormalities may *not* be significant in CFS.

In the Lake Tahoe epidemic, 80 per cent of patients had brain MRI lesions.[65] In California, endemic (isolated) cases also were 80 per cent positive. These were compared with 21 per cent positive in healthy controls. Non-specific changes in the brain cause MRI spots as one gets older, and this has led to doubts about MRI findings in CFS patients. However, Dr Cheney looked at positive MRI scans in different age groups.[66] In ill teenagers with CFS he noted that 50 per cent were positive, which cannot be the norm in a healthy teenage group.

What is striking, looking at varying figures for MRI abnormalities in ME/CFS, is that figures were highest when a group of patients were tested who had been involved in a *localized outbreak*, and the MRI figures are also higher when the patients studied have been diagnosed with CFS using the stricter 1998 criteria (*see Chapter 3*), which exclude psychiatric symptoms.

However, with brain scans that demonstrate *function* rather than *structure*, abnormalities are more likely to be significant and robust.

SPECT Scanning

SPECT scanning is sophisticated technology that demonstrates the uptake of a radio-labelled substance that is injected into the bloodstream. The uptake of the test substance may depend on blood perfusion; various studies of the brain in ME/CFS have consistently shown abnormalities. However, abnormalities of brain perfusion are also seen in many psychiatric disorders, and it is important to understand that *blood perfusion reflects the function and metabolism of the tissue being looked at.*

The most striking study using SPECT on ME/CFS patients was published from London by Dr D Costa's team.[67] The CFS patients were compared with both healthy controls and patients with a diagnosis of depression. Although there were areas of reduced perfusion in both CFS and depressed people, there was a significant reduction of blood perfusion in the *brainstem* in the CFS group, not present in the healthy nor the depressed controls.

Papers from the US by Dr Schwartz and colleagues[68, 69] found areas of reduced uptake in 81 per cent CFS patients (*see above*), the most common sites being the lateral frontal cortex, temporal cortex and basal ganglia (the cortex is the layer over the surface of the brain; the basal ganglia are much deeper structures). In a study using SPECT to compare findings in patients with CFS, AIDS dementia, and major depression, abnormalities in uptake were found in all groups. The authors suggested that the location of abnormalities in all groups could account for the symptoms of cognitive dysfunction and depression, and that the defects on SPECT could represent dysfunction in the nerve cell – in cell membrane, cytoplasm or the nucleus.

They also found a similarity in the patterns of abnormality seen in CFS and AIDS dementia patients, and suggested 'a similar origin for the neurological dysfunction' in these conditions, and that their findings are consistent with a hypothesis that CFS could result from a low-grade chronic viral encephalitis.

SPECT scanning has also been carried out on children. In a recent study[70] abnormalities of SPECT were found in 13 children with CFS (1994 criteria; *see Chapter 1*) ranging in age from 7 to 18. Defects in perfusion were seen in various areas, but there is no mention of brain stem abnormalities in this study. It is possible that in many SPECT studies, the area of the brain stem is not specifically looked at.

PET Scanning

Positron Emission Tomography is another objective technique that looks at function, as it measures the uptake of radio-labelled *glucose*, which reflects metabolism.

In a study from Italy[71] 12 patients with CFS, who did not have any psychiatric disorder, had PET scans and were compared to 6 healthy controls and 6 patients with clinical depression. The results showed significantly low metabolism in the right frontal cortex and *also in the brain stem* of the CFS patients, compared to the healthy controls. Comparing patients affected by CFS and depression, the depression group had severely reduced metabolism in the frontal cortex, but none in the brain stem.

This PET study confirms the findings by Dr Costa's team (*see above*) that there is an abnormality of perfusion and metabolism in the brain stem in many patients with ME/CFS, not found in patients with depression. The hypothalamus (*see below*), an important part of the brain which is involved directly in the control of sleep and the autonomic nervous system, is situated in the brain stem.

STUDIES OF NEURO-ENDOCRINOLOGY IN ME/CFS

Of all brain abnormalities reported in the past 10 years, the most striking and consistent are those of *neuro-endocrine function*. Neuro-endocrinology is the study of chemical substances produced by nerve cells that act on other cells, also called neurotransmitters or, if they act on glands such as the thyroid, adrenal or sex organs, commonly know as hormones.

The studies undertaken so far show that the underlying disturbances originate from the *hypothalamus*, a small but vitally important part of the brain that lies at the base of the brain stem at the level of the mid-brain. In layman's terms, you could call the hypothalamus the 'mission control centre' of the autonomic nervous system. Neuro-hormones looked at so far are:

- **5-hydroxytriptamine** (*5-HT*, also called serotonin). This a very important neurotransmitter which is reduced in action and availability in moods of depression.
- **Prolactin, growth hormone (GH), dopamine, antidiuretic hormone (vasopressin)** – abnormalities have been found in the production all these brain hormones.[72,73]

A study of hypothalamic function by Professor Behan of Glasgow looked at water balance in ME/CFS:[74]

'One way of testing hypothalamic function in humans is to use a water loading test. ME patients, given a large volume of water to drink, cannot excrete the water via the kidneys as quickly as normal. Antidiuretic hormone (ADH), which tells the body to conserve water, is controlled from the hypothalamus. In many ME patients the hypothalamus cannot switch off ADH, so the body mistakenly keeps the excess water, leading to water retention. This may explain weight gain in ME. Studies of people with Irritable Bowel Syndrome found they also often had water retention, and the mechanism in women with PMT is the same.'

Behan went on to relate that some young ME patients had been seen with Parkinsonism, which usually gets better in a year. Iceland researchers also found a higher than expected incidence of Parkinson's disease among survivors of the 1948 Akureyri outbreak.

Some of the most clinically important studies have been looking at the stress hormone *cortisol* in ME/CFS.

The *hypothalamic-pituitary-adrenal axis (HPA)* is the system that controls the response to stress in humans. The first published investigation into cortisol and the stress response in CFS came from Dr Mark Demitrack and colleagues in the US,[75] who demonstrated an impairment of the HPA in patients with CFS, with mild hypocortisolaemia. This is due to a reduced production of cortical-releasing hormone (CRH) from the hypothalamus.

CRH acts on the pituitary gland, which releases adrenocortical-releasing hormone (ACTH), which acts on the adrenal glands to produce cortisol.

The adrenal cortex hormones are vital to life. A rare condition, Addisons disease, where the adrenals fail to produce cortisol, is fatal if untreated. It is rarely seen now, but used to be commonly caused by tuberculosis. Low adrenal function results in low blood pressure, weakness and fatigue, tendency to faint, low blood sugar, reduced sodium and water in the body, and collapse in response to stress. However, the symptoms of some people with ME/CFS do not indicate Addisons disease, and any reduction in cortisol levels are mild compared with true adrenal insufficiency.

However, the impairment in the HPA means that people with ME/CFS may be very sensitive to stress (*see Chapter 8*); this may explain the tendency to dizziness, sensitivity to slightly low blood sugar levels, and postural hypotension often experienced, especially when subjected to any physical or mental stress.

Further studies of the HPA in ME/CFS have been carried out in the UK by Professor Ted Dinan at St Bartholemew's Hospital, London, Professor Peter Behan from Glasgow, and their colleagues. They have shown a blunted response of the HPA and reduced 24-hour urine excretion cortisol levels in response to various challenges.

However, a placebo-controlled study trial of low-dose hydrocortisone treatment in the US[76] concluded that there were no significant benefits of cortisone therapy for CFS, and also that cortisone therapy, even in low dosage, suppressed the body's production of ACTH, which would dampen down the body's natural cortisone production and outweigh any possible improvement in fatigue.

THE AUTONOMIC NERVOUS SYSTEM AND BLOOD PRESSURE CONTROL

The first significant research paper on this found an association between 'neurally mediated hypotension' and CFS.[77] Patients with CFS responded to a tilt-table test by a drop in blood pressure, and were advised to increase salt intake, and some were prescribed fludrocortisone, an adrenal hormone that conserves sodium. At follow-up, 76 per cent patients felt improved. However, further work needs to be done to prove the possible role of fludrocortisone in CFS, and at the present time people with ME/CFS are advised they should *not* ask their GPs for fludrocortisone treatment.

A paper by Komaroff and Freeman investigated the role of the autonomic nervous system in CFS.[78] Various tests included the tilt-table test – 25 per cent had a drop in blood pressure – and recording the heart rate when lying down, sitting and standing, and a breathing test. Overall, the researchers concluded that 'CFS patients showed alterations in sympathetic and parasympathetic nervous system functioning' (these are the two nervous system pathways of the autonomic system).

ABNORMALITIES OF ACETYLCHOLINE

Acetylcholine (a.ch) is another very important neurotransmitter, both in the brain and in the peripheral nervous system. A disturbance in a.ch function in the brain could cause nausea, sweating, rapid heart beat, postural drop in blood pressure and sleep disturbances. Acetylcholine controls all the parasympathetic nervous system, and is responsible for REM sleep. A supersensitivity – or upregulation – of acetylcholine receptors on cells is present in depression.

Acetylcholine also regulates the production of growth hormone (GH). Deficiency of GH can lead to muscle weakness, among other symptoms.

Organophosphate insecticides paralyse, then kill insects, and in large enough doses can kill humans (*see page 278*). In chronic OP poisoning, acetylcholine receptors are affected. A study from Glasgow[79] tested patients with CFS and healthy controls; the same tests were carried out on 10 men who developed symptoms similar to CFS following a documented history of chronic OP exposure. A drug, pyridostigmine, which stimulates GH production via the a.ch pathway, was given to all subjects. Both the CFS and the OP patients showed an exaggerated response to pyridostigmine, compared to the healthy controls, results which suggested 'similar mechanisms involving the acetylcholine neuro-endocrine axis are involved' (in CFS and in OP poisoning). The research also pointed to an upregulation – or supersensitivity – of a.ch receptors on nerve cells.

In a further study in Glasgow, three tests of neuro-endocrine function were carried out patients exposed to OPs and on healthy controls.[80] The abnormal results in the OP group were the same as those found previously when patients with CFS were given the same tests, and Professor Behan noted that the symptoms of chronic OP poisoning are identical to those of CFS.

A drug, galanthamine hydrobromide, which might help some ME/CFS symptoms, is an acetylcholinesterase-inhibitor (that is, it inhibits the enzyme that breaks down acetylcholine). A treatment study of galanthamine[81] found an improvement in symptoms of myalgia, fatigue and sleep in over 60 per cent of CFS subjects. The most striking improvement was in sleep, however many patients had side-effects, especially nausea. These results support the theory that a cholinergic defect is involved in CFS.

Vestibular Symptoms

Quite a lot of people with ME/CFS report problems with balance – some so severe and accompanied by tinnitus (ringing in the ears) and vertigo that they are diagnosed with Meniere's syndrome. These symptoms are caused by a disturbance in the *vestibular* system of the brain, which is controlled by nerve centres in the brainstem which have connections to the eyes, ears, incoming sensations from joints and muscles, and to other parts of the brain. Some doctors dismiss these disabling symptoms as being psychological, however there are objective signs of vestibular dysfunction in some patients: for example, a simple test of balance with the eyes closed (Romberg test), or a specialized test looking at eye rotation movements.

A study of vestibular dysfunction in ME/CFS[82] tested 11 patients who met the CDC criteria for CFS and who had symptoms of dysequilibrium and/or dizziness. The tests measured vestibulo-ocular, vestibular-spinal and visual-vestibular reflexes. The abnormalities found suggested that the cause of the symptoms lies centrally in the brain, not in the vestibular nerves or any part of the body such as the muscles or joints.

Multiple Sclerosis and ME/CFS

Both MS and ME/CFS are neurological disorders, although ME also can have muscle abnormalities. ME/CFS patients may sometimes have neurological signs and symptoms which could lead to a misdiagnosis of MS, and some MS patients may be diagnosed ME/CFS in the early stages.

However, there are similarities and clear differences:

Similarities

- Peak onset at age 20–40, affecting women predominantly.
- Fatigue (central origin) and weakness – MS patients complain of severe fatigue.
- A variety of neurological symptoms which may come and go.
- Both can be precipitated by a viral illness or immunization.
- Emotional lability is common in both.
- Abnormalities in MRI scans, and cerebrospinal fluid can be found in both, though MRI abnormalities are different (*see below*).
- Diagnosis is essentially clinical, with most investigations proving normal.

• These illnesses tend to follow a relapsing-remitting course and become chronic.

Differences

• ME tends to occur in outbreaks or clusters as well as isolated cases, pointing to an infectious origin. Clusters of MS are rarely seen.

• ME has myalgia and arthralgia (pains in muscles and joints), MS does not have these.

• MS symptoms must be disseminated in time and space for a diagnosis.

• MRI abnormalities (small hyperintensive spots) are mainly periventricular (situated centrally in the brain) in MS, but (if present) subcortical (below the surface cortex) in ME/CFS.

• Sensory changes in MS are usually fixed, and take the form of numbness and/or pins and needles; in ME/CFS, the sensations are burning and move from place to place.

• Autonomic disorders commonly seen in ME/CFS (such as changes in sweating, gut function, hormones) do not occur in MS.

• MS typically has neurological symptoms that are backed up by objective abnormalities: double vision, nystagmus (jerky eye movements), paralysis of the eye muscles, abnormal reflexes, ataxia, brainstem signs, bladder and bowel sphincter problems. ME/CFS tends to have diverse neurological symptoms that are not backed up on examination.

• MS tends to affect brain, spinal cord and cranial nerve nuclei, but not peripheral nerves or muscles.

• MS does not have fevers, sore throats, or tender glands (Dr Charles Poser)[83].

Cognitive and Psychological Problems

Possibly the most crippling symptom, especially in the long-term patient, is the loss of intellectual abilities, collectively known as 'cognitive dysfunction'. This is what causes many people with ME/CFS to lose their jobs, and many young people to miss out on taking important school exams and going to college or to university. Physical disablement is hard enough but can be coped with; many other people with loss of function of limbs, even spastic quadriplegics, can function intellectually and hold jobs, compute, create and contribute some wage-earning activity to society.

When someone of normal or above average intelligence finds that their memory, concentration, comprehension, even speech is disturbed by this disease, is it any surprise that many are depressed and anxious? As well as cognitive dysfunction, emotional disturbance is common with ME/CFS, not only depression, but acute anxiety, 'panic attacks' and sometimes euphoria and mania.

Depression and anxiety are such common symptoms of ME/CFS that some psychiatrists reason that many cases that have been labelled ME or CFS may be suffering from untreated depression.

However, depressive symptoms are common in people with any chronic illness. A depressed person 'suffers from lowering of mood, reduction of energy, and decrease in activity. Capacity for enjoyment, interest and concentration are impaired, and marked tiredness after minimum effort is common' (from latest *International Classification of Diseases*). But this is not an accurate description of someone with ME/CFS, who is typically well motivated, enjoys things he is capable of and does not have sustained lowering of mood. Depressive symptoms are directly associated with exhaustion and feeling ill after exertion, and usually improve with rest. (*For more about depression in ME/CFS see Chapters 3 and 9.*)

A doctor who has an interest in psychological problems in people with medical illnesses has written:

'Diminished ability to think, concentrate or remember may be caused by an organic mental disorder, and are not useful symptoms for making a diagnosis of a major depressive episode in the medically ill. Since fatigue and loss of energy are so commonly caused by physical illness, these vegetative symptoms cannot be used to make a diagnosis of major depression.'[84]

An Australian study in 1990[85] carried out a range of psychological tests to compare 48 CFS patients with controls who had major depression. The pre-illness rate of psychiatric disorder was no higher than in the general community. In addition, the pattern of psychiatric symptoms was found to be significantly different to that of the depressed control group, and severe depression was rare.

The researchers concluded:

'There is no evidence from our well-defined sample to support the hypothesis that CFS is a physical variant or expression of a depressive disorder. Instead, our study supports the hypothesis that the current psychological symptoms of CFS are a consequence of the disorder, rather than evidence of antecedent vulnerability.'

In one survey of people with multiple sclerosis it is estimated that 'the lifetime risk of depression is 40–50 per cent, and that cognitive deficits are present in 60–70 per cent patients'.[86]

In another study of people with MS, it was found that increase in emotional disturbance coincided with increasing disease activity. Another similarity between ME/CFS and MS is that severe disabling fatigue affects 80–90 per cent of patients with MS.

And a study of cognitive performance in patients with MS, and with CFS, found that both groups of patients had similar difficulties with processing efficiency.[87]

TESTS OF COGNITIVE FUNCTION

A study in the UK in 1990[88] measured sensory-evoked and auditory event-related cognitive potentials in 37 ME/CFS patients and in 25 healthy controls. (A 'potential' means measurement of an electrical change in the brain, which results from a stimulus – sound, peripheral nerve, or visual stimulus.) There were no abnormalities in the sensory pathways of vision or sound in the ME/CFS patients. However, cognitive potentials which measured attention, and efficiency of information processing (identifying two different sounds, and responding to them) were abnormal in the ME/CFS patients. 'The abnormalities indicate attentional deficits in some patients and speed of information processing in others. The prolonged latencies observed in these patients have not been observed in patients with depression, in many other studies.'

A later UK study[89] assessed 57 patients with ME/CFS by a range of cognitive function tests, plus evaluation of symptoms and mood by questionnaires. The results found that CFS people had problems in attention, retrieving information from memory and psychomotor impairments, and were oversensitive to visual stimuli. The authors said 'performance impairments do not reflect depression, or any non-specific global impairment of cognitive or psychomotor function.'

Northern Nevada Epidemic Data

Following an outbreak in Nevada, US, various tests were carried out on brain function.[90] Cognitive function was impaired in 19 out of 20 patients. The most marked and frequent defects were in attention-concentration, problem-solving, kinesthetic ability and verbal memory.

MRI scans were done on 15 of these patients and 16 controls. There were abnormalities in *all* patient scans and one control. The researchers concluded:

'The striking distortion along with the abnormal results of MRI scans in these patients suggest a pathological process in the brain. The pattern of focal and lateral impairments is more consistent with that of an *atypical organic brain syndrome* than of anxiety and depression.'

A further study, entitled 'Cognitive function is impaired in patients with CFS devoid of psychiatric disease',[91] found that overall performance of patients was below normal, from a range of tests. The controls used were healthy people who did not exercise. The CFS patients were subgrouped into those with and without current or previous psychiatric illness. The presence or past history of psychiatric illness did *not* make the performance any worse.

In these and other tests of cognitive function, the main impairments were on attention, retaining new information, and short-term memory.

Electro-Encephalo-Gram

Dr Jamal (who did the single-fibre EMGs, *see page 64*) found EEG abnormalities in 85 per cent of 20 PVFS patients tested.[92] These changes suggested a patchy disturbance of cerebral function.

There have been many more published studies about the brain in ME/CFS than I have had space to write about. Much of the literature in the past six years on ME/CFS has been about the possible role of psychological factors in many cases of CFS. During the next few years there will be more evidence that CFS is multifactorial, and that not all cases are the same. It seems increasingly probable that the core clinical features of ME and CFS, namely abnormal severe fatigue plus neuro-psychological and cognitive problems, can be arrived at by different causes – post-viral, stress, immunizations, and exposure to environmental toxins, especially organophosphates – all resulting in the same type of syndrome.

The word *syndrome* means a collection of symptoms that gives a recognizable picture of illness. It also, in Greek, means 'similar roads'! So these differing triggers and causes would all appear to arrive at, by similar routes, a common place – chronic fatigue syndrome. Hopefully, ongoing research will explain the differences in the routes, and what is going on at the arrival places of fatigue.

Chapter 3

ME, CFS and Psychiatry

Back in the 1980s, the illness described by Dr Melvin Ramsay (*page 89*) was called myalgic encephalomyelitis or post-viral fatigue syndrome, and although there was a lot of ignorance about it, those that understood ME recognized it to be a chronic, potentially disabling disease. But the situation is now quite different. The medical establishment in the UK, and indeed throughout the world, has decided that the name ME is not appropriate and should be abandoned (*see Royal Colleges' Report, page 99*). The illness is now called chronic fatigue syndrome (CFS), and is seen by many doctors to be a mainly psychiatric condition.

The purpose of this chapter is to try and explain why there is at present so much polarization of views about the nature of ME/CFS, with misconceptions among doctors and confusion and anger among patients. Arguments in the medical world are about whether this illness is primarily psychiatric or is a condition with an underlying organic basis. Other comparisons used are 'physical or psychological?', or (in the tabloid press) 'a real illness, or all-in-the-mind?'! At the end of the day, these arguments are unhelpful to patients and can sometimes lead to mistakes in treatment. It is important to remember that the suffering of people with psychiatric disorders such as major depression or schizophrenia can be far worse than any so-called physical illnesses. An attitude that disparages psychiatric illnesses is cruel, and not worthy of people who live in an enlightened society.

But, sadly, psychiatric illness still carries a stigma, and people who develop ME have fought hard to get their illness taken seriously by health professionals, the Government and the general public.

It is no longer rational to try to separate mind from body, because we all know that the two are interdependent. Bodily disorders can have profound affects on mood and sleep, for example the secondary depression that arises from long-standing pain and disability. Conversely, disordered emotions can lead to bodily ills, for example people who are grieving over the death of a spouse are more prone to illness.

Medical research in the areas of neurology and psychiatry is finding increasing evidence of objective abnormalities in the brain in many illnesses labelled as psychiatric. A more useful word when referring to illnesses that have a proven 'organic' or 'physical' basis is *biological*. The medical specialities dealing with the brain, until now separated into *neurology* and *psychiatry*, are increasingly likely to be called *neuro-psychiatry*, or *neuro-endocrinology* (which means the study of chemicals and hormones involved in brain function). Psychiatrists may call themselves social psychiatrists, and be more concerned with the social, family and emotional aspects of mental disorders. Or they may specialize in biological psychiatry, looking at what is going wrong with brain function, for example neuro-endocrinology.

This merging of neurology, which was about the workings of the brain and nervous system, with psychiatry, which was about behaviour, thoughts and emotions, will hopefully mean that conditions such as ME/CFS, post-traumatic stress disorder and epilepsy will become better understood and more socially acceptable.

History of ME and CFS

NEURASTHENIA

In the middle of the 19th century, neurasthenia was a fashionable condition. It was described by Dr George Beard, a neurologist from New York, as a condition of nervous exhaustion.[1] He wrote:

'Even the slightest and most transient disturbances of the nervous system are the result of correspondingly slight morbid changes of the brain or spinal cord, or of the peripheral nerves. I admit that this view is speculative, but I feel assured that it will in time be confirmed by microscopic and chemical examinations of the nervous system.'

Proposed causes included hereditary predisposition and 'pressure of bereavement, business and family cares'.

He said that the diagnosis 'is obtained partly by the positive symptoms, and partly by exclusion'. Symptoms he described included:

'General malaise and debility of all the functions, weakness in the back and spine, fugitive neuralgic pains, hysteria, insomnia, disinclination for mental labour, severe attacks of headache, and at the same time gives no evidence of organic disease.'

The main treatment prescribed was rest, also '… all possible tonic influence on the nervous system – air, sunlight, water, food, rest, diversion, muscular exercise ...' He also advised nervous-system stimulants such as strychnine, phosphorus and arsenic, plus general electrization – the application of weak electric currents to the head and spine. (Perhaps a forerunner of electro-convulsive-therapy, still used for intractable severe depression?)

The point of describing neurasthenia is to show that a condition that resembled ME/CFS was recognized as an illness in the mid-1800s. However, by 1900 psychodynamic explanations were given to many symptoms that had been attributed to physical illness, as a result of the work of Sigmund Freud and others, and the science of psychiatry was born. Neurasthenia came to be regarded as a psychological condition, and went out of fashion.

EFFORT SYNDROME

During the First World War, many soldiers were invalided out of the front suffering with 'Effort Syndrome' – they collapsed, many suffered acute paralysing anxiety and became unable to sustain physical effort. Some were sent home to mental institutions. Effort Syndrome also had a shameful aspect to it: some soldiers were branded as cowards. Some medical historians now believe these soldiers had a form of neurasthenia.

ATYPICAL POLIO

Various outbreaks of an illness that resembled polio, but left many victims with a lingering condition that resembled neurasthenia, began to be recorded in the 1930s. The first such was 'atypical polio' in Los Angeles, 1934. Other outbreaks associated with polio were those in Iceland in 1948 and Durban in 1955. Recent studies of a new condition, *post-polio syndrome*, which has many clinical features identical to ME, have revived an interest in the possible association between polioviruses and ME.

MYALGIC ENCEPHALOMYELITIS

The names changed and evolved, such as 'epidemic neuro-myesthenia', and in 1956 Dr Melvin Ramsay published his first article in the *Lancet* about eight cases in the Royal Free out-break,[2] and called it *benign myalgic encephalomyelitis*. Dr Ramsay later dropped the word 'benign' after observing how disabling and protracted the illness became in many patients.

The illness Myalgic Encephalomyelitis first appeared in the non-medical press in the mid-1980s, although a few dedicated patients had already formed an organization in 1976 whose purpose was to provide information and encourage research (*the ME Association, see Appendix A*). Meanwhile in the US a simi-lar if not identical illness was called CEBVD (Chronic Epstein Barr Virus Disease), and was also highlighted in the media.

CHRONIC FATIGUE SYNDROME

The most significant name change came in 1988, and it is really since the adoption of a name that concentrated on only one symptom – *fatigue* – that the problems have begun. Many researchers believed that both CEBV and ME were incorrect names, since there was no evidence of persisting EB virus, nor of inflammation in the brain and spinal cord (encephalomyelitis). So, in the absence of a better name at that time, *chronic fatigue syndrome* was adopted at a meeting of doctors in the US in 1988.

The original working case definition for CFS (1988) required:[3]

1. the presence of persistent or relapsing, debilitating fatigue or easy fatiguability, in a person with no previous history of similar symptoms. The fatigue should be severe enough

to reduce daily activity to less than 50 per cent of the
pre-illness level, and does not resolve with bedrest. The
fatigue should have been present for at least six months.
2. exclusion of other conditions, including psychiatric disease and drug abuse
3. the presence of at least six of these symptoms plus two
physical findings (fever, sore throat, glands) or, if no physical
findings, at least eight of these symptoms:

- mild fever
- sore throat
- painful lymph nodes
- unexplained muscle weakness; muscle pain
- prolonged post exertional fatigue
- headaches of a new type
- joint pains
- neuropsychological symptoms
- sleep disturbance.

As you can see, many of the features specified by Dr Ramsay
are present in the CFS 1988 criteria – post-exertional muscle
fatigue, cognitive problems, muscle pain.

Then, in 1991, some British doctors who were not happy
with the American CFS criteria, had a meeting at Oxford and
published new guidelines about CFS. These are known as the
Oxford Criteria for chronic fatigue syndrome:[4]

- a syndrome which has fatigue as the main symptom
- the illness has definite onset
- the fatigue is severe, disabling and affects physical and
mental functioning, and is present for at least six months for
50 per cent of the time

- exclusion of medical conditions, organic brain disorders and certain psychiatric disorders: schizophrenia, eating disorders, drug abuse
- depression and anxiety disorder *are not exclusions*.

The Oxford criteria also allow a subgroup to be defined:

- *Post infectious fatigue syndrome:* An illness which fulfils the above criteria, developing after an infection which has been confirmed by laboratory evidence.

However, in practice this subgroup is not used or mentioned in research studies, which is regrettable, since many patients with CFS report a viral infection at the onset, and it would be useful to see if those patients whose illness is triggered by an infection have different characteristics from those with a gradual onset.

Now compare the Oxford criteria with the *cardinal features of ME*, as described by Melvin Ramsay:

1. Abnormal **muscle fatigue** after relatively trivial exertion, with prolonged recovery.
2. Various **neuropsychiatric** symptoms, loss of memory, concentration and comprehension, and disturbances of sensation.
3. **Variability** in severity of symptoms from week to week, day to day.
4. A tendency to become **chronic** over many months or years.

The Oxford criteria for CFS do *not* require the person diagnosed with CFS to have problems with concentration and memory, nor abnormal muscle fatigue or pain, nor fatigue made worse by exercise, nor symptoms that vary from day to day.

But the Oxford CFS *can include people with fatigue due to depression*, or stress such as athletic overtraining, or 'burn-out' from overwork.

Finally, a further modification of the US 1988 criteria was published in 1994 by Drs Fukuda and others[5] – these are, at present, used internationally for diagnosing CFS (*see page 108*). The main difference between the CFS criteria of 1994 and 1988 is that minor psychiatric disorders – anxiety, non-psychotic depression and somatization – are not exclusions when making the diagnosis of CFS. The resulting major differences in descriptions of the illness mean that research studies of CFS patients diagnosed using the Oxford or 1994 (Fukuda) criteria may include people who have stress, psychosocial or various psychiatric reasons for being very fatigued. This means that maybe only a proportion of people diagnosed CFS by these criteria have the same illness as that described by Dr Ramsay.

Many articles have been published about the incidence of depression and anxiety in people with CFS. The first influential one in 1991[6] stated that depression occurs in 50 per cent of CFS, and other minor psychiatric disorders in about 25 per cent. These figures led some doctors to believe that CFS is a psychiatric disorder. The apparent high incidence of psychiatric diagnoses in CFS results from two things:

1. having *many medically unexplained symptoms* can count towards a score for psychiatric illness
2. many of the symptoms required by the CFS criteria are also symptoms common in depression, such as fatigue, sleep disturbance, muscle and joint aches, and problems with concentration and memory

SOME OF THE CONSEQUENCES OF THE NAME CHANGE TO CFS, AND THE CURRENTLY USED DIAGNOSTIC CRITERIA

- CFS now covers a broader range of conditions causing fatigue, not only ME.
- Concentrating on one symptom – fatigue – which is part of everyday life, and is also present in many illnesses, has meant that many neurological symptoms and disabling aspects are ignored or denied.
- Including cases whose fatigue is due to depression, anxiety, stress or 'burn-out' dilutes (even disregards) the potential severity of some patients' illness.
- An *apparently* high incidence of co-existing psychiatric conditions in people with CFS has led to many problems for patients. Examples are: qualifying for Social Security benefits and ill-health pensions, because the illness is mistakenly perceived by many doctors and officials as being mainly psychiatric. Ill children are being forced to return to school before they are well enough to cope.
- Conflicting results in research studies, because different criteria are used and characteristics of patient groups used in research may not be the same.

Depression and CFS – Could They Be the Same?

No one can deny that many people with ME/CFS get periods of depression, anxiety and despair. But many other chronic illnesses induce depression, for example cancer, heart disease, multiple sclerosis, arthritis and Parkinson's disease, to name a few. I have already pointed out that some of the symptoms of ME/CFS are common in depression.

Another problem is that if a doctor already believes ME/CFS to be a psychiatric illness with no underlying pathology, then he or she will interpret the patient's symptoms as psychosomatic, including unexplained pain, muscle weakness and 'foggy brain'.

Symptoms ME/CFS Has in Common with Psychological Disorders

DEPRESSION
- Lethargy and fatigue.
- Sleep disorder.
- Inability to function.
- Problems with memory and concentration, brain-fog.
- Aches and pains in muscles.
- Feelings of sadness or hopelessness.
- Loss of appetite and/or weight change.

ANXIETY
- Shortness of breath.
- Dizziness.
- Diarrhoea.
- Chest pains.
- Panic attacks.
- Numbness or tingling sensations.
- Nausea.

However, there are clear differences:

ME/CFS Symptoms Not Common in Depression

- Fever or sore throat.
- Painful or swollen lymph glands.
- Muscle weakness.
- Post-exertional malaise.
- Muscle pains and twitching.
- Sudden onset with no situational cause.
- Neurological disturbances.

And the depression experienced is different:

Depression	ME/CFS
Low motivation	Motivated to do things
Exercise improves symptoms	Exercise significantly worsens symptoms
Low self-esteem	Self-esteem intact
Suicidal thoughts	Usually no persisting suicidal thoughts
Low mood constant for several weeks	Low mood lasts a few days
Patient underestimates cognitive performance	Patient overestimates cognitive capabilities
Memory not impaired by interruption	Memory impaired by interruption

More often the patient with ME/CFS experiences bouts of extreme frustration, because of not being able to do things, rather than true depression. The 'depression' may be a few hours' or days' uncontrollable weepiness, like an inconsolable anguish. This 'emotional storm' may be associated with sweating, malaise, increased pain and feeling generally awful, indicating that it results from general relapse. The weepiness and other symptoms may settle after a few days' rest (see also Chapter 9).

WHY ARE THE ESTIMATES OF DEPRESSION IN CFS ARTIFICIALLY HIGH, AND INCONSISTENT?

The incidences of depression and anxiety in CFS have ranged from 22 per cent to over 75 per cent in different published papers.[7] As already stated, the patient groups studied may differ in their levels of psychiatric disorder, depending on what criteria were used to diagnose their ME or CFS.

There may be other variables, for example whether the patient is in a stable state or a severe relapse; what the main symptoms are; the level of disability and impairment of daily activities; and whether the ill person has good practical and emotional support. It is really essential that future research on all aspects of ME and CFS uses clearly described groups of patients, and sticks to one set of diagnostic criteria, so that published papers can give consistent information.

But the rate of psychiatric disorder can also depend on what method is used to interpret the patients' answers. Psychiatric diagnosis does not depend on physical examination nor laboratory tests, but uses standardized questionnaires, known in the trade as 'tools'. There are many of these, for example an interview called the Diagnostic Interview Schedule (DIS) – a structured psychiatric tool developed in 1991 which has often been used to find out how much psychiatric illness is present in a sample of patients with CFS. The problem is that DIS was designed to be used in general community surveys, and not for medically ill people!

Another psychiatric tool is called Semi-Structured Clinical Interview (SCID), and this uses more sources of information than DIS to get a true assessment of a patient's problems. In an interesting experiment,[8] a sample of patients with CFS (1994 criteria) were assessed first using the DIS interview, and then the SCID.

The researchers found that 50 per cent got a psychiatric diagnosis using the DIS, whereas when the same group was assessed using SCID, only 22 per cent qualified for a psychiatric diagnosis. So whether or not you as a person with ME/CFS are judged to have co-existing psychological illness may depend on what test is used!

Another consequence of using the much broader criteria for CFS (Oxford and Fukuda) has been to increase the apparent incidence of CFS in the population. So much so that the prevalence of CFS using the original 1998 criteria was 7.4 cases per 100,000 population, whereas using the revised criteria (Fukuda 1994) the latest prevalence is estimated as 2,600 per 100 000 – or 2.6 per cent. If this were the case, every GP would have up to 40 patients with chronic fatigue syndrome on his or her list. This figure was obtained by doing a random survey of a general population, but the people who appeared to meet the criteria for CFS were not assessed medically to exclude other illnesses.

As with many changes in fashions, many of the influential opinions about ME and CFS have crossed the Atlantic from the US. Although in the UK doctors have been urged to call the illness CFS, there are rumblings of more changes in the US. Many patient support groups in the US are campaigning to get rid of the name CFS and to find a better one.

A well-known and respected CFS clinician and researcher from Boston, Professor Anthony Komaroff, when speaking at the ME Association's AGM in October 1995, said

'...I share your views on CFS, not only because it has become a waste-basket disease, but because fatigue is a universal experience, and it trivializes the illness. I think CFS is a terrible name, and I'm partly responsible for it. I would have said 5 years ago [1990] ME was a bad name because there was no evidence at that time of any inflammatory process of the brain or spinal cord. I actually think ME is getting to be a better name, but I'm reluctant to keep changing the name of this darn illness before we understand it better.'

PUBLICATIONS THAT HAVE INFLUENCED OPINIONS ABOUT ME AND CFS IN THE UK

THE NATIONAL TASK FORCE REPORT ON CHRONIC FATIGUE SYNDROME, POST VIRAL FATIGUE SYNDROME, MYALGIC ENCEPHALOMYELITIS (PUBLISHED 26TH SEPTEMBER 1994)

Early in 1992 the ME organizations asked the UK Department of Health to send guidelines to doctors advising on the diagnosis and management of ME. The Department responded by saying they did not have enough information and suggested a Task Force should be set up to investigate all aspects of the illness and to prepare a Report. The Task Force that resulted from this suggestion was set up on the initiative of Westcare (an ME charity based in Bristol). After preliminary meetings and applications for funding, the Task Force was formally established on 1st September 1993 with membership comprising 13 doctors with a wide range of experience and research into the illness. Medical disciplines represented were virology, immunology, general medicine, psychiatry, neurology, paediatrics, general practice, epidemiology, pharmacology and psychology. Advice and contributions to the final Report also came from many other doctors and from representatives of the patient organizations.

Although at the outset it seemed that agreement could not be reached from the widely differing opinions about ME and CFS, the Report was able to reach a consensus view on most issues, and to provide a balanced overview about these illnesses. The Chairman's foreword sums this up:

'We have tried to summarise areas of agreement, disagreement and ignorance and to express ourselves for the most part in plain and relatively non-technical language. Our report does not claim to be definitive; indeed we hope it will soon be superseded. Instead, we have written what we see as a temporary guide until research establishes or refutes the hypotheses involved and until better treatments become available.'

The TaskForce Report on CFS/PFVS/ME covers all aspects of ME/CFS, and is available from Westcare (155 Whiteladies Road, Bristol BS8 2RF; tel. 0117 923 9341) and costs £9.95 including postage and packing.

'CHRONIC FATIGUE SYNDROME': THE REPORT OF A JOINT WORKING GROUP FROM THE ROYAL COLLEGES OF MEDICINE, PSYCHIATRY AND GENERAL PRACTICE

This was published on 4th October 1996, largely as a response to the Task Force Report.

This 'Royal Colleges' Report' has received much criticism from patients and from some doctors, but it has also had a significant influence because it is supposed to be authoritative, representing the views of the highest echelons of academic medicine.

The Royal Colleges' report was *positive* in saying:

- *CFS is a genuine and disabling illness*: 'whatever label is chosen it is essential that the doctor accepts the patient's distress as genuine. No patient should ever feel their credibility is doubted. There is no place for such statements as "there is nothing wrong with you" or "it is all in the mind," just as there is no place for such statements as "you have ME – there is nothing I can do."'

- *it is often badly managed by doctors*
- *there is a need to improve diagnostic and management services*
- *it is poorly understood*
- *the syndrome has physical and psychological dimensions*
- *there is need for good research.*

The report is criticized because it:

- *does not describe the main symptoms.* It mentions fatigue, and depression, but any doctor who has never seen a case of ME/CFS would learn nothing about how to recognize a typical patient from this report.
- *fails to portray the potential seriousness* of the illness, and makes no mention of the severity and chronicity of about 10 per cent of patients
- *the selection of published studies quoted is heavily biased to psychiatry*, whereas good research on neuro-endocrinology, infection and muscle abnormalities is ignored or glossed over
- *management advice emphasizes the role of psychological and social factors*, and ignores possible biological abnormalities. There is no mention of subgroups.
- *recommends management should be by GPs*, but then says there is

no need to provide any basic guidelines about CFS to GPs!
- *the section about CFS in children* implies that the illness is psychological, and recommends that all ME/CFS children should be sent back to school
- *the report is complacent about funding for research*, which at present is all funded privately, compared to the US where Congress now takes CFS seriously and national funding for research has been granted.

However, the apparent psychiatric bias of the Royal Colleges' Report as a whole, with scant information about underlying organic pathology, is easier to understand when you look at the membership of the working group of authors:

Of 16 authors, 15 are doctors.

Of 15 doctors there are eight social psychiatrists, six physicians and only one GP (who is an academic). And, in spite of the clinical evidence that ME/CFS is an illness of the brain, there was no neurologist, nor neuro-endocrinologist. In spite of the frequent onset following infection, there was no microbiologist or immunologist in the group.

In summary, the conclusions and recommendations in the Royal Colleges' Report have done nothing to help the considerable problems still being faced by people with ME/CFS – the difficulties in getting a correct diagnosis, confusing management advice, hospital referral facilities, refusal of benefits and the management and education of affected children.

In some parts of the UK these things are worse for patients now than they were before publication of the Report.

People who have this chronic disabling illness, their relatives, support organizations and many GPs and paediatricians were extremely disappointed with this eagerly awaited report. We all hope that there will be a follow-up sequel from the

Royal Colleges in the UK in the next few years – one that
includes input from a much wider group of researchers and
also from patients themselves, and that this will provide a more
informative and useful view of the complexities of ME/CFS.

Subgroups of CFS

It is clear that in order to provide evidence of the underlying
biological abnormalities in most cases of ME/CFS, and to show
that there is much more to this illness than 'fatigue', we need
to see sound research into *subgroups* of clearly defined patients.
For example:

- some patients have symptoms of depression or anxiety,
  many do not
- some patients have abnormalities of metabolism, some have
  none
- some cases of CFS have no post-exertional malaise
- a few have involvement of the heart
- there are immunological changes in some, but not all cases
- the onset in some is post-infectious, others from immunization, yet others from pesticide exposure
- some cases have a gradual onset with no triggering event
- sometimes there are clusters or mini-outbreaks in a school
  or village, and yet most cases appear to be isolated.

What most people afflicted by ME/CFS really want is recognition that their illness is real and disabling, and deserving
of the same respect and care from doctors as people diagnosed with arthritis or multiple sclerosis. Second to that,
they would really like someone to find a cure! These things
are far more important to most patients than arguments about
pathology.

In the mean time, while scientists and doctors and patient support organizations argue, there is quite a lot that most people with ME/CFS can do to help themselves, plus some recently published therapies that can greatly improve some, if not all patients. The same fundamental principles of, firstly, diagnosis, then education about the illness, then self-help, also apply to people with MS and rheumatoid arthritis. Many other chronic conditions are still searching for a cure.

Case Study – Janet's Story

Here is another case history. The name has been changed but she told me her story only a few weeks ago.

Janet's story illustrates a case of severe and chronic illness. Her symptoms support the view of many people with ME that their illness is much, much more than 'fatigue'.

Janet was aged 34 with two teenage children and a full-time administrative job when she became ill. In 1989, she had had a flu immunization because she had a history of severe asthma and was vulnerable to getting chest infections. A few weeks following the flu jab she developed a bad virus infection, which was complicated by pneumonia, requiring hospitalization, steroids and antibiotics. After this she did not recover properly. She returned to work but had recurrent fevers, sore throats, enlarged glands and malaise. She struggled, with repeated time off, for three months, then had to give up work completely. She has never been able to return to work.

Over the next year her condition gradually deteriorated, with not only severe fatigue and malaise, but worrying neurological symptoms, including poor balance, numbness of the right side and tingling in her right hand, and stumbling gait. She also developed ringing in the ears and oversensitivity to sound. Her memory and comprehension deteriorated, so she became unable to read or follow a play on TV.

She had noticed strange episodes of tingling and numbness down her left side, even before this illness developed, but had paid no attention to them.

Although she had suffered from classic migraines before becoming ill, Janet now developed very severe headaches 'all round the head', with vomiting. She also suffered from painful muscle spasms in her limbs. Her sleep became worse and worse, so that she was basically awake all day and night, with only short periods of very disturbed sleep. 'My brain never switched off.'

Janet was thoroughly investigated by a physician, who diagnosed ME. After two years she started to have blackouts, and was admitted to a specialist neurological unit for tests. Various investigations (electro-encephalo-grams, MRI and SPECT scans) showed abnormalities in her brain function, but ruled out other conditions such as multiple sclerosis. The specialist said the abnormalities pointed to an 'organic brain disturbance' but were not typical of any known condition. She was also referred to a neuropsychiatrist for assessment, but cannot remember anything about what happened at that interview.

Over the eight years of her illness, Janet has had only one remission, which lasted from December 1996 until spring 1997. She has no idea what led to the improvement, during which time she no longer felt ill and 'poisoned' and could go for walks. Just as mysteriously she relapsed overnight, with no identifiable cause, and is now worse than at any time since 1989. In the early years of the illness she 'had a few good days, but the brain symptoms were the worst thing – I used to have a good brain, but I lost my memory, and used wrong words when speaking.'

Another unusual feature was that her periods stopped when she was 39, however blood tests did not indicate the menopause. During the short remission early in 1997, she had three normal periods, which have now stopped again. She continues to suffer from severe intractable insomnia, which has not responded to treatment with sedative tricyclic antidepressants – 'they made me feel very peculiar and even more awake', sleeping pills, or to being more active by day when she is able. But her worst symptoms at present are 'feeling horribly ill all the time, a lot of nausea, and severe pains in my legs and hands, as well as the headaches.' In 1996 she had all her mercury fillings removed, and felt a little better for a few months after, but this has not led to significant recovery.

Although she feels ill all the time, Janet tries to stay mobile, gets dressed every day and tries to get out of the house at least once a week. She feels the cold badly, and cannot walk far. She has also lost a lot of weight. She has the support of her partner (her children by now having left home).

Janet believes that past ill-health may have predisposed her to developing ME – 'I was very ill as a baby, I was born severely underweight and had to be in an oxygen tent. I had asthma for years, very badly, and had several hospital admissions requiring oxygen and huge doses of steroids. What is so strange is that since getting ME I no longer have asthma attacks.'

In spite of her ongoing illness and resulting disabilities, this courageous woman remains calm and accepting, and optimistic that things will improve. She also has a very supportive GP, who visits regularly and is prepared to try any treatment that might help.

Chapter 4

Diagnosis of ME/CFS

A diagnosis of ME or CFS is still based on taking a good history, and exclusion of other conditions which may give similar symptoms. There is, as yet, no one reliable laboratory test for CFS, although recent research is pointing to a few possibilities (*see Chapter 3*).

There are many people who read about ME and CFS in books or newspapers and then decide this is the reason why they feel tired. Such self-diagnosed people may in fact have something quite different and which could well be treatable. There may also be some people who genuinely suffer from the condition, but are afraid to seek a proper diagnosis in case they are dismissed by the doctor as having 'an imaginary illness'. Yet others may even have the classic symptoms but decide they just need more 'true grit' and push on with their lives until they collapse.

It is really important that if you, or anyone you know, has symptoms of fatigue severe enough to disrupt daily life, you or they go to a doctor to find out what is wrong. If your GP is unsure or is unfamiliar with the features of ME/CFS you should be referred to a specialist who understands this type of illness.

A proper diagnosis is really essential.

Why?

- Other conditions confused with ME or CFS may be treatable. You may not have ME/CFS at all.
- You need a diagnosis in order to apply for time off work or a change to part-time work, to apply for Social Security benefits, home help, retirement pension, etc.
- If you are at school, you need the diagnosis to allow you to rest at home when ill, without your parents being prosecuted for your non-attendance. (Yes, this does happen to parents of children with ME/CFS, hopefully less often now that the illness is better recognized.)
- You need to know if you have a genuine illness in order to stay sane. To be told that you are really ill, and not inadequate or lazy, is a wonderful relief and may save some from suicide.
- Through knowing what is wrong you can start to reorganize your life, come to terms with the illness and plan for recovery.
- Getting a diagnosis is, for many, the starting point of improving. Battling on in ignorance of the problem is a sure way to get worse.
- You need all the support and understanding you can get. It is hard for your doctor, family and friends to supply this when they do not realize that you are really ill.
- Through getting a diagnosis you can be put in touch with other patients through self-help organizations.
- If you have *not* got ME/CFS, you will be very glad to know it.

The diagnosis is made on the history, and lack of objective signs of other disease. There are sometimes abnormal signs on physical examination, and there are a number of laboratory tests which may help confirm the diagnosis – but which, if normal, do not rule out ME/CFS.

A list of symptoms typical of ME is given in Chapter 1. The cardinal symptom is fatigue, unrelieved by rest, made worse by exercise.

These days most doctors prefer to use the term CFS, and certainly for purposes of qualifying for pensions, or in legal disputes, or in research studies, the diagnosis needs to based on the following criteria:

DIAGNOSTIC CRITERIA FOR CHRONIC FATIGUE SYNDROME (FUKUDA *ET AL.* 1994)

Major Criteria

- Unexplained, persistent, or relapsing chronic fatigue that is of new or definite onset (not lifelong).
- Fatigue is not due to ongoing exertion.
- Fatigue is not substantially alleviated by rest.
- The fatigue results in substantial reduction in occupational, educational, social or personal activities.

Minor Criteria – at least four of these should be present

- Self-reported impairment in short-term memory or concentration severe enough to cause substantial reduction in occupational, educational, social or personal activities.
- Sore throat.
- Tender cervical or axillary lymph nodes.
- Muscle pain.
- Multi-joint pain without joint swelling or redness.
- Headaches of a new type, pattern or severity.
- Unrefreshing sleep.
- Post-exertional malaise lasting more than 24 hours.

Exclusion of Other Medical Illnesses, including Drug or Substance Abuse, and Major Psychiatric Illness

For a diagnosis to be made, the case must fulfil all the major criteria plus four or more of the minor criteria. Each minor criterion must have persisted or recurred during six or more consecutive months of illness and must not have predated the fatigue.

When you go to your doctor, or to a specialist, do prepare some sort of history of your illness in writing, in advance. Write down:

- when you last felt well
- all infectious illnesses you have had, especially any that occurred around the time of onset of symptoms
- anything else that happened to you just before the onset
- if anyone in your family or work circle was ill at the same time, and if any of them developed symptoms of ME/CFS
- your main symptoms that bother you now
- if the symptoms have been constant, or intermittent
- how your illness has affected your lifestyle – work, family life, income, social activities
- how much exercise you could take when you were well, and what you can do now without ill-effects
- anything that seems to make you better.

This preparation will help the doctor, and save you from forgetting important information at the time of consultation – most people with ME/CFS have a bad memory which is worse when under cross-examination!

If possible, take with you a relative or close friend who knows you very well, and who can add his or her observations about any changes in you since the illness, should your mind become a blank.

If your illness has begun shortly after a viral infection (sometimes up to six weeks later), and you have classical symptoms, then the diagnosis is fairly easy. It is much more difficult in someone who has become unwell gradually, with no obvious precipitating infection. For these people it is especially helpful to try and remember past infections or bouts of unwellness, which may be as seemingly trivial as a 24-hour tummy bug while abroad.

If your doctor tells you he or she does not believe that any illness called ME or chronic fatigue syndrome exists, you should remind him or her of the Report on chronic fatigue syndrome that was published by the Royal Colleges in October 1996 (*see page 99*).

Your doctor will enquire about childhood illnesses, previous health, operations and drugs taken, especially antibiotics. Also about the health of your parents and siblings, and family history of allergies, undue infections, or ME-type illness.

A full physical examination should be carried out, including blood pressure, examination of heart, lungs and abdomen, a search for enlarged glands, and tests of neurological function and muscle power.

There is rarely extreme muscle wasting, but there may be some loss of muscle bulk, especially of the thighs. This is usually symmetrical. Objective tests of the nervous system (neurological tests) will usually prove normal.

Simple tests of muscle power may also prove normal. However, if muscles are exercised – such as the patient squeezing a rubber ball for one minute, or being sent to climb 40 steps (if able), the muscles used may be found to be weak, the weakness lasting several hours or several days.

Muscle tenderness is common, and fingertip feeling of the thigh or upper back (trapezius) muscles often finds points of great tenderness. These are called trigger points, and are also typical of the related condition – fibromyalgia.

A key factor in arriving at a diagnosis of ME or CFS is the exclusion of other diseases which might be causing fatigue. Briefly, these would include chronic infections, endocrine diseases, nervous system disorders, cancer, muscle diseases, auto-immune disorders and primary psychiatric illnesses. However, the presence of symptoms of mild depression or anxiety may not count.

There are a number of blood tests which should be carried out, as well as urine testing, and then possibly more specialized investigations to exclude other conditions (*see Appendix B*). However, muscle biopsies, electromyograms and brain scans are *not* routine tests, but may be used as part of some research programme.

Some Conditions That May Be Confused with ME/CFS

- Fibromyalgia.
- Myesthenia.
- Early auto-immune disorders such as rheumatoid arthritis, lupus, Sjogren's.
- Multiple sclerosis.
- Major depression.

FIBROMYALGIA SYNDROME (FMS)

Fibromyalgia is another condition where the causes and patho-logical processes are poorly understood. Its main symptom is muscle stiffness and pain, with acute tenderness at focal points called 'trigger points'. These are often where a muscle joins a tendon, and there are classical places for these trigger points, used when making the diagnosis. Many people with fibromyalgia see rheumatologists with an initial diagnosis of arthritis. People with fibromyalgia also get very exhausted, and tend to have poor sleep with frequent waking.

There is said to be a significant incidence of psychiatric disorder in FMS, mainly major depression, however the figure is probably no higher than is seen in rheumatoid arthritis.

The increased sensitivity to pain may be partly caused by disturbance of sleep, with a relative lack of the restorative type of sleep.

However, fibromyalgia differs from ME in some respects – it does not have the post-exertional muscle weakness and malaise, muscle twitching, the marked cognitive dysfunction, or sore throats and tender glands that you see in ME and CFS, nor does it usually have a clear post-viral onset. Some doctors believe fibromyalgia is a form of chronic fatigue syndrome, while others make a clear differentiation between them. The treatment for fibromyalgia is graded exercise plus low-dose tricyclic anti-depressants at night. Some patients do well on this regime, but many do not, and remain disabled by pain and fatigue for years.

ARTHRITIS AND OTHER SOFT TISSUE DISORDERS

Many people with symptoms of ME/CFS have pains in muscles, joints and other soft tissues. Sometimes the early stages of rheumatic conditions can be mis-diagnosed as ME or CFS. If there is any doubt, blood tests usually rule these out, but an opinion from a rheumatologist may be needed.

MYESTHENIA GRAVIS

This is an uncommon auto-immune disease of muscle, in which there is a fault at the neuro-muscular junction with a chemical called acetylcholine. The reason it could be confused with ME is that in myesthenia there is severe exercise-induced weakness. The earliest symptom may be of double vision caused by weakness of the eye muscles, then patients get weakness of the limbs and of the muscles used for chewing, and even loss of voice. However, myesthenia can be diagnosed by specific tests, and can be successfully treated, using a drug called pyridostigmine which inhibits the enzyme that breaks down acetylcholine – that is, pyridostigmine is an anticholinesterase inhibitor, the same drug given to troops in the Gulf War to counter the effects of organophosphates in nerve gas (*see page 278*).

At present, a study is under way in the UK that is finding evidence of a problem in peripheral acetylcholine transmission, and this could explain why some patients with ME, who have severe muscle fatiguability, appear to have an overlap with myesthenia.

MULTIPLE SCLEROSIS

The similarities and differences between ME/CFS and MS are discussed in Chapter 2.

DEPRESSION

Although superficially some people with ME/CFS may appear to be suffering primarily from a depressive disorder, there are usually clear differences. A full discussion about the overlap and pitfalls of misdiagnosis of ME as depression can be found in Chapter 3.

Some doctors, especially hospital specialists, are now including a psychiatric assessment as part of the overall process of diagnosing a patient with severe fatigue. If you have symptoms suggestive of a depressive illness or anxiety disorder as well as severe fatigue, then exclusion of a treatable psychiatric condition is obviously sensible. In certain cases, for example applications for occupational pensions, when a documented thorough assessment of the applicant is required, a psychiatric opinion may be mandatory, in addition to the usual investigations.

My personal experience is that most psychiatrists are familiar with ME/CFS, and can provide support and understanding to a condition for which there is no quick treatment or cure! Since psychological problems tend to develop with most chronic illnesses, it can be very helpful for an expert to 'tease out' and separate secondary issues from the original illness. It can also be very reassuring for an ill and possibly confused person with ME/CFS to be told 'you are basically sane, but you do have a disabling and distressing illness which is making your life miserable' or something along those lines. And, if there is a component of depressive illness, of if the psychiatrist decides that most of the symptoms are due to a depressive disorder, this can be treated.

Do remember that a psychiatric appointment allows much more time with the doctor than is usually given by a GP or any other speciality, and that psychiatrists are trained to listen to their patients. I think it is a pity that there is (natural) reluctance on the part of people with ME or CFS to have anything to do with psychiatrists, because of the perceived stigma of possibly having a 'mental' illness. If you had heart symptoms, or bad gut problems, with ME, would you object to seeing a cardiologist or a gastro-enterologist?

Once a doctor has seen a patient with ME/CFS, the symptom picture is not forgotten. It is fair to say that many doctors are unsure about recognizing the illness, or even believing in it, until they know one of their patients, one of their family or a colleague who develops it; this experience usually dispels any scepticism.

Under the Patients' Charter, you have a right to a second opinion if your GP does not believe in a diagnosis of ME or CFS. One problem is that referral outside your health district costs money, and most Health Trusts are reluctant to pay this unless they can be convinced it is the interest of the patient. Such a referral outside your area is called an ECR (extra-contractural referral).

The differential diagnosis of ME/CFS, and a suggested routine of investigations, are given in Appendix B; this may be of interest to doctors and other health workers.

Chapter 5

Plan of Management

You cannot go to your doctor and come away with a prescription for a drug which will cure ME/CFS. However, for most people the illness does gradually improve over a period of time, but there is no 'quick-fix'. It seems that those who rest early in the illness have a better chance of recovery, although this theory has not been tested statistically.

Present estimates are that about 20 per cent of people diagnosed with ME or CFS recover within two to three years. The majority of patients make a partial recovery, then live for many years with energy levels that may vary and with some restrictions on exercise capability. This is an illness which usually has ups and downs, and if you can learn to manage your life within your limits then you are unlikely to stay at your worst all the time. There is a difference between the 'recovery' that means complete and lasting cure and a return to all pre-illness activities, and the 'recovery' that means getting back to some sort of satisfactory life, while still having the symptoms of ME/CFS for some or all of the time.

Many people with other chronic disabling conditions manage to start living again by making adjustments and adaptations in daily life. It may not be possible to go back to work full-time to the pre-illness job, nor to return to playing football or climbing mountains, but the secret of recovering a satisfying life is to maximize what you can do, and to let go of what you can no longer do.

There are broadly three categories to describe the course of the illness:

1. a minority, roughly 20 per cent, gradually get better, then stay better. This is most likely to happen within two years. These people make a 'full recovery'.
2. the majority, about 60 per cent, have remissions and relapses (the remissions may last for several years), but never seem to shake the disease off permanently. They can be said to make a 'partial recovery', for example to about 60 to 70 per cent of pre-illness function, and many manage to work part-time and/or run a household, but still have ME symptoms for a lot of the time.
3. a small number, about 20 per cent, have no remissions and remain disabled for years.

Prognosis is the medical term used to try and make a prediction of the likely course of an illness in an individual. One of the problems for someone diagnosed with ME or CFS is to predict the prognosis. Why do some lucky ones recover in a few years, while a few become severely and chronically ill?

Early in 1996, a group of doctors who all had experience of people with ME and CFS got together to discuss what factors might influence the prognosis. This Expert Group was convened to advise the Chief Medical Adviser of the UK Government Department of Social Security about prognosis and chronicity in CFS. Although there were inevitably some differences of opinion over the main features of the illness and the best course of management, some potentially useful conclusions were reached:[1]

'Chronic fatigue syndrome is a complex condition which is not fully understood ... Because of this, it is not possible to define concrete sets of favourable or unfavourable prognoses in each case there often be conflicting favourable and adverse factors interacting to determine the overall outcome.'

GOOD PROGNOSIS
- A definite history of acute viral illness, with no previous psychological disorder.
- Clinical features showing a tendency to recovery.
- Early diagnosis, which eliminates other disorders and identifies treatable psychiatric disorder.
- A management regime which addresses physical, psychological and social issues.
- A management regime which strikes a balance between overactivity and deconditioning, works towards functional improvement, and deals with maintaining factors such as sleep disturbance or depression.

POOR PROGNOSIS
- A gradual onset with a background of psychological and factors.
- An onset following a severe infection, e.g. meningitis.
- Severe and unremitting symptoms for more than four years.
- Delayed diagnosis or self-diagnosis.
- A management regime which overemphasizes too much rest, or too rapid return to activity, or does not treat any associated psychological or sleep disturbances.

So far, no research study has shown any proven factors in prognosis, however there are various factors, known from the experience of patients over many years, which can clearly influence outcome:

- age
  - children and young people under 20 have a better chance of good recovery, even though the illness can be very severe in teenagers

- length of illness
  - once a person has had symptoms for four years or longer, with no improvement, the likelihood of recovery is poor

- type of illness
  - those who have severe symptoms, with muscle pains plus neurological symptoms, may be more likely to become chronically affected

- onset
  - people with a gradual onset, with psychiatric symptoms as well as fatigue, have less chance of remission or recovery, unless the psychological part of the illness is treated or improves. Those whose illness is triggered by severe infection (e.g. meningitis or encephalitis) or a vaccination, especially hepatitis B, or acute organophosphate exposure, tend to do badly.

- social factors
  - lack of personal and emotional support may predispose to secondary depression and low self-esteem, which can inhibit recovery

- ongoing stress from family or relationship problems may prevent recovery
- financial hardship causes stress (anxiety over bills, etc.) and may force the patient to be too physically active – e.g. not being able to pay for help with shopping and cleaning, and thus preventing proper pacing of energy

- management of the illness
  - late diagnosis may result in the patient trying to fight the condition by inappropriate exercise, or to struggle on at work and become more ill. Too much bed rest for too long and complete lack of activity can result in problems in rehabilitation. Any co-existing depressive disorder that is untreated will delay or prevent improvement.
  - inappropriate exercise programmes at the wrong time can lead to demoralization and worsening of symptoms, especially in patients with predominant muscle symptoms.

One of the characteristic features of ME/CFS is the tendency to relapses and remissions – or, if you prefer, flare-ups and improvements. Very often these appear to be completely unpredictable. Sometimes a relapse can happen after years of apparent recovery. So what causes relapses, and what factors are known to maintain the illness?

An event that can trigger the onset can also be something which triggers a relapse.

Things that can bring on a relapse:

- too much physical activity on one day, or sustained over several days
- getting a new infection – for example a cold, tooth infection or a urine infection

- an emotional shock such as a family row, sudden bereavement, or arguments at work
- mental overwork and stress, for example if preparing for exams
- a major life stress such as divorce, bereavement, moving house (which is also physically exhausting)
- sudden climatic change
- physical trauma, such as a car accident, surgery
- immunization
- exposure to chemicals such as organophosphates (OPs) or new paint (*see Chapter 14*).

Apart from relapses and remissions along the way, there may be other, perhaps more subtle and continuous factors which keep the illness going, which are not so obvious.

Maintaining factors – things that may prevent overall recovery:

- continuing overactivity – not being able to rest when necessary to replenish energy
- too much bed-rest after the acute stage. This can lead to loss of muscle tone, unfitness, weakness of heart and circulation, dizziness on standing and an inability to start any exercise without bringing on symptoms
- sleep disorder – inability to get to sleep, repeated waking up, poor quality sleep, with nightmares, reversed sleep pattern with sleepiness in the day
- on-going exposure to chemical pollution (*see Chapter 14*)
- poor diet, or untreated food allergies
- social isolation, loneliness, depression or despair, which may result from being housebound or living alone
- on-going emotional stress – at home, at school, or at work

- lack of emotional and/or practical support. This may be a cause of overactivity.
- financial worries.

Some of the things on these lists may be unavoidable, but you can do something about many of them. While I do not subscribe to a fashionable 'New Age' belief that it is possible to cure every illness if you adopt the correct way of thinking, I do believe that emotions and thoughts can influence what happens in our bodies. It is known that any physical illness can be made worse if the person is also depressed. Although it is not a scientifically proven fact, I am sure that the experience of being unloved and unvalued as a human being can contribute to a lot of ill-health in our modern society. If you are a person who has always cared for others and given out a lot of love at the possible neglect of yourself, you may have become more vulnerable to developing depression, exhaustion, or ME/CFS. A useful word for such a person is 'depleted' – of both emotional and physical energy. Such a person may also be more susceptible to infections and other illnesses.

So it is extremely important that someone who has been diagnosed as ME/CFS should try and restore depleted energy, especially during the acute stage of the illness. When you are ill you need to spoil yourself a bit, to give yourself those good and natural things you would wish for a loved one. Part of this may involve finding ways to improve self-esteem, and if love is not forthcoming from family or friends, then an ill person has to find it in himself or herself. It is not always realistic to expect other people to provide total practical and emotional support. With this illness it is no good lying back and waiting for a cure.

Keeping a Diary

If you want to be able to monitor your illness, get some clues about what causes relapses and look at your progress over a period of time, then I strongly advise you to keep a diary. This can be updated each week, but recording something each day is better (this makes it easier to spot possible cause-and-effect connections). It is useful to record: Times of waking up, getting up, activity in morning, time of lunch, activity in afternoon (including sleep or bedrest), time of evening meal, activities of evening, time of going to bed; also the sort of night you had, and how ill or well you feel on a scale of, for instance, 1 to 5. There are other things to record, depending on what seems important, such as emotions, energy levels, muscle pain, appetite, symptoms such as nausea, migraine, sore throat, etc. If you suspect you have food allergies, then a diary of what you eat and drink at each meal is obviously going to be helpful. It may not be easy to make a connection between an event or eating something, and new or worse symptoms two days later, without keeping a diary.

Another good reason for keeping a record over a period of months is that it is hard to remember exactly how you were six months ago, and while there may be ups and downs the general trend is more likely to be one of very gradual improvement, which will only become obvious when you refer back to the diary.

The decision to keep a diary is an individual one. If you are too ill to write, perhaps your carer can keep some sort of a record for you.

The aim of any plan of management should be to encourage the body to mobilize its own healing forces. We have an amazing capacity for healing and repair of damage in our bodies;

unfortunately, for all sorts of reasons this healing force is often suppressed by the sorts of things listed above.

Your state of health results from the balance between things that decrease your healing energy and those things that promote recovery.

Energy

Having ME/CFS has been likened to being a battery that cannot hold its charge. The battery may appear to be fully charged, but the light becomes dim very quickly when the torch is used. Another analogy I find helpful is to compare your store of energy to a bank account. When you are in overdraft (negative bank balance) you cannot spend energy or money without increasing the overdraft. When your bank balance is positive (or 'in the black' as opposed to 'in the red'), you may feel confident about spending money.

But if your bank balance, though positive, is only £50, not £500, then spending money rashly quickly puts you back into overdraft. If you then continue to spend money, the day will come when your bank stops issuing you with any. Similarly, if with ME/CFS one day you feel better, and think you have a lot of energy, so go out and spend the little you have, you will quickly be exhausted. If you overspend your energy day after day, your body will eventually call in the overdraft and you may go into serious relapse and be unable to move.

In planning a strategy for learning to live with ME/CFS and eventually recover, it is best to do it in stages and have an order of priority. In deciding how much to rest or how much to increase activity, it may be useful to consider what stage of the illness you may be in. Dr Alan Franklin, a paediatrician, has suggested three stages:[2]

Stage 1 – Toxic stage – symptoms severe or increasing. The patient feels ill all the time. Common symptoms are muscle pain and twitching, nausea, sweating, flu-like malaise, weakness, sore throat, sleeping most of the time. Any attempt at exercise is difficult or counterproductive.

Stage 2 – Convalescent – still some symptoms but the patient does not feel ill all the time. Activity can be increased, but with great caution. It is at this stage that many people with ME/CFS feel better, then go and do too much too quickly. A minority of patients may stay in this stage for years, and not make any progress because they alternate between doing too much, then crashing and feeling ill again.

Stage 3 – Recovery – exercise can be gradually increased with confidence, with minimal symptoms. However, even in this stage relapses can be triggered by any of the factors on page 24.

Mental Activity

Brain exercise has the same limitations as physical exercise, and the same principles should be applied, especially for children and students returning to part- or full-time study.

The operative word for getting the right balance between exercise and rest, at any stage of the illness, is *pacing*. More about this in Chapters 6 and 7.

There is not yet enough evidence that the following suggestions will be helpful in every case, however reducing exertion and pacing activities seems to be essential for everyone. Other lines of management have all helped some people. The advice offered is not aimed at achieving a total cure, but rather to lessen the severity, encourage more remissions, and help you to achieve some gradual recovery and to live more comfortably with the condition.

It is not much use spending money and time on various therapies, many of which may be of uncertain value, and at the same time continuing to live on an overdraft of energy, so reorganizing life so you throw out what is unnecessary and concentrate on what is important will help you to plan a strategy for the near future, and also to allow for ways of conserving energy.

THINGS TO DO TO HELP YOU COPE WITH THE ILLNESS

- Organize your lifestyle to allow more rest, and better pacing of activity.
- Stop activities which are unnecessary and wasteful of your energy.
- Improve the quality of your sleep.
- Accept your limitations.
- Get help and possibly treatment for depression, if present.
- Improve your nutrition, avoid low blood sugar.
- Keep warm at all times.
- Avoid chemical pollution.
- Treat any allergies.
- Have more fresh air and daylight.
- Try and sort out sources of anxiety such as lack of money. Apply for any financial benefits you may be entitled to.
- Do not be shy about asking for help from friends or neighbours.
- Apply for things to make life easier (walking aids, etc. – *see Chapter 18*)
- Contact other people with ME/CFS for support, if you feel isolated, but do not compare yourself with others.

Some will be more ill, some better; all have ups and downs like you.

In learning to cope with ME/CFS, half the battle is won if you can accept that you just cannot live at the same pace as you did before you became ill. To do this you need to realize that your worth is not measured by achievements in terms of being busy, earning money, athleticism or even being good at anything.

Remember, you will probably improve.

The following chapters will talk about these things in more detail.

Of all these suggestions, **physical and mental rest, balancing rest with activity, and good nutrition** are probably the most important.

Chapter 6

Rest and Sleep

Energy Management

As mentioned in the previous chapter, a person with ME/CFS is like a battery that cannot hold its charge. You can buy a more efficient battery, but you have to make do with the human body. Rest is all about recharging the batteries.

The production and use of energy has somehow gone wrong in someone suffering from ME/CFS or chronic fatigue, for reasons which are still not clear. The power stations in each living cell (called mitochondria) may, in some patients, have a 'spanner in the works', which may be due to a piece of virus or to some toxic chemical (*see page 59*). The parts of the body with the highest requirement of energy are in muscles and the central nervous system, so this is perhaps why these systems produce the most symptoms.

When you use muscles, a by-product of the energy reaction is lactic acid, a build-up of which causes pain. This pain and stiffness normally goes away in a day or two in a healthy person. But in some ME/CFS people with muscle symptoms, lactic acid builds up after relatively little work, and the recovery period takes longer than in healthy muscles (*see page 147*).

Many patients find out by experience that more can be achieved in a day by doing only a little at a time and having frequent rests, than by pushing on to the limit and then having to have a long rest. The problem in managing exercise and rest is that by the time you feel exhausted, you may have passed the stage at which a short rest would have recharged you and it may take several days of rest to recover. If you stop before this point, recovery may only take a few hours.

ESTABLISHING A ROUTINE

It is helpful to think of your available energy as resembling your available cash – in a bank balance. Lots of rest builds up your bank balance of energy. Each morning you will have a certain level of energy to use before you go into the red. If you have almost depleted the account the previous day, you may start out with the impression that you have plenty of energy in the bank, but will quickly find that you were only just in the black, and go overdrawn early in the day.

Each day you (and only you) have to decide how best to spend your energy quota. Often it has to be spent on 'basic house-keeping' – eating, dressing, excretion, maybe shopping or cooking. If you want to do something extra – for example attend a social event, do some part-time work, or do your Christmas shopping – you allow for this by taking extra rest beforehand, and do not complain if the next day you are in overdraft!

However unwell you may be, you are likely to have a daily pattern to your energy – some wake up feeling reasonably human, but steadily run down as the day progresses. These people need to plan to do essential things early in the day, to make most efficient use of what energy there is. Others wake up (if they have slept) feeling they would rather be dead, and by later on they may improve. For them, things to be done should be arranged for the latter time of day. It is worth telling friends and colleagues when to call, and when not to bother you. This saves the awkwardness of being incoherent on the phone to someone you'd otherwise love to talk to.

If you are well enough to think of working full- or part-time, and this can be arranged, it obviously pays to try and organize your working hours to suit your best time of day, and to be able to rest during the day if necessary. This will be less stressful on both you and your colleagues, and also be more efficient. Having said all this, I do realize that there are people with ME/CFS who find no pattern to their levels of energy at all. However, if you keep a diary of ups and downs and what you have been doing, then some sort of pattern may well emerge.

LEARNING TO REST

The more you rest early on in the illness or during a relapse, the quicker you will improve.

Resting, and the giving up of a lot of activities which were part of a busy life, requires discipline. In the past decade we have been bombarded with exhortations to take exercise in order to be healthy. The streets and parks are full of joggers; friends always seem to be planning 'activity' holidays such as skiing, sailing, or walking. We are conditioned now to think that if you sit all day in a chair you will become ill or get furred-up arteries, and for a healthy person this may be true.

Success tends to be measured by visible achievement; keeping busy is reckoned to be good for morale. As a colleague of mine said recently, people with 'boundless energy' are much admired, almost as though having boundless energy is some-how morally desirable! Just look at self-improvement books in a bookshop – 'how to make money/how to be successful/how to succeed in business' as though these are the only things in life that matter! Women who successfully (on the surface) juggle high-powered careers with running a home and caring for children are admired – but at what cost? Does it really matter if your garden is overgrown, your clothes secondhand, or you cancel your social engagements?

If you have ME/CFS or other fatiguing illnesses, you must unlearn all these conditionings. You will have to learn to be more of an observer and listener instead of a do-er or talker!

Do try and think of the giving up of activities as something *positive* to do, rather than *negative* ('being lazy'). Rest should be regarded as positive, constructive treatment rather than just as 'doing nothing'. In restructuring your life you will find you have to have a 'spring clean' of priorities, and in fact some aspects of life become much simpler, because there will be fewer choices to have to make. For example, if you do not have the energy (or money) to buy clothes, you will not have to endure exhausting hours and indecision in clothes shops!

Contentment and happiness can come from very simple things. With a debilitating illness the secret of coping is to lower your sights, *to move the goalposts a lot nearer*. Then you will be able to score an achievement more often, with a great deal less effort. Then a walk to a local shop can be as exciting as a weekend walking in the country. A beautiful sunset can be as pleasurable (and cheaper) as a trip to the cinema.

It is important to accept the things you cannot do, and to make the most of what remains. Also to remain optimistic about the future, and to continue to believe that improvement is possible. During the time that you are ill you must not be too proud to ask for help where needed. Most people like to give and to help and are waiting to be asked. There may be a forgotten relative who could help, or a lonely neighbour who would be happy to do some shopping or look after the children some-times. It is worth asking your doctor, or local Citizen's Advice Bureau, what sorts of help are available, until you are better.

Do remember that your health is more precious than money, and that none of us is indispensable at work. The office, patients or students will all be there when you get better. So will the possibility of doing other things, should you have to give up your job through illness. Many unemployed people, without ME or CFS, also have to learn to cope without a job in the present economic climate.

The decisions involved in reorganizing life are individual and personal. It is usually a question of sorting out the priori-ties, and the top priorities have to be to look after your health and welfare, and to plan for some sort of recovery.

I used to have a scarlet sweatshirt with a motif which read: *Non Omnia Possumus Omnes* – Latin for 'It is not always possible to do everything.' Even though I am largely recovered from ME/CFS, I still have to have to remind myself of this. It is a good motto for anyone with diminished energy, from whatever cause, struggling to get through the day.

WHAT IS MEANT BY REST?
1) Bed Rest
Total bed rest is not a good idea, except when in a severe relapse, or in the acute early stage – although not everyone has a sudden or severe start to the illness. However, staying in bed 24 hours a day should ideally not continue beyond a week or two. If possible, even during periods of complete rest you should walk to the bathroom, and sit out in a chair for a short time each day. Lying flat all the time in bed is also not advisable beyond a few days, because this can lead to loss of postural control of blood pressure. When we sit up or stand from a lying

position, the heart and blood vessels need to compensate to prevent most of the blood collecting in the lower half of the body due to gravity. If the compensation reflex is not working, the person feels dizzy or faints when assuming an upright posture. The other chief hazard of prolonged rest in bed is that unused muscles quickly lose their tone and strength. A patient with any illness who lies in bed will lose muscle strength after about two weeks.

The consequence of prolonged rest in bed is that a person with ME/CFS finds it very difficult to start any gentle exercise again when he or she feels better. The combined effects of prolonged rest on postural control of the circulation, on muscle tone and power, and heart and lung function, is known as '*deconditioning*'.

A sportsperson who for whatever reason goes for some weeks without the accustomed hard exercise will feel 'out of condition' when he or she takes up the sport again. For the first few occasions of playing tennis, or running, etc., he or she will get quickly out of breath, have a racing heart, and experience sore, achy muscles the next day. This is how a person with ME/CFS feels, after a long period of bed rest, even just walking round the house, and because of the abnormal response to exercise of muscles in some, it takes much longer to overcome such deconditioning than for an unfit athlete.

Another potential effect of too much bed rest is that the joints, especially knees and elbows, may become stiff and contracted. If you are ill enough to be spending all day in bed, and if this is likely to be for weeks, then it is essential to do some very simple and non-strenuous movements each day. Every joint should be moved through its full range, and gentle stretching of the whole body should be attempted, as is done by a cat on waking. This can be done yourself or by a carer.

SUGGESTED MOVEMENTS

- *Shoulders:* Lift each arm forwards, up beside the ears, back as far as possible, and down. Then take the hand behind the back and reach up.
- *Elbows:* Straighten each arm completely, then bend so that the hand touches the shoulder.
- *Wrists:* Keeping the forearm still, make a circle with the fingertips.
- *Fingers:* Curl them up so the fingertips touch the palms, then straighten them out and spread them wide. Squeezing a soft rubber ball several times is a useful way to maintain the grip.
- *Neck:* Starting with the chin on the chest, make a slow circle of the chin in both directions, so that the neck bends forwards, then sideways, then backwards, to the other side then forward again. Try to touch the left ear to the left shoulder, and the right ear to the right shoulder.
- *Hips:* Lying prone or on one side, take the leg backwards, return to starting place, then take it sideways. These movements need not be great, but are important to prevent the hips becoming stiff and bent.
- *Knees:* Bend the knees fully, then straighten the legs as completely as possible.
- *Ankles and feet:* With each foot, point the toes down then bring them up as far as possible, then circle the foot in each direction.
- *Back:* It is important to have good back support while sitting in bed. Lying on your front for a while each day should extend the back. Back tension can be eased by lying on one side, then curling the knees up near the chin for a few minutes, then unfolding again and arching the back for a few minutes.

The object of these movements is to prevent stiffness or deformity of joints. Most patients will be doing enough each day for this immobility not to become a problem – having a bath, drying, putting on clothes, walking round the house. Even if you have to spend much of the day in or on the bed, you should change out of your nightclothes into something else which is warm and comfortable during the day.

It does not take much extra energy to do enough movements to keep the joints supple, and maintain the ability to stand and walk, while still having enough rest. The other reason for moving around is to keep the circulation going to the extremities, which tend to get cold anyway.

2) Rest During the Day

If you are up and dressed in the daytime, you may well need to take rests during the day. Such rest periods should be real mental and physical relaxation, *not* getting into bed to watch TV, or to catch up on phone calls! Many doctors and other health professionals discourage going to sleep during the day, saying that this will lead to poor sleep at night. However, a period of between 30 minutes and 2 hours lying down, warm and comfortable, with no mental stimulation or noise (other than quiet music possibly) may lead many to drop off into a light sleep or 'catnap'. Personally, I find I get much more out of a day if I do this after lunch when possible, and this recharges the batteries for the second part of the day. It's worth remembering that the northern European way of keeping going all day does not apply in Mediterranean countries, when an afternoon 'siesta' is normal behaviour.

Generally speaking, anyone who has a fatiguing illness, not only ME/CFS but conditions like arthritis, heart disease or multiple sclerosis, finds that alternating activity or work with rest is absolutely essential. This is the basis of *pacing*, which is a useful term that encompasses such sensible energy management. The most important rule of pacing is *stop before you become exhausted*.

It is also important to aim for some increased activity after the initial period of illness – that is, when sore throat, fever, muscle spasms and sweating have diminished. Fear of exercise-induced symptoms may prevent a sufferer from ever trying anything new. Do remember that mild symptoms of muscle aching, dizziness and fatigue are inevitable when starting even gentle activity after bed rest lasting more than a few weeks. Mild symptoms will settle quickly, and should not be a reason to collapse back in bed. Even if you inadvertently overdo things during a slow increase in activity and have ME-type 'post-exertional malaise', this will not harm you, and with rest these symptoms will settle again.

3) Sleep

This is the best form of rest. During sleep the rate of repair of body tissues is greatest, especially during the quiet, non-dreaming stages of sleep. Animals and children sleep the clock round when they are ill. Many people with ME/CFS complain that they seem to need too much sleep, especially during acute phases or relapses, but it is all right to sleep as much as you can; it will do nothing but good. If you don't sleep well, you cannot get well.

It is common to have 'hypersomnia' at the beginning of the illness or during a severe relapse, but in the chronic stage, poor and disturbed sleep usually develops and can be very difficult to overcome. It is bad enough to feel ill and exhausted during the day, but to go to bed and then have a disturbed, sleepless night only makes you feel worse.

Poor sleep may be due to brain disturbance at the level of the sleep centre, part of the hypothalamus. There appears to a loss of part of the sleep cycle which shows up on an elec-tro-encephalo-gram (EEG) as 'alpha rhythm', the very deep dreamless phase of sleep. Another part of sleep, called 'rapid eye movement' (REM) is preserved, and may give many vivid, unpleasant dreams. Other things can disturb sleep:

- muscle pain and/or twitching
- restless legs
- oversensitivity to noise
- palpitations, sweating, nightmares
- breathing difficulties or not breathing (sleep apnoea)
- panic attacks, and a racing brain that just will not switch off even though you are exhausted.

If you sometimes spend some time awake during the night, have some distraction at hand, such as a radio or silly book, and also something to eat. Try not to fret about being awake; this wastes energy and stops you relaxing.

Suggestions for helping you to sleep:

- go to bed before you become exhausted, and allow time to relax, maybe with quiet music/the radio or an easy book
- avoid watching TV until late, as this stimulates the brain and prevents you going to sleep afterwards. It is best to turn off the TV at least one hour before you plan to go to bed or sleep. For example, no TV after 9 p.m., then settle down with the light off by 10.30.
- make sure your bed is comfortable. If the muscles are very sore, put a quilt, duvet or sleeping bag under the lower sheet. The mattress should be fairly soft but not sagging.

I have found a good quality latex foam (non-inflammable) mattress better than a sprung one, and also better insulated, hence warmer, but this is a personal preference.

- if you are spending a lot of time in bed, consider investing in a washable sheepskin to lie on. Make sure you are *warm* enough. Chilliness increases muscle tension. A hot water bottle or heated pad next to an aching part of the body is useful. *If you use an electric blanket, this must be switched off before you go to sleep.*

- essential oils, in the bath or gently massaged into the limbs, really do help. If you can get someone else to do this for you, even better. You can find out more about the properties of various oils by consulting an aromatherapist or reading a book on the subject. It is important to use only oils that are calming or relaxing – those that are stimulating should be avoided. Lavender is ideal: it relaxes and calms muscles and balances body energies.

- avoid exciting or distressing TV, books or arguments in the evening. Emotional responses seem to be heightened in this illness, and a tragedy seen on the evening news can keep you awake all night.

- do not go to sleep hungry, for you will wake up a few hours later feeling terrible. An old-fashioned hot milky drink, such as Horlicks or chocolate, with a banana or biscuit, taken last thing at night, helps to prevent night hunger.

- make sure the bedroom is properly ventilated; an airtight, stuffy room does not provide enough oxygen, and may increase indoor air pollution.

- ear plugs are a boon if you are extra noise sensitive; they muffle street noises, courting cats, ticking clocks and snoring spouses. The best are the soft wax ones, which soften in the ear, fit snugly, and are non-irritant. (They are also useful on a noisy train or bus, or in any situation when noise is an irritation. In summer they help if you are sitting in the garden and a neighbouring lawn mower starts up.)
- avoid having lots of electric cables passing across or near the bed head, and if possible switch things off at the plug before sleeping, except for a bedside light. Electro-magnetic energy fields may not affect those who are well, but ill people seem to be extra sensitive to them, and sleep disturbance may be one of the effects. The worst culprit for this is a transformer-plug, such as that used for an answerphone.

Sleeping pills are in theory best avoided, as they can lead to dependence on them. However, if you have insomnia night after night, and also have tense painful muscles, then taking a mild sedative for a few weeks does no harm. Once you start to feel a bit better you may be able to do without them, or take them on the odd night only. A short-acting one like temazepam 10 mg (you can break the tablet in half) should give 6 to 7 hours of sleep and not make you groggy in the morning. Zopiclone is a newer type of sleeping pill that is less addictive than temazepam.

Some anti-depressants are sedative, and some more so than others. For intractable sleep disturbance, which is such a common symptom of ME/CFS, a low dose of an antidepressant such as amitriptyline, 10–20 mg to start with, at night can be useful. It is also good for pain relief, and indeed is prescribed for intractable pain in other conditions. Sleep disturbance is a common feature of a condition which resembles ME/CFS called fibromyalgia, and good results have been obtained in a trial of low-dose tricyclic antidepressant (amitriptyline). No formal study has been done yet on its usefulness in ME/CFS. Some cannot tolerate side-effects of antidepressants, but side-effects are less in very low doses and wear off after 10 days or so. (*See also page 184.*)

4) Mental Rest

It is very important to have mental and emotional rest as well as physical rest. Brain fatigue is as real as muscle fatigue, and for many people who have had the illness for more than two years, the mental fatigue and loss of concentration and memory are far more disabling than physical exhaustion. It is the brain fatigue and loss of cognitive functions that prevent so many intelligent, motivated people from getting back to work or to their studies.

Most of us have a constant chatter of thoughts whizzing around in the brain while we are awake. Healthy people can cope with thinking about several things at the same time. The problem if you have ME/CFS is that if the short-term memory is defective, you have forgotten what you were about to do (or say or write) a few seconds or minutes later.

The intellectual functions affected by the disturbance to the brain – whether as a result of altered neurotransmitter function (brain chemical messengers), cytokines from an over-active immune system, low-grade viral infection or reduced blood flow (and no one really knows what it is yet) – are:

- loss of short-term memory
- poor concentration
- inability to learn and retain new information
- easy distractibility
- muddled speech – using the wrong words for things, not

being able to form a sentence
- loss of ability to do simple arithmetic
- poor comprehension when someone speaks to you
- not being able to cope with several people speaking at once
- loss of the ability to understand the written word
- not being able to follow a TV programme or film
- confusion and muddled thinking
- forgetting how to do complex procedures that were once automatic, such as changing gear in a car, or making an omelette.

It is no good trying to force your brain to cope. Many of the brain circuits and terminals are out of order; some days more circuits will function than others. Computer experts talk about 'virus' interfering with computer function. They also talk about computer files being 'corrupted', though I really don't believe there is any corruption involved in the brains of people afflicted with ME/CFS!

Even though, at present, I have largely recovered from the physical debility of ME, I have found, like many others, that the cognitive malfunction is still a great nuisance. On a bad day or after writing at my computer for more than one hour, if someone telephones me, various things can happen:

a) I can't remember, half an hour later, who has called, and what he or she has said
b) I am unable to remember what I was in the middle of doing when the phone rang
c) I may be unable to speak coherently until my brain recovers from talking on the phone.

Ways of helping to cope with poor brain function:

- Make lists – of things to be done, people to phone, shopping.
- Become obsessive about putting things in their rightful place each time.
- Keep your lists in a special place!
- Be strict about distracting noises – turn off the radio or TV before speaking on the phone.
- Do not overload your brain – do not try and read with the radio or TV on.
- Do one thing at a time, and finish it before thinking about the next thing.
- Plan plenty of rest periods for your brain.
- If you are studying, or writing, only work for a limited time, then either rest and meditate, or do something quite different that does not need the brain, such as the washing up or watching birds in the garden.

Remember that physical exertion can affect brain function. So if you are writing or studying for an exam, you should hold back on physical exercise. Most school pupils recovering from ME/CFS find that they cannot learn anything at school if they are doing sports or even walk every day to school. It is as if you have to choose whether to use energy for the brain or for the muscles!

A lot of problems are caused by not being able to make memories properly. You cannot get a memory out of the filing cabinet in your brain if you never filed it properly in the first place. So a visual imprint of a book sitting where you put it is not filed in the brain. Then, if you have also lost the association of things and places, it is not surprising to find the book in the fridge, sausages in the bedroom and your pile of clean under-wear on the hall table!

The frustration of losing things, and the names for them, is very wasteful of mental energy, and for previously mentally agile patients this can be harder to bear than the physical fatigue.

If mental confusion comes on quickly during the day, it may signal the need for some food and/or a rest. It feels as though someone has suddenly pulled the electric plug out! Some people with ME/CFS manage to stay in a job by negotiating flexible hours and arranging for a couch to rest on if their energy suddenly runs out. It is just as important to stop before you get tired when working with your brain, as it is to stop physical activity.

There are also various techniques for learning mental rest, including meditation, hypnotherapy, or listening to relaxation tapes.

In the early stages of the illness or during a relapse, the symptoms that result from doing too much develop within a few hours or the next day. With recovery, the time lapse from overdoing it to getting the symptoms (which prove that you shouldn't have done it) gets longer and it becomes more difficult to relate cause and effect. The muscle pain, weakness, sweating or feeling awful may not happen until two days following the imprudent exertion. If you are still keeping a diary it may show you what has caused the relapse. With recovery, the length of time needed to come out of a relapse should get shorter, maybe one week of rest instead of three months; maybe one day instead of a week.

Beware – during the time of gradual recovery it is very tempting, when feeling so wonderfully well (comparatively), to do something stupid like running for a bus or shifting furniture. I know some people whose sudden extreme exertion has put them back to bed for months.

Do remember that, when you have this type of illness, all your functions need to be adjusted so as not to waste precious energy. You need to work out new patterns of behaviour, and to do this effectively you need to listen to what your body and mind are telling you.

'One way of looking at the illness is to see it as our body going on strike, and demanding new terms and conditions of employment. Most people with ME are by nature highly energetic and other people tend to look to them for support and enthusiasm. ME seems to thrive on these patterns of behaviour.'

(FROM AN ARTICLE BY A PATIENT)

Becoming ill with ME/CFS, or any fatiguing illness, is a clear message that something is wrong. The illness has forced you to come to a full stop, and fighting what is happening is the worst thing you can do. So give in gracefully; stop fighting yourself and the world. Rest and let the world go by for a time. Unless you do this at the start, the illness may become chronic. After a period of time, when the severe symptoms have abated, you can start gradually to push out your boundaries and to extend your capability to physical exertion. However, this has to be done very carefully, and at the right time (*see Chapter* 7).

Chapter 7

Exercise and Rehabilitation

One of the things that told me clearly I was ill, before I had even heard of ME, was my *changed* response to any exercise. Before getting the infection that triggered my illness, if I felt tired and low in spirits I used to go for a long walk, or dig the garden, such as at weekends after a busy working week. This exercise would always cheer me up, provide me with a good night's sleep, and refresh me for the next week. After developing ME I found that even the most gentle exercise would completely shatter me, sometimes the next day, and led to my feeling ill, hurting all over and crying for no reason. This dramatic alteration in the response to what is considered healthy exercise is the most classic symptom of ME, and should distinguish it from other fatigue syndromes. It is often referred to as *'post-exertional malaise'*.

Something that does not seem to be understood by the people who want to call this illness 'chronic fatigue' is the difference between the fatigue felt by a normal person after a game of tennis or a 12-mile walk, and that felt by someone with ME/CFS after minor exercise: The former is described as 'healthy tiredness', refreshes the mind, improves appetite and leads to a good night's sleep. The muscles may ache, but are relieved by a hot bath and sleep. This sort of healthy fatigue is beneficial for many people with depression. The post-exercise fatigue typical of ME is quite different, and needs to be experienced to be understood – it is not just tiredness, it is feeling horribly ill, collapsed, as though poisoned, with visible muscle twitchings, intense pains in the muscles and maybe joints; nausea, sweating, insomnia and nightmares; maybe elevated temperature and recurrence of sore throat and tender, enlarged glands. This fatigue (an understatement) is not relieved by a good night's sleep.

Is Exercise Good for ME/CFS?

How I wish that something as simple as gradually increased daily exercise could cure everyone who has ME/CFS. Exercise is an emotive word, and the advice generally given by experienced patients is *do not overexercise*. But the reality is not as simple as that – whether exercise is appropriate or not will depend on various factors.

(1) THE TYPE OF ILLNESS
In some cases there may be no problem with muscle function. The illness described by Dr Melvin Ramsay (*see page 89*) has 'abnormal muscle fatiguability' and post-exertional malaise and muscle weakness as its core symptom. But if you take the most recent diagnostic criteria for chronic fatigue syndrome (*see Chapter 4*) you can see that some people who qualify for a diagnosis of CFS, and are certainly ill, fatigued and disabled, may not have any muscle symptoms. As was explained in Chapter 3, it seems probable that within the label of CFS there are *subgroups*, and that not everyone diagnosed CFS has the same illness that was described in earlier epidemics.

A research study published in 1995 showed that some, but not all, people with CFS have abnormal production of lactic acid during exercise.[1] Ninety-six patients who met the Oxford criteria for CFS (a broad criteria that may include people with psychiatric illness; *see Chapter 3*) underwent exercise on a bicycle ergonometer for 15 minutes at a rate worked out individually. Thirty-three subjects had abnormal lactate response (measured in blood) to a level of exercise that should not cause anaerobic metabolism in normal people. What was also interesting was that the subjects who had normal response to exercise were more likely to qualify for a psychiatric diagnosis.

What this study demonstrated was that a subset of people diagnosed CFS have abnormal muscle metabolism. It would be interesting to carry out the same exercise and lactic acid test using only patients who have symptoms of early abnormal muscle fatigue and pain following minimal exertion – that is, the illness described as ME by Dr Ramsay.

(2) THE STAGE OF THE ILLNESS

Exercise may be detrimental during the early acute phase or during a severe relapse, when there are symptoms of feeling feverish, sore throat with enlarged, tender glands, nausea, severe muscle pain with visible twitching, and malaise.

Once the severe symptoms have settled, and provided that there is no major sleep disturbance, a cautious increase in exercise is a good idea.

(3) PRESENCE OF OTHER PROBLEMS

If the person has a sleep disorder, with disturbed sleep and frequent waking, increasing activity is unlikely to succeed. This is because repair and regeneration of muscle fibres only takes place during restorative sleep.

Also, if severe depression is present it may be impossible to increase exercise levels. Anyone with ME/CFS who wants to improve function by gradually increasing exercise is advised to get help for sleep disturbance and depression first.

(4) THE TYPE OF EXERCISE

Exercise means different things to different people. At one extreme is punishing exercise such as running and playing squash, in which a fit person pushes him- or herself to the limits of endurance and uses anaerobic metabolism. There is no evidence that jogging prolongs life; it certainly wears out joints and running shoes. Heart attacks can happen to apparently fit young to middle-aged people during squash or running, including the American man who popularized jogging in the first place (Jim Fixx). Doing vigorous exercise while recovering from any viral infection could be hazardous, as the heart muscle may be affected by any virus. I do not recollect anyone reaching the age of 100 attributing his or her long life to jogging – more usually it's attributed to a gentle lifestyle, with a daily trip to the local pub!

The other extreme is the exercise involved in getting out of bed and putting on clothes, which may cause exhaustion in someone acutely ill with ME/CFS. For people who cannot exercise because they are too ill, what might be more appropriate would be movement and activity, rather than exertional exercise.

The general understanding of *aerobic exercise* is something like cycling, fitness training, running, dancing, etc. In fact, any exercise that increases heart rate and breathing and can be sustained for several minutes is aerobic exercise – that is, exercise where the muscles burn oxygen.

By contrast, *anaerobic exercise* is exercise that continues beyond the point when oxygen is used, at which point glucose is burned to make energy – lactic acid is the painful by-product. A rapid sprint, such as over 100 metres, relies on anaerobic metabolism, with compensatory oxygen use in the recovery period. Given that many people with ME/CFS have very inefficient aerobic muscle metabolism anyway, doing any violent exercise such as sprinting or playing squash is out of the question, and would be most unhelpful.

A Study of the Benefits of Increasing Exercise

A study was carried out at St Bartholomew's Hospital, London in 1996[2] that showed that a carefully tailored programme of gradually increased aerobic exercise can benefit some, but not all, people diagnosed CFS. From outpatient clinic attenders who met the Oxford criteria for CFS, 66 patients entered the programme of graded aerobic exercise. Of these, 47 patients completed the year-long study, and 36 people reported a significant improvement in function at the end of the year. It is not known how many of the 36 actually went back to full-time work or full former life activities.

Unfortunately this useful research was hyped up in the press and translated into headings such as 'Exhausted ME Victims Advised to Run for their Lives – a vigorous new regime of graded exercises for sufferers of chronic fatigue syndrome' (*Observer*, 26th October 1997). In fact when I spoke to Dr Peter White, the psychiatrist in charge of the study, he explained that for some subjects who took part, the starting point was to sit up out of bed, then work towards walking across a room. The type of exercise used in this study was walking, although one patient in the trial, who used to be a runner, became able to jog for 2 miles at the end of her programme. However, this woman probably did *not* have the abnormal muscle response to exercise that is so typical of ME.

It is important to remember that improving function does not equal getting back to pre-illness levels of exercise. Many people with ME/CFS are already functioning at or near their 'ceiling' of fitness, and I believe that graded exercise programmes are useful mainly for people with chronic fatigue syndrome whose potential improvement is hampered by deconditioning of the heart, lungs and muscles, and who could become more active with proper guidance.

The best types of exercise for anyone with ME/CFS who feels that a cautious increase in activity is worth trying are yoga, walking, and gentle swimming. What actually got me back into improving my activity level was singing! I realize it is not for everyone, but I had been a regular choral singer before becoming ill, and after two years of illness and isolation I decided to rejoin a small choral group and took singing lessons. It was hard work at first, and I could not remain standing during rehearsals or throughout concerts. But I believe that the work of using the diaphragm (the most important breathing muscle) properly, plus learning voice control, together with the fun of making music with friends, helped me turn the corner. In fact, serious singing is aerobic exercise, and I still find I am exhausted the day after a long rehearsal followed by a live concert.

(5) THE FREQUENCY OF EXERCISE

It is no good for anyone who is ill and has been resting and not doing any exercise for some time to expect to be able to suddenly walk half a mile, or take up a sport. Programmes of graded exercise only do any good if the exercise is tailored to the individual's ability, starts at a very low level, and is increased very slowly, step by step. Apart from the likelihood of the patient being very unfit, it is a much more difficult and a slower process to get the heart and breathing and muscle power (which are, of course, all inter-dependent) toned up again in someone who has been inactive due to ME/CFS, compared to someone who has been inactive for some other reason such as having a leg in plaster. If you are someone with ME/CFS who has muscle weakness, pain and twitching following any mild exercise, then it will be difficult to build up muscle strength by physiotherapy or hard exercise.

Cognitive Behaviour Therapy (CBT)

An alternative explanation of long-term disability in chronic fatigue syndromes was first published by some British psychiatrists in 1991:[3]

'Looking specifically at CFS, it is plausible that an initial infective trigger may begin a cycle in which attributional and cognitive factors fuel avoidant behaviour. The initial symptoms, in particular fatigue and myalgia, engender a state of 'learned helplessness' ... and may trigger or exacerbate the mood disorder that is found in many patients. Avoidant behaviour sustains symptoms, by decreasing activity tolerance and increasing sensitivity to any stimulation, as does associated mood disorder. Re-exposure to activity causes more symptoms and more fear. The result is a vicious circle of symptoms, avoidance, fatigue, demoralization and depression and the clinical picture of CFS.'

The treatment proposed by these psychiatrists, CBT, therefore consists of:

a) treatment of depression (if present) with antidepressants
b) gradual planned increase in activities including exercise, agreed with the patient

c) cognitive therapy to help the patient change his or her perception of the illness, to give the patient more confidence, and to break the association between activity and symptoms.

The results of the first trial on CBT to be published showed that two-thirds of patients felt better after 6 weeks. However, there were no controls to compare with, and there was little long-term follow-up to see if improvements were maintained. There was an association noted between lack of improvement/worsening and patients who believed that their symptoms were due to physical disease, as well as those who had positive VP1 (enterovirus in blood).

The most recently published paper is about a study carried out by Dr Michael Sharpe and colleagues at Oxford[4] The sample of 60 patients met the Oxford criteria for CFS, and were randomly divided into two groups:

1. one group of 30 patients were told they had CFS, received medical care, and also attended 16 weekly sessions for CBT over 16 weeks. The therapy asked the patients to rethink their beliefs about their illness and to try a gradual and consistent increase in activity and problem-solving approaches to personal relationships and work.
2. the second group of 30 patients were also told they had CFS, had general medical care alone, and were advised to do as much as they felt able to.

The average baseline disability levels of both groups were the same (mean score was 71, on the Karnofsky scale, which is a scale of function in daily life). The main outcome measure was in function. Assessments were made before treatment, at

5 months, then at 8 and 12 months. At 12 months, 73 per cent of the CBT group achieved a score of 80 or more on the Karnofsky scale, compared to 27 per cent of those who had medical care alone.

However, other things, such as symptoms, were not assessed. Overall, 60 per cent of the CBT group rated themselves as much improved, compared to 23 per cent of the medical care-only group. There was also improvement in depression and a reduction in the number of days spent in bed in the CBT group.

CBT as a therapy is not new. It has been used for some years to help patients with other chronic illnesses, including chronic pain and rheumatoid arthritis. Having reviewed all the available information about CBT from published studies and from talking to therapists and to patients who have been treated with it, the Alliance of ME/CFS patient organizations has written:

'We welcome the use of cognitive behaviour therapy where it is intended to help patients develop improved strategies for coping with their illness. However, we have some reservations about the way in which CBT has been interpreted or administered in some patients with ME/CFS, and believe it has a number of drawbacks – some of which were omitted from the [Royal Colleges'] report [*see page 99*].

In our experience, CBT does not provide a cure for ME/CFS but it can help to bring about an improvement in the quality of life for selected patients, and might assist complete recovery in a few. We are enthusiastic about the type of CBT being used in centres such as Harold Wood Hospital, Essex, where the emphasis is on helping severely affected patients cope with their physical and mental limitations. CBT can also produce undoubted benefits in patients where psychological problems or abnormal illness behaviour are delaying any potential recovery process.

At the same time, CBT has a potential for misuse, and an inflexible programme applied to all patients with ME/CFS could cause a worsening of both symptoms and disability. Consequently, CBT should only be administered by health professionals who fully understand this illness and treat patients with respect.'

It is important for both patients with ME/CFS and for health professionals considering CBT to distinguish between improvement in function and quality of life, and complete cure. A valuable result of CBT for some patients could be to 'iron out' the 'boom or bust' pattern of so many patients, by establishing a daily schedule of activity and rest. For many this will mean doing less at first, and getting a baseline of activity that can be sustained without producing extra symptoms. Only then is the patient encouraged to increase activity, gradually. A good piece of advice is: 'do no more on a good day than you do on a bad day.' By proper pacing of activity and rest, ideally the patient should be able to sustain a daily lifestyle without having crashes!

Before I ever heard of 'cognitive behaviour therapy', I believed that one simple way to tell the difference between someone with chronic fatigue due to stress or depression and someone with muscle fatigue caused by ME/CFS, was an exercise test such as the following.

The Bull in a Field Test

Place the subject under test in a field. Introduce a fierce bull into the field and shut the gate. The subject provokes the bull (using a cruelty-free scientifically tested stimulus). The activity and symptoms of the subject are monitored for 24 hours.

The subject with fatigue due to stress or depression will be seen to run briskly across the field, and get over the gate; the next day he will feel less depressed as a result of the surge of adrenaline and endorphins associated with the hard exercise.

The subject with ME/CFS fatigue will be seen to stagger or maybe run across the field and collapse by the gate; if alive and not mauled by the bull, the next day his symptoms of muscle exhaustion and pain will be much worse, he will complain of feeling ill and 'fluey' and he may be depressed and weeping.

This test has not been scientifically proven!

Dangers of Prolonged Bed Rest

Avoidance of exercise, such as prolonged bed rest beyond the initial acute stage of ME/CFS and other post-viral fatigue conditions, can lead to problems:

- deconditioning of heart, lungs and muscles
- possibly some psychological problems, and belief that one is becoming a permanent invalid
- lack of use leads to muscle weakness and loss of muscle bulk and tone
- lying flat for too long causes poor blood pressure control when getting up, with dizziness
- initial attempts to exercise after a period of bed rest will probably result in weakness, unsteadiness, and muscle aching in unused muscles.

But too much exercise can be followed by a relapse. So what is the best middle course for someone with ME/CFS to follow?

Dr Darrell Ho-Yen, consultant microbiologist at Inverness, who has studied a large number of post-viral fatigue patients, has pointed out that there are various subgroups of patients, and this may affect how quickly they recover and how they respond to exercise.[5] It is evident when looking at any form of management of this illness that each patient must be assessed individually, as what helps one may be useless for another. There is no doubt that complete rest in the first weeks or months of a post-viral illness is helpful. Pushing oneself to exhaustion while convalescing from any infection delays recovery, and may result in longer or more severe illness. It is during the chronic stage that a *gentle* increase of daily activity may be advisable.

Dr Ho-Yen has written:

'Patients' experiences do not show that avoidance of exercise is maladaptive. It is proposed that the recently ill often try to exercise to fitness, whereas the chronically ill have learned to avoid exercise. Recovery is more likely to be achieved if patients learn about their illness and do not exhaust their available energy.'

Available energy is the key to planning how much to do. As you hopefully gradually improve, you will slowly increase your bank balance of energy. It takes a long time, and one day of over-optimistic exertion may push your energy balance back into overdraft for weeks. If the gradual increase in activity is done at the correct pace, then for some people doing more may actually increase their daily available energy.

How Much Exercise Is Safe?

After trying out some new activity or exercise, see if the activity produces gentle healthy tiredness, or if it leads to malaise and pain. However, even if only mild tiredness is produced, the patient needs to be very cautious and slow in increasing the activity.

Unfortunately there is no easy predictor of whether an activity is going to harm you. The only thing to do is to try something; if it proves to be harmful, rest until recovered, then try it again – but *only do half as much*. Learn to read your body carefully to distinguish between symptoms of healthy tiredness, and those that threaten a relapse. Another important way to achieve more activity is to stick to a daily schedule of rest and activities, and to vary the activities during the day so as not to exhaust different muscle groups or your brain.

For example, if during one day you aim to do a total of 2 hours' paper work, plus half an hour of gentle walking (maybe an ambitious day for some people), plus 4 hours of bed rest, it will work out better if these activities are split up and rotated – such as 10 minutes' walk, one hour rest, half an hour on paperwork, etc. Much more is achieved this way. Some people with ME/CFS manage to return to a job by negotiating staggered hours of work, with rest during the day.

You (if you have ME/CFS) will find that *your body is the best judge* of how much, how often and what type of exercise to do. If you have features of fever, muscle twitchings, spasms and muscle weakness, your body is telling you its muscles need rest. After a period of rest (not necessarily total bed rest), if the muscles stop complaining and you feel less ill you may be able to start some gentle daily exercise. If you get some warning symptoms after the experimental exercise, it was probably too much. The secret is to stop *before* you start to feel tired.

If you gradually increase the amount you can do and find that you can cope with it, you may nevertheless eventually reach a limit beyond which you just cannot go, without a relapse – no matter how motivated you are. This limit must be determined by you and your body, not by a well-meaning physiotherapist, psychiatrist or friend. The limit will vary; it may be quite high during a period of remission, but may be drastically reduced following some adverse factor such as catching a cold, exposure to chemicals, or physical or emotional stress.

Some Research on Exercise in ME/CFS:

There are cardiac abnormalities in the acute phase of most viral infections, which largely disappear after 6 weeks. A study of heart function at rest and with exercise in CFS was carried out by Canadian researchers:[6]

'On graded exercise testing, 20 of 32 healthy subjects achieved target heart rates, compared to only 4 of 31 patients ... Patients with CFS have normal resting cardiac function, but markedly shortened exercise capacity, slow acceleration of heart rate, and fatigue of exercising muscles long before peak rate is achieved. The data are compatible with latent viral effects on cardiac pacemaker cells, or their autonomic control, and skeletal muscle tissues.'

The authors noted that the patients were strongly motivated to exercise, and to gain further insight into their symptoms.

Belfast doctors investigated aerobic work capacity in patients with CFS.[7] Thirteen patients were compared with 13 healthy controls and 7 people with irritable bowel syndrome. The CFS group had a reduced exercise capacity, a lower peak oxygen consumption, higher heart rate at submaximal levels of exertion, and higher blood lactic acid levels during the final stages of exertion. The authors concluded that reduced exercise capacity could be due to unfitness, but that similar findings occur with muscle damage.

A study published in 1996 found abnormal oxidative

metabolism in CFS patients. This study of muscle metabolism was carried out on 22 patients with CFS and 15 healthy controls who were sedentary and did not do regular exercise.[8] They were tested one week before, then two days after maximal exercise (to exhaustion) on a treadmill. Muscle oxidative capacity was measured as the maximum rate of resynthesis of phosphocreatine (one of the chemicals used up in the energy cycle) after exercise. It is a measure both of oxidative muscle metabolism and of recovery. The results showed a significant reduction in the capacity of oxidative metabolism in the subjects with CFS compared to sedentary (and therefore unfit) controls.

There are other forms of exercise besides walking and swimming which might be considered suitable for people recovering from ME/CFS, such as Yoga and T'ai Chi.

Yoga

Yoga is beneficial for circulation and breathing, and seems to improve blood flow to the extremities and hence oxygenation of tissues.

However, any posture that requires prolonged muscle action should be avoided, as should upside-down postures. The Yoga for Health Foundation (*address in Appendix A*) runs short residential courses where yoga is taught to people with various disabilities. They also hold regular courses specifically for people who have ME/CFS. The yoga used on these courses is extremely gentle and can be used even by patients unable to stand up. The single most useful exercise to learn in yoga is how to breathe correctly, and this can be done at home, sitting or lying down.

T'ai Chi Chu'an

T'ai Chi is a very ancient, gentle martial art, performed as a series of traditional movements that are intended to unite body and mind. It was developed many centuries ago and is widely practised in China, Japan and other countries round the world for health, meditation and enjoyment.

The movements in T'ai Chi are gentle and flowing – no force or sudden muscular effort is used at all. It can be learned by people of any age, weak or strong. Each muscle is changing between use and relaxation; there is improvement of muscle tone, of circulation of the blood and lymphatics; there is gentle movement of all joints. It is good for maintaining muscle tone. There is calming of mind and body, and deep regular breathing.

It is recorded that a T'ai Chi master, a Mr Liang, learned the art in middle age, after many operations and prolonged illness. He not only confounded doctors, who had predicted his imminent death, but was still practising at the advanced age of 77 to preserve his health.

T'ai Chi is recommended for people who are getting better or are in remission, especially those whose muscle weakness or pain is not so severe. Once learned it can be performed at home as well as in a class. Even doing a few movements for a few minutes between spells of lying down can be beneficial.

To summarize the last two chapters, here is a quotation from the *Self-Care Manual for patients with CFS*, written in 1991:[9]

(1) Lifestyle
'Rest is best' ... most patients report that rest is the best therapy. You must restructure your life so that it is possible to stop what you are doing when your body says 'stop'.

Most patients report that restructuring their life is the most difficult task, but is ultimately a rewarding lesson that many enjoy sharing with others.

Adjust your daily schedule to accommodate your body rhythm. Follow a fixed schedule of retiring and arising at the same time each day.

Each day you are given a finite amount of daily energy. An inner sense of trial and error will tell you how much energy you have each day and when you must stop.

You will feel your best by pushing almost to the limit of your daily energy allowance. At the least get up, bathe and dress each morning. Don't regularly exceed your daily energy allowance or you will risk relapse.

Laying down and resting during the day can earn you extra energy towards your daily limit; mental stress and emotional strain sap energy and lower your daily energy allowance.

Save your energy for important things, hire others to do housework. Get a cordless phone.

2) Exercise

Daily exercise of some kind is essential to prevent deconditioning. On the other hand, never exercise so much as to exceed your daily energy limit or risk relapse. If able, embark on a gentle walking programme. Begin with just a minute or two each day, then try five, then seven, and so on. You may be able to try swimming or cycling later ... progress gradually. Some exercise each day may actually give you more energy for the next day. The trick is in knowing the limit of what is therapeutic as compared with what is harmful.

A Case History of someone who tried a rehabilitation course:

Mrs S J was aged 42, with two children aged 14 and 11, when she became ill. Following a year or so of unremitting family stresses, which included a daughter with a serious illness, she had a presumed viral infection from which she did not make a proper recovery. The virus caused headaches, sore throat and malaise. Several weeks later, Sarah was still unable to return to her work as a clinical psychologist, and her GP suggested she had a 'post-viral syndrome'. Four and a half months later, still suffering from easy fatigue and malaise, she tried to return to work part-time, but had to give up work completely.

One year after the viral illness, Sarah was still unwell.

Her symptoms were:

Easily exhausted, recurrent low mood, post-exertional malaise and muscle weakness, aching legs and inability to stand for long. She also found she used the wrong words when speaking and had poor memory and concentration. On many days she was unable to read or follow a TV programme. Her GP by now had made the diagnosis of post-viral fatigue syndrome (PVFS, another name for ME). It was at this time that Sarah heard about the residential rehabilitation courses organized by Westcare, a Bristol-based charity for ME/CFS sufferers (*see Appendix A*). She really wanted to do something for herself to try and recover, so she booked on a Westcare course.

Sarah told me about her concerns before going to the course:

- she was wary of having to 'come out' about her illness in front of a group of people
- she wondered if the money would be well spent
- she had misgivings about leaving her family for five days, with her daughter being ill.

I asked what happened on the course:

'I shared a cottage with another woman of similar age and level of illness. Each day there were two group sessions, with either a counsellor, or the Occupational Therapist, doctor or nutritionist. Each patient had individual sessions with the OT and a counsellor during the five days. The counsellor talked about issues of accepting the illness, dealing with losses, and ways of dealing with emotions. The OT talked about energy management, baseline activity, goal-setting, pacing and dealing with setbacks. We were encouraged to rest or have short walks between the sessions. The idea was not that we would go home recovered, but rather that we had learned about developing a personal strategy for living that could help each of us to achieve some sort of improvement in the condition. Of course when you get home, all the problems are still there! But you can make a daily schedule and try and stick to it.'

Sarah's condition and energy levels gradually improved over the next two years. She is now able to work for 14 hours a week, do a range of physical activities, and needs only one brief rest per day.

Chapter 8

Stress

The word 'stress' is quite fashionable nowadays, and is blamed for much ill-health. But what is stress?

It is comfortable to think that stress is an outside event which just happens to us – the unexpected car crash, the terrorist attack, floods and earthquakes. With this point of view we can believe that we have no control over how much stress we receive. We can say: 'Life has treated me badly, that is why I have become ill.' Or 'There are too many demands on me, I am exhausted – I have to strive so hard at work.' These attitudes are of people who see themselves as victims.

Just as fever is not caused by germs, but by the body's reaction to infection, so stress itself need not cause ill-health; it is the *reaction of body and mind to stress* that determines if a person is affected by life's events.

Stress means anything which disturbs the equilibrium of mind or body. The tendency of the living person is towards stability, whether of body temperature, blood sugar, or the emotions. So 'stress' has a broader definition than that of a difficult job or a demanding family. It can be extreme heat or cold, hunger, trauma, infection, exhaustion, fear.

Dr Hans Selye, Professor of Experimental Medicine and

Surgery at the University of Montreal, began in the 1930s to study the effects of stress on living things. He was the first to show that the adrenal gland cortex produces cortisone in response to any disturbance to the body. Selye performed careful experiments on rats, using exposure to severe cold as the stress. He observed three stages in the animals' response to repeated exposure to cold:

1. Stage One – a shock response to the first exposure to the stress, followed by a reaction, and then recovery.
2. Stage Two – on repeated exposure the animals appeared to adapt and become resistant to the cold. In this stage, the adrenal glands enlarged, in response to a stimulus from the pituitary gland (located below the brain). The changes in the animals to counteract the stress became more permanent. *The rats appeared to be coping.*
3. Stage Three – exhaustion. The rats gradually failed to thrive; in those that died, post-mortem investigations showed that the adrenal glands were shrunken and had ceased functioning.

Selye called these events the *general adaptation syndrome*. These stages are similar in humans:

1. the first exposure to stress produces an outpouring of cortisone and of adrenaline to prepare the body for 'fight or flight' – the initial arousal state. If the stress passes, this reaction settles the body returns to its status quo.
2. repeated stressing leads to a stage of adaptation, and the arousal changes become more or less permanent. The person may appear to adapt, but general health declines. There are chronic symptoms such as migraine, asthma,

rashes, blood pressure changes, heart problems, mental
symptoms, and poor blood sugar control. The body cannot
remain constantly trying to adapt to stress without showing some damage.

3. there is a breakdown in the adaptation process. The result
is collapse and exhaustion. This may take the form of a
heart attack, nervous breakdown or perhaps a major illness such as cancer. The breakdown may occur following
an apparently minor stress, which acts as the last straw.

The second stage of the General Adaptation Syndrome is the
one in which most GPs see their patients, with a whole range
of chronic non-life-threatening illnesses. At this stage, if the
stress is removed recovery can take place.

With ME/CFS, the viral infection which appears to trigger
it off may be the 'last straw' for a chronically stressed system.
Not all patients have been stressed before developing
ME/CFS, but the stress may not have been obvious – intensive
athletic training can injure the immune system, yet the subject
would have believed him- or herself to have been supremely
fit! Maybe this is why many people with this illness are those
who were very physically active pre-illness.

But maybe the chronic stress was not emotional, nor overwork; perhaps it was exhaustion brought on by raising small
children, or maybe chronic low-dose exposure to a chemical
toxin such as organophosphates (OPs, *see page 278*).

There are many stressors, but what is essential if you reach
the stage of adaptive exhaustion and become seriously ill, is to
accept where you are, to stop struggling to adapt, and to allow
the adrenal glands and immune system to recover.

Suffering from ME/CFS is of course a continuing new stress.
The patient is fighting to get back to work, to get a diagnosis,

to cope with daily functions such as maintaining enough income to eat, to look after a family while ill, etc. Some cope better with the stress of chronic illness than others; some have emotional support and helpful doctors. Others may live alone, or be accused of malingering by GP and family. Practical support is the first major way to reduce stress. Other ways are: Relaxation, learning to breathe properly, meditation, and counselling to gain insight into the reality of becoming ill, and the possibility of getting better.

The symptoms of ME/CFS appear to be greatly influenced by both mental and physical stress. Although the illness may result from a viral infection or some other trigger, there is also a psychological dimension to ME and CFS. *All* illness has a psychological dimension.

Research into causes and treatment of ME/CFS can be hindered by the artificial division of disease into 'physical' and 'psychological'.[1] The mind and the body operate as one unit. A structural disorder in the brain can manifest in psychiatric symptoms – such as after a mild stroke. Unexpressed psychological distress can manifest as physical symptoms (e.g. abdominal pain); this is called 'somatization' in psychiatry. It is fashionable and acceptable nowadays to attribute ill-health to stress. But in northern European cultures it is not socially acceptable to attribute symptoms to mental illness.

So management of ME/CFS requires not only physical rest but also mental and emotional rest, and sometimes treatment of mental as well as bodily symptoms.

In ME/CFS there is increased sensitivity to stress. In health, the body's response to stress is an activation of the hypothalamic-pituitary-adrenal pathway of hormones, resulting in an out-in various ways. Taken to extreme, the response becomes a full-blown panic attack. The heart rate is raised, with palpitations, out of proportion to the stimulus of anxiety or minimal physical effort; the breathing is often disordered, with feelings of breathlessness or of a weight on the chest; nightmares, sleep disturbance and panic states are common. ME/CFS patients are frequently exhausted, sweat profusely, have unstable blood sugars; the peripheral circulation is often poor, and body thermostats don't work. They are oversensitive to noises, smells, touch and pain, and are emotionally unstable.

All these symptoms can reflect an overactive sympathetic nervous system (a part of the nervous system controlled by the hypothalamus). In a study by Dr Paul Levine and others, the researchers found average plasma noradrenaline levels were higher in 20 CFS patients when compared to normal controls – both when lying down and standing. The authors suggest that patients with CFS have a *dysregulated adrenergic system*, a theory that could unify the diverse symptoms of the illness. The hormone noradrenaline, released in response to a 'flight or fight' situation, causes rapid heartbeat, palpitations, flushing and sweating. These symptoms may respond to self-relaxation techniques such as meditation, autogenic training, self-hypnosis, etc.

Meditation

Meditation is a technique for getting very high quality mental rest; but it is not only the mind that is quiet. Transcendental meditation, for example, produces a state of profound physiological rest of the body, at the same time as increasing mental alertness. Some people may be put off meditation because they have wrong ideas about it.

POPULAR MISCONCEPTIONS ABOUT MEDITATION

Meditation is thought to require effort to control the mind, and thus to be difficult and mentally taxing.

It is supposed to be appropriate only for a particular lifestyle – of mystics and religious people who withdraw from the world – or that taking it up means you have to join a sect or convert to a new religion.

Most people do not know about any of the bodily benefits of meditation; they think it is only for spiritual growth.

HOW CAN MEDITATION HELP ME SUFFERERS?

There are different techniques of meditating, also other ways of learning deep relaxation such as self-hypnosis, or by listening to relaxation tapes.

The effects of meditation have been extensively studied on subjects during transcendental meditation (TM). The physiological changes during TM indicate a state of quietness of the sympathetic nervous system, i.e. the opposite of the 'fight or flight' arousal state:

- the heart rate is decreased, the blood pressure lowered, and breathing is slower
- oxygen consumption by the whole body is reduced
- blood flow to tissues increases, leading to better removal of the waste products of metabolism and a lower level of lactic acid in the blood
- long-term meditation is found to decrease resting cortisol levels even when not meditating. This calming of adrenergic activity is the opposite of Selye's stress response, and must be beneficial for ME/CFS.

- regular practice of TM increases stability of the autonomic nervous system
- there are demonstrated electro-encephalo-gram (EEG) changes during TM, indicating more ordered brain function
- sensitivity to noise is reduced, and there is improved temperature control.

Relaxation Techniques

There are classes for learning relaxation, and there are a great many relaxation tapes available. They range from simple instructions for physical relaxation to guided imagery. The patient who is too ill (or poor) to attend classes will gain a lot of benefit from obtaining a relaxation cassette and listening regularly at home.

Case History
The following story is told by a lady who has had ME/CFS for 18 years, and illustrates the importance of rest:

Miss W T, aged 66 (in 1987), retired

'I was first ill in 1970, when I was 49. It was thought at the time to be a virus infection – there were a number of funny viruses around at the time. There were years of relapse and recovery, years of weak legs, years of apparent good health, and a steady decline starting in the winter of 1982–83 until the summer of 1985 (when I started to adapt my life instead of trying to fight it). Since then the only relapses have been when I was in hospital for tests and forced to exercise for physiotherapy or testing. For the last two years I have been able to live at barely 50 per cent of normal life.

My symptoms, worst in relapse:

Muscle weakness, causing problems with standing, walking,
carrying
Fatigue
Pain and jumpy legs at night
Sensitivity to noise
Inability to concentrate for long
Sleep disturbance – brain may race and I cannot relax, or I may
go to sleep, then wake up feeling disturbed by a bad dream
Very sensitive to changes of temperature
Words get muddled
When I am very tired, I am clumsy and irritable, and my face
goes a nasty yellow-grey colour.

Medical tests done were all normal, apart from muscle biopsy
which slowed slight abnormality. Psychological interview was
normal!

Diagnoses:

1970, 1972, 1976 – 'virus infections'

1984 – 'nothing wrong with you'

1985 – damage to nerve in muscle, unknown cause

1986 – nothing neurologically wrong – advised to see a
psychiatrist

Later 1986 (same muscle biopsy) – damage to muscle, could
be due to earlier virus?

1987 – ME (after 17 years!)

I worked out that the muscle weakness dated from the old
virus infection (1970), but doctors would not listen to me. In
1986 I heard a radio talk about ME. It sounded like me. I sent
off to the ME Association for more information. I became more
convinced. Later I found a consultant who is familiar with ME,
who confirmed the diagnosis, without doing further tests.

In the light of my experience during the last four years, I cannot stress too much the need for rest, and for adopting a lifestyle in keeping with one's limitations. Right from getting the initial virus I wanted to keep going and was encouraged to be as active as possible as soon as possible. Since my troubles really started in about 1984, doctors have continually told me to keep going, and even when I was diagnosed as having irreparable damage and told by my GP to adapt my lifestyle and keep within my limits, the neurologist was still assuring me that I must not rest, I must keep as active as ever possible.

It was during the time that I was fighting against the weakness, and dragging myself about in an effort to keep going, that my condition deteriorated so fast and so permanently. As soon as I modified my life and listened to what my body was saying and kept within my limits whatever anyone said, it was amazing how the deterioration slowed down and almost stopped.

The ME Association theory is that rest in the initial stages can be a big factor in recovery. I never had that rest. And now,

I cannot help wondering whether, if I had been advised to rest even in 1984 instead of being instructed to keep going, I might not have the permanent damage which has now occurred.'

Chapter 9

Depression and Anxiety

There can be few people with ME/CFS who have not travelled down into the dark valley at some time during their illness. Symptoms of depression are common in ME/CFS, and only those who have experienced depression or despair can really understand what it is like. However, here I refer to depression as a symptom, rather than as a diagnosis in itself.

The diagnosis of depression or anxiety disorder, and the confusion or overlap of these with ME/CFS, has been discussed already in Chapter 3. In this chapter I am talking about the experience of feelings of depression. There is a difference between depression and unhappiness/sadness. The latter is usually the result of bereavement, difficult circumstances or perhaps the inability to adapt to a situation. If someone grieves for a deceased loved one, their sadness is normal; but if the sadness continues for a long time after one would expect the grief to have settled, it may turn into depression. Many people who are physically ill for any length of time get periods of feeling low in spirits, of grieving over the loss of many activities and friends that were part of the pre-illness life.

There are other emotions that can be disturbed if you have ME/CFS. It is fairly common for sufferers to feel uncared for and unappreciated and this can, in an extreme form, lead to *paranoid beliefs and behaviour*. Problems in comprehension of what other people are saying or doing, confusion and memory disturbance can combine to distort the reality of what is going on around the patient.

Another fairly common mood disturbance is that of *anxiety*, which if severe can take the form of a *panic attack* with features of overbreathing, nausea, restlessness, rapid pulse, fear and anguish. Again, difficulties with awareness, communication and poor memory may combine with common anxieties about things like finance, a relationship, something important that the patient has forgotten to do, being unsure of the ability to find the way (home, round a shop, or wherever), with the result that the natural anxiety spirals upwards into a full-blown panic attack. I believe this has something to do with too much adrenaline, or oversensitivity to adrenaline, but whatever is going on in the body, it is a horrible experience.

The worst panic attack I can remember experiencing was when I was driving somewhere and became confused while trying to find the correct exit from a complicated motorway junction. The more confused I got, the less I could see or interpret the signs. In the end I drove round and round and pulled over onto a hard shoulder, in a state as described above: quite petrified, sobbing, gasping for breath and shaking. In the end a passing motorist stopped and sat with me until I calmed down. I have found on this occasion and others (such as when navigating a busy railway station) that *eating something* – a bar of chocolate or a banana – seems to 'switch off' the storm and allow me to calm down and start to think more rationally.

This leads me to state that I believe that attacks of acute anxiety and panic can be triggered by exhaustion, whether of mind or body, together with low blood sugar, in a vulnerable person in certain circumstances such as acute stress. I am also sure that the apparent frequency of 'anxiety disorder' (a psychiatric term) in people with ME/CFS is partly explained by the loss of normal cognitive functions, such as memory and concentration, confusion and sometimes loss of spatial recognition. When these cognitive defects happen in a person who was formally coping with all of life's hazards and changes, they cause fear and worry. For example, having no recollection of doing something such as turning off the cooker can make you extremely anxious while you are out. It seems that if you are unwell or relapsed it is very difficult to make decisions, and the inability to make decisions means you cannot resolve problems, and the awareness of this lack only compounds the difficulties of daily living.

A friend of mine who has battled with this illness for years explains, 'When I feel well enough I try to drive to the local shops. But I find organizing myself and coping with the trip is like strategic planning to go into a battlefield. The brain processes involved leave me exhausted before I get there' – and this is a person who used to be a practising GP and a capable wife and mother of three children!

Depression as an illness affects most bodily functions. The sleep pattern is usually disturbed, with early morning waking and mood lowest at the beginning of the day and improving later. A depressed person may be cold and slow-moving, the appetite is poor, there is lack of motivation, and an inability to experience pleasure in anything – the symptom called *anhedonia*.

However, in ME/CFS depressive symptoms are not usually constant, and may be present for a few days or a few hours only. As with MS, emotional symptoms in ME/CFS usually correlate with disease activity, most commonly associated with general relapse, worsened by overexertion, and improving with rest. This is the converse to a depressive disorder with psycho-logical origin (*see page 29*), where exertion improves mood.

Someone with ME/CFS suffering from *emotional lability* may experience black despair, non-stop weeping, and suicidal feelings for a few days, then wake up one morning feeling fine. Or they may be irrationally happy, laughing and excited (maybe over nothing more than waking up without pain) one day – this euphoria leading to delusions of ability and too much activity ... and what happens the next day? The patient crashes with a bump into the state of weeping and exhaustion. This up-and-down emotional behaviour is not the same as a state of depression, when the patient usually has a persisting low mood for weeks.

The best way to lessen the highs and lows is to live within a daily routine of rest and activity, so your energy is used wisely, as advised in Chapters 6 and 7.

Another source of depression is the natural grief reaction to loss – of your former active self, of a job, friends, sporting activities, maybe of a spouse. This loss is not unlike that of someone who retires or is made redundant after many active years in a fulfilling job. There is inevitably a sense of not being needed; the world carries on very well without you, a world in which we are judged by what we are seen to do and achieve.

This secondary depression is common to all chronic disabling conditions, especially when the future is uncertain, and is bound up with anxiety and fear about the future. And part of the reaction to finding yourself ill is, naturally, anger. Anger, if kept inside and not expressed, turns into depression, with loss of self-esteem.

It is natural to be angry at developing a life-changing illness, and having to abandon, even temporarily, plans for the future. But because the person feels 'flattened', and is inactive and maybe inarticulate, the anger is overlooked and very often suppressed.

Expressing anger in a constructive way is often used as part of psychotherapy for all sorts of mental problems; however, if you are resting and saving your energy to do essential things you will not feel like hitting pillows or shouting to vent your rage. Some people are angry with themselves, if they are led to believe that they have developed ME/CFS because of 'bad' living or past mistakes. You would be surprised to know how many people feel guilty about being ill. The belief that sickness may be some sort of retribution brought on oneself is common, though not openly admitted.

If you have ME/CFS and depression, the loss of self-esteem is unfortunately reinforced by the loss of ability to work or function normally. Talking about these fears and grief with a trained psychologist or counsellor can assist an ill person to come to terms with the symptoms and the life changes.

However, sometimes there may be a more sustained period of severe depression, when short-term remedies do not help. The patient may be in black despair for days or weeks, unable to see a way out of it, and while in this state has no chance of improving energy levels or other symptoms. There is commonly a feeling of isolation, that one is cut off from other people and from experiencing any contact with beautiful things. An unhappy person may be moved to tears by beautiful music or a glorious sunset. A really depressed person will hear or see such things and feel absolutely nothing except perhaps despair because his or her contact with them is gone.

With this sort of depression there is often lack of motivation, insight or judgement. The general purposelessness of life is seen in contrast to the apparent industry and contentment of other people.

The really frightening thing about severe depression is that you hate being in that blackness but cannot climb out of it. Well-meaning friends suggest that you snap out of it, or read a good book, or think of the world's starving children. But when in this state you often cannot read, listen to the radio, or even speak on the phone.

Why Are Symptoms of Depression Common in ME/CFS?

There are a number of reasons why depression can afflict people with ME/CFS:

- all *viral infections* cause some degree of depression
- *cytokines* are the chemicals which help to limit a virus infection. When interferon (one of the cytokines) was used to treat patients for another virus, the side-effects complained of were of fatigue, muscle aches, and depression. Many ME/CFS symptoms may be caused by continued production of cytokines by the immune system reacting to something. This happens in auto-immune conditions such as rheumatoid arthritis.
- if the brain is affected in ME/CFS, then quite a lot of neurological functions are interfered with. Transmission of impulses between nerve cells takes place via chemical messengers called *neuro-transmitters*. (Antidepressant drugs change the balance of these chemicals, and so influence mood – *see page 184*.)
- the brain's chemical reactions need various amino acids (derived from proteins), vitamins, and enzymes in order to work. Nutritional deficiencies due to poor diet, poor digestion or malabsorbtion may contribute to depression. If a person

with ME/CFS has recurrent diarrhoea and poor food absorption, this will increase the risk of depression because of a shortage of amino acids and B vitamins. (Depression is an early symptom in cases of starvation, and beri-beri – vitamin B_1 deficiency.)

No one has invented a way of doing a biopsy on the living brain. So, unlike muscle tissue which can be studied with an electron microscope, brain cells that might be affected by a virus or by the action of cytokines retain their secrets, and we don't understand exactly what is going wrong. However, some brains from people with ME who have committed suicide have been found to have enterovirus in the tissue.[1]

Depression should be seen as yet another nasty symptom, rather than to do with the personality of the patient. Many ME/CFS sufferers are people with no previous history of emotional disturbance, and their changed behaviour can be alarming both to their relatives and themselves. Uncontrollable tears, terrible black depression, despair, panic, suicidal thoughts – all these can be felt by someone previously regarded as well-adjusted and in control of his or her emotions. Such a miserable wreck can also become cheerful, laughing or manic, this transformation taking place overnight or even within a few days. All these emotional ups and downs are quite devastating to patients, and also to their friends and families.

Mood changes are common in many brain disorders. For example, people who suffer from multiple sclerosis or Parkinson's disease, or who have had a stroke may develop emotional changes such as depression, anxiety or irritability.

And in ME/CFS there are other factors which may tip the scales between just coping and becoming severely upset:

- *exhaustion*, which may precede a relapse
- *low blood sugar*, which is treatable
- *hormonal* changes, for example premenstrual depression
- *food or chemical allergy* reaction
- *a problem with a relationship* (family, children or friend)
- *occasions* like Christmas or special anniversaries, which make many people depressed especially if they are lonely or ill
- *dark winter days*
- *malnutrition*, for example if on a strict diet.

When people or events make you upset, learn to tell yourself, 'It doesn't matter, this can't hurt me.' Living with any illness can strengthen the inner resources and lead sufferers to be less dependent on the opinions and approval of others. A friend told me, 'I try not to react to upsetting things now, nor to get overexcited or overjoyous. I have reduced the level of all emotional reactions and just let things wash past me, and it is easier to cope.'

It is easy for friends and family to cause hurt. You find out who your real friends are; others melt away because they feel threatened by the illness. They do not know how to approach someone who has changed and whose mood may be unpredictable. The upset from such hurt can be lessened if you have a strong belief in yourself, and if you can realize that your *unique special self (soul, spirit) is still intact and special*, in spite of being ill and losing friends.

Those with experience of depression can often recognize when they are going down again. Before the thing has got hold of you and you don't have the will or insight to sort anything out, try looking to see if there is anything pulling you down which you can maybe change, or at least comprehend.

Checklist for Low Mood

- Are you overdoing things? Extra rest and sleep, and letting go of striving, may help.
- Are you eating enough, and of the right things?
- If you are female, is your period due soon? If so, you know this will pass.
- If you have had symptoms pointing to yeast overgrowth, could you be having a flare-up, and need to check your diet?
- Have you eaten something you normally avoid to which you may be hypersensitive, such as wheat? If so, this reaction will pass.
- Is there some extra chemical around, such as gas or new paint? If you cannot avoid it, take extra vitamin C and wait for the reaction to settle, or consider removing yourself from the situation, if possible.
- Is it a time of year when you have felt bad before? Many people find a seasonal pattern to their ups and downs. There is not much you can do about the earth turning, but you know it will go on turning and bring you to a better month. If it is winter, maybe a full-spectrum lamp will help.
- Weather can also influence mood. Damp weather with low pressure seems to affect a lot of people, and may be associated with increased negative ions and moulds in the air.
- Is your low mood the result of some personal upset? If so, try and talk about it to someone you trust, instead of bottling it up.

It can happen that just when you think you have really got this illness sorted out and are functioning more and coping well, then crash, down you go into a spell of depression and nothing you do seems to pull you out. This happened to me during the first few years of being ill, when I was trying to increase my exercise tolerance, and thought I was doing very well! I was very depressed for weeks, but came through it.

What helped me most was (a) getting more physical and mental rest, and (b) using either sleeping pills or low-dose tricyclic antidepressants to ensure nights of good sleep. Each bout of depression I got always followed a period of extra activity, mental or physical, and came with other symptoms – fever, sore throat, sweating, muscle twitching and pain, etc. This leads me to believe that a lot of ME/CFS depression or other emotional disturbance is due to a flare-up of the disease process.

So what encouragement can be offered to people going through a low patch? The following ideas may help carers as well as patients, and if you have ME/CFS and are at present well enough to read and understand this, then store this information up against a future bad time:

- remember that *you, a unique special person, are the same person underneath*. The essential you is intact, even when you feel disintegrated and cut off from the world. Try to see the depression as an awful symptom to be borne patiently until it passes.
- *this time of blackness will pass.* Be very patient with yourself; remember that seasons come and go and so do moods.
- *do not feel ashamed of being as you are.* Depression is a symptom of the illness, and may need treatment. Many talented and special people before you have survived periods of deep depression (such as famous composers, and Spike Milligan, who has written a very useful book about depression).
- make a list of all the people you have ever known who love you, and care about what happens to you. Do this while you

are less depressed, and take this list out and refer to it if you have a bad time. These people *still* care about you while you are depressed.

Allow those people who love you to give you their affection even if you cannot give anything back at the time. The thoughts and prayers of others can sustain you during a long bad patch. Michael Mayne, a recent Dean of Westminster who has had ME, said 'When I was depressed I found I could not even pray, so I had to allow others to do the praying for me.'

Some of you may live alone, and say that you have no one who cares about you. There is probably someone, maybe at a distance, who could be contacted by phone or a written note. Could any friend fail to respond to a simple plea, such as 'I'm going through a very bad patch just now – please think of me, or phone me, or come and see me'?

The majority of those other people out there who appear to be happy and stable have probably gone through depression at some time in their lives. Those most able to understand and give support are those who have been in the dark valley and know what it is like. Such people could be contacted through your local support group, local church, or one of the national ME organizations' telephone help-lines.

Try and give yourself treats, or allow others to pamper you. A problem, of course, is that you may be in physical relapse and not strong enough for outings. A trip outside just to sit in the garden might be more appropriate.

One of the classic features of depression is the loss of self-esteem. By trying to give yourself treats you are reinforcing your affection for yourself. There is nothing wrong with loving yourself. Loving yourself is not the same as selfishness, it means accepting and caring about your individual personality with all its faults and weaknesses, just as you accept the imperfections of a loved one.

Laughter is good medicine for any illness. Norman Cousins, in his book *Anatomy of an Illness* tells of how, when confronted by sudden, severe, life-shattering arthritis he withdrew from life and watched comedies on videos for days. He laughed his way back to health.

One way to boost self-esteem is to manage to complete a small task each day. There is no point in setting impossible goals that you cannot achieve without collapse, so the task needs to be something within your grasp. Perhaps writing a short letter, tidying a drawer, a small patch of weeding – according to your ability.

The positive feedback from accomplishing something, especially if you see the result, can give a small boost each day. A certain degree of apathy may need to be overcome, but it is amazing how once the initial effort is made, the concentration required overcomes the misery for a time. Do not set a goal which is beyond your powers; if the task is unreasonable you will give up half-way through, and this can be counterproductive.

Should You Take Antidepressant Drugs?

Antidepressants have helped many people with ME/CFS. While they do not effect a total cure of the underlying illness, they may enable a patient who is making no progress and who maybe has severely disturbed sleep to improve the quality of sleep and energy levels, and stabilize mood swings. Some sufferers, however, do not tolerate any of this type of drug, or else have found no benefit. Often when they are not tolerated the drug has been prescribed in too high a dose.

It is important to remember that trying a course of anti-depressants does not necessarily mean that you have a major psychiatric illness, nor that you are stupid or lacking in moral fibre. If depression takes hold, no amount of will power can change the chemical reactions in the brain! If you were to break a leg, would you rely on will power and grit to deal with the pain or to immobilize the leg while it healed?

If your doctor, whether GP or specialist, seriously believes that a certain antidepressant might be helpful, it is really important that first you start with a very low dose, and secondly that give the treatment a good trial – at least four weeks – before deciding it is not for you.

TRICYCLIC ANTIDEPRESSANTS

These were originally developed as antihistamines to treat allergies. The chemical formulae of the tricyclics, the antihist-amines used to treat hay fever and skin allergies, and the pheno-thiazines used to treat schizophrenia and mania are very similar. In fact tricyclic antidepressants are sometimes used to treat chronic skin problems.

Tricyclics work by altering the available levels of some neurotransmitters, with effects not only on mood but on the transmission of other nerve impulses. So it is not surprising that brain functions in general may improve, such as memory, concentration, sleep patterns and sensitivity to pain and noise. They are often prescribed to reduce pain in other conditions. As these drugs also have antihistamine effects, they may modify some allergic symptoms as well.

Possible side-effects usually pass within two weeks, and will be more tolerable if the initial dose is very low. They may include dry mouth, blurred vision, difficulty passing urine, consti-pation, low blood pressure, dizziness, irregular or slow heart beats, nightmares.

Most side-effects settle after the first week or two, especially if the dose is increased gradually.

The starting dose should be *much smaller* for someone with ME/CFS than is normally prescribed for a patient with clinical depression. For example, *amitriptyline* can be started with 10–20 mg each evening, then gradually increased every two weeks to 25, 50, or 75 mg, or until there is good sleep with minimal side-effects.

Other tricyclics used for ME/CFS are *prothiaden*, *trimipramine*, and *doxepin*.

There are also other tricyclics, but the most useful types are those that are sedative and reduce anxiety.

The important thing to remember about tricyclics is that they do not work overnight like aspirins or sleeping pills. It will be at least two weeks before you see any real improvement in mood. Before that, most people benefit from better sleep and reduced pain and anxiety, a great relief if there is marked insomnia and agitation as well as depression.

If you have unpleasant side-effects at the start of treatment, especially any heart symptoms such as missed beats, tell your doctor. Some of the newer tricyclics have fewer side-effects.

SSRIS

The other main type of antidepressants are called *SSRIs* – *Selective Serotonin Re-uptake Inhibitors*. These include fluoxetine (trade name Prozac), sertraline (trade name Lustral) and paroxetine (trade name Seroxat). These work in a different way to tricyclics, but the end effect is to increase available 5-hydroxytriptamine – 5HT, also called serotonin. SSRIs are taken in the morning, and tend to be stimulant rather than sedative. They also may produce side-effects: nausea, sweating, dizziness, insomnia, shakiness and occasionally mania or feelings of unreality. Even if taken in the morning, insomnia and vivid dreams may be an unwanted problem.

For ME/CFS, this type of antidepressant is usually prescribed in small doses. However it is difficult to get below half the normal dose (25 mg sertraline, or 10 mg fluoextine or paroxetine) because the preparations come only in 50-mg or 20-mg tablets respectively. Fluoxetine (Prozac) is available as liquid, 20 mg per 5 ml, so much smaller doses could be used.

The only published double-blind controlled trial of anti-depressants in CFS was for Prozac, and found no overall benefit in mood or energy levels.[2]

MAOIS

The third type of antidepressant to mention is *MAOIs – Mono-Amine Oxidase Inhibitors*. These alter the levels and availability of noradrenergic brain hormones, rather than altering serotonin as the tricyclics and SSRIs do. MAOIs have side-effects and interactions with various foods (foods that contain tyramine, such as cheese, marmite, beef extracts, wines and some beans) which may a cause sudden rise in blood pressure. For these reasons, MAOIs are rarely used outside the super-vision of a hospital specialist. However, a newer type called moclobemide (trade name Manerix) has fewer unpleasant side-effects, and has been used successfully on some ME/CFS patients.

A problem for many ME/CFS people is that they have an altered sensitivity or reaction to any drug that acts on the brain. I know two people who became manic after three days on a tiny dose of tricyclic, with total insomnia – the opposite effect to what would be expected!

WHEN DEPRESSIVE SYMPTOMS ARE SEVERE

If the depressive symptoms are severe and constant for more than a short time, then a diagnosis of clinical depression is probable, especially if the patient has suicidal ideas. In this case, it is really important that expert help is sought, and the GP may get an urgent psychiatric opinion. If major depression co-exists with ME/CFS, antidepressant treatment using the full therapeutic doses may be needed. Nobody can start to make any recovery from ME/CFS (or many other conditions) if severe depression is present and untreated.

If you are improving in both mood and energy while on antidepressants, **do not suddenly stop them**. Even if you think you don't need them any more, you need to reduce the daily dose very gradually under regular medical supervision. Sudden withdrawal could put you right back to where you started from, or make you even worse than you were in the first place.

Sadly, there is a small but steady toll of people with ME/CFS who find they just cannot bear life any more, and take their own lives. This is really tragic, though understandable. Major depression has a high death rate, and is a potentially fatal complication of any illness, and must be taken seriously. *So please, if you as a person with ME/CFS, or someone you know, is seriously depressed and has thought or talked of suicide, do get medical help, and don't refuse treatment or hospital admission if this is advised.*

If you are not taking any nutritional supplements already, consider the following, all of which are necessary for good brain function:

- vitamin B complex (or as part of a multivitamin), containing at least 20 mg each B_1, B_2, B_6

- vitamin C, zinc, magnesium
- amino acid complex, especially there is poor intake or absorption of protein foods.

Psychotherapy

The term is used here rather loosely, and refers to the sort of skilled help that can be given by a psychiatrist, a psychotherapist, a counsellor, or anyone else trained in this field.

Psychotherapy proper is not suggested for someone in the early acute stage of illness, nor during a relapse, because there is just not the energy available for the talking and self-understanding that is part of the therapy. Digging up past painful experiences does not help an ill person; better help comes from a skilled listener, and dealing together with problems of the present moment.

Learning to live with a debilitating illness is difficult. One of the first steps to coping is accepting the illness and coming to terms with the limitations it imposes.

Anger and grief are perfectly normal reactions to developing a condition such as ME/CFS. If these emotions can be expressed and admitted, instead of being suppressed and driven inside, then the patient has a better chance of maintaining a degree of sanity, and of coping with further relapses or depression.

Often, family and friends really want to help a person with ME/CFS, who they see is devastated by the symptoms and loss of normal life, but they may not have the skills needed to help psychologically.

COGNITIVE BEHAVIOUR THERAPY

CBT has already been described in Chapter 7. Another closely related type of treatment is Cognitive Analytic Therapy (CAT), in which the therapist together with the patient work on ways of accepting and adjusting to what is happening now. Sometimes this also means changing one's perceptions of what is going on in life. It means dealing with reality rather than a fantasy. Whatever the titles or techniques of therapy, the aims are always:

- to support and affirm the patient whatever the distress
- to help the patient improve self-esteem and confidence
- to look for other ways of coping with the symptoms
- to look for ways of minimizing the impact on emotions
- to work with the patient towards finding new ways of day-to-day living, so that energy is managed better
- to encourage the patient to feel more in control of the illness.

To my mind, an important benefit from any form of psycho-therapy should be that the patient no longer feels a victim of the ME or fatigue syndrome. People who feel they are victims tend to withdraw from the world, and also to keep on finding something or someone to blame for what has happened to them.

Loneliness

I have talked about grief and anger and their role in contributing to depression. Loneliness is a feeling that hurts a lot of people when they are ill, even those living in a family situation. Chronic illness may lose you friends, but it need not; a lot depends on how you view your friends and family. For example, if you become jealous of the health of others, this shows, and drives them away.

Self-pity, moaning about how unfair life is, and seeing your-self as a victim all lead in the end to resentment. *Much of life is unfair and difficult for every human being!* You may have a strange illness; other people have different problems. Many people in the world are starving to death as you read this. Feelings of resentment, envy and self-pity can only make the illness worse, and they get between you and friends and lead to loneliness.

Past hurts and grievances, if they are hung on to, eat away inside. All sorts of barriers that stop you loving other people, and keep their affection from you, can spring up from jealousy and resentment. Loneliness is partly a state of mind. People can feel lonely surrounded by a crowd in a city, or not feel lonely while apparently isolated in a deserted landscape.

Solitude is something different, and can be very rewarding if it is viewed positively. With so much noise and overcrowding in the modern world, solitude and peace can be hard to find, and if you are in the stage of convalescing or recovery from ME/CFS, you may find solitude a more comfortable state, and that increasing exposure to people and noise is hard to cope with.

I do not write these things as an outsider with no understanding – I have had experience of the pit of despair, I still experience loneliness, envy of friends and relatives who are fit and active, and anger. However, I think it is natural to feel these things. What is destructive is either not to acknowledge these emotions, or to feed on them. Once you are aware of them, express them – on paper or out loud when alone! – then throw them away and replace them with more useful thoughts.

Here are some words by the writer Kahlil Gibran, taken from his little masterpiece *The Prophet*. They speak clearly about unhappiness and the pain of depression:

...OF JOY AND SORROW...

When you are joyous, look deep into your heart and you shall find it is only that which has given you sorrow that is giving you joy.

When you are sorrowful, look again in your heart, and you shall see that in truth you are weeping for that which has been your delight.

Some of you say, 'Joy is greater than sorrow,' and others say, 'Nay, sorrow is the greater.'

But I say unto you, they are inseparable.

Together they come, and when one sits alone with you at your board, remember that the other is asleep upon your bed.

...OF PAIN...

Your pain is the breaking of the shell that encloses your understanding.

Even as the stone of the fruit must break, that its heart may stand in the sun, so must you know pain.

And could you keep your heart in wonder at the daily miracle of your life, your pain would not seem less wondrous than your joy;

And you would accept the seasons of your heart, even as you have always accepted the seasons that pass over your fields.

And you would watch with serenity through the winters of your grief.

RECOMMENDED READING
The Road Less Travelled by M Scott Peck (Arrow Books, 1990)

Chapter 10

Orthodox Treatments and Hazards

Drugs

People with ME/CFS should be cautious about taking medicines, for various reasons. Many sufferers become hypersensitive to drugs, and in some there may be a problem – if the liver is at all affected – in breaking down and disposing of a drug. Treatments that act on the nervous system may produce quite bizarre effects, sometimes the opposite of what is intended. A good rule is to ask your doctor about any medicine you may be prescribed. You need to know exactly what it is – its name and purpose, the symptoms it is supposed to treat, how to take it, and for how long. Report any reaction or side-effect as soon as possible. Various self-medications that can be purchased over the counter, which may previously have been harmless, may now cause side-effects or allergic reactions.

Drugs You Should Try to Avoid

TRANQUILLIZERS

Tranquillizers include drugs such as Valium, Librium, Ativan, and medium- to long-acting sleeping pills. These can be addictive, can make depression worse, and do not do anything to correct underlying brain disturbance.

ANTIBIOTICS

Broad-spectrum antibiotics should be avoided unless a course is essential for an infection. Ideally, proof of a bacterial infection should be obtained first, such as by a urine culture or throat swab. If an antibiotic is needed, hopefully your doctor will prescribe one specifically for that infection, for a limited length of time. It is a good idea for someone with ME/CFS who develops an infection to take measures to boost his or her natural resistance to infections by taking extra vitamin C, zinc and vitamin A, and getting extra rest and plenty of fluids. If you need antibiotics it is important to complete the course, because if you stop taking it when you feel better, the bacteria may develop resistance to that particular antibiotic.

Restore the friendly bugs in your gut, which will have been depleted by the antibiotic, by taking probiotics (*see page 255*) for at least two weeks after the antibiotics are finished.

Septrin

Following reports of adverse reactions to Septrin (which is a combination of two antibiotics: trimethoprin and sulphamethazole), leading not only to ME but various other condition, its use has been restricted to certain specific infections, and it is unlikely to be routinely prescribed for urinary tract infections, as used to be the case.

STEROIDS

If you are already taking cortico-steroids (cortisone, prednis-olone or similar), *do not stop taking them*. Consult your GP or specialist about the need for them. Steroids may cause tempo-rary improvement of symptoms in many conditions, including asthma, rheumatoid arthritis, ulcerative colitis and polymyal-gia. However, this dramatic improvement happens because the body's own supply of cortisone is boosted artificially; this can dampen down the symptoms which result from allergic reac-tions (such as asthma) or from auto-immune diseases. Short-term benefits are outweighed by the longer-term effects of steroids: laziness of the adrenal-cortex glands in making one's own cortisone, which leads to poor response to stress and infection, and to increasing dependence on the steroid drug as the source of cortisone. Other longer-term hazards are depres-sion, osteoporosis, gut ulcers, weight gain, cataracts and high blood pressure. Taking steroids dampens down the body's natur-al response to infection and could mask infections such as TB.

A person who has been on steroids for more than a few weeks must not suddenly stop them. If long-term treatment is to be stopped, the dose has to be lowered very gradually over a period of time, and under medical supervision.

There *are* conditions where steroids save lives, and for some people life-long replacement steroid therapy is essential. How-ever, steroids are *not* recommended for people with ME/CFS. In view of the findings of low-cortisol response to stress in ME/CFS, with symptoms suggesting mild low-adrenal func-tion in some patients, a trial was carried out in the US to see if low-dose hydrocortisone therapy could be useful.[1] But the results found little benefit in terms of fatigue and other symp-toms, and this, together with secondary suppression of ACTH (the pituitary hormone that stimulates the adrenals to produce

natural cortisones), led the author of this study, Dr Stephen
Strauss, to conclude that cortisone replacement therapy is not
indicated in CFS.

ORAL CONTRACEPTIVES
See Chapter 16.

ANAESTHETICS AND SURGERY
All anaesthetic agents are drugs with powerful effects on
the central nervous system. Any after-effects may be more
severe for a patient with ME/CFS. I know of two cases where
the effect of a muscle-paralysing drug (routinely used in anaesthesia after you have gone to sleep, to allow a tube to be safely
passed down the airway) has taken an abnormally long time to
wear off after the operation. Since early research into abnormalities of transmission of acetylcholine in ME/CFS are
demonstrating problems, both in the brain and in the peripheral nervous system (*see page 76*), it is not surprising that a
routine anaesthetic may cause problems. Obviously there are
occasions when surgery is essential. It is important to tell the
anaesthetist you have ME/CFS, and describe any problems
you may have with muscles, walking, co-ordination and brain
symptoms. Then he or she can make adjustments and use the
most appropriate drugs, in lower doses if necessary.

Of course, any operation is stressful and may bring on
some kind of relapse. If it is unavoidable, then try to make provision for extra care and rest in the convalescent period, and
take extra vitamin C, zinc and vitamin A for a few weeks after
surgery. A useful homoeopathic remedy that restricts bleeding
and promotes healing is *Arnica*. It is harmless, can be bought at
any chemist, and is helpful for any trauma including bruising
(*see page 238*). It is probably wise to postpone non-urgent

surgery if you are severely ill or in a relapse, but remember that hundreds of people with ME/CFS do have operations safely each year.

Local Anaesthetic
Many people with ME/CFS report increased sensitivity to local anaesthetic. It may be a reaction to the adrenaline which is often combined with the anaesthetic, and it is wise to ask the surgeon to use a local anaesthetic that does not contain added adrenaline. Several instances have been recorded of patients collapsing or losing consciousness after local anaesthesia for dental procedures. On the other hand, many muscle biopsies have been performed for ME research with no ill-effect from the local anaesthetic. So the reactions experienced in the dentist's chair may be partly due to stress caused by dental treatment, or to the dose used, or to the site of injection being closer to the brain.

You may find that the health of your gums is better after improving your diet and increasing your vitamin C intake. But tooth abscess or any chronic mouth sepsis must be treated, with penicillin and dental surgery if needed, as any septic focus in the body damages health and will delay recovery.

Mercury Toxicity – Is it Relevant?
Another reason why some ME/CFS patients report a relapse following dental work involving fillings may be to do with mercury sensitivity. This is a very controversial topic. Although the use of mercury amalgam is being abandoned in some European countries, there is a reluctance in the British dental profession to look closely at mercury's hazards.

WHAT ARE THE FACTS?

We know that mercury is extremely poisonous. In dentistry it is used in a mixture with silver, tin, copper and zinc, containing about 50 per cent mercury. Once this amalgam has been installed in a tooth, there is no proof that some of the mercury does not escape in the form of vapour and enter the body. When the fillings are ground, as is done when chewing, some mercury does escape as vapour, and this can enter the saliva and be swallowed, where it can be converted into methyl mercury by the action of bacteria in the mouth and in the gut. Methyl mercury is much more toxic than elemental mercury.

Because there is more than one metal in the mouth and there is liquid in the form of saliva, a small but measurable electric current is continuously generated in the mouth. This is something that gradually corrodes the amalgam, together with foodstuffs and chemicals and physical wearing away by chewing. All amalgam fillings gradually deteriorate; some have to be replaced after five to ten years. So where has the mercury gone?

The electric potentials between teeth and their surrounding saliva can be measured using a *milliammeter*. Some of the symptoms possibly due to the electric current in the mouth, which has been measured as 900 mv or more, include a metallic taste in the mouth, increased salivation, irritability, pins and needles or pain in the face, and severe depression. The roots of teeth, particularly in the upper jaw, pass close to main nerves, and the impulses passing along nerves can be affected by local electric currents.

Research has demonstrated that mercury can affect central nervous system functioning, and also has a bad effect on the immune system. It was demonstrated in 1984 that removal of amalgam fillings resulted in a rise in circulating T lymphocytes, whose numbers fell when the amalgam was reinserted. This may be due to hypersensitivity to amalgam fillings. There is certainly plenty of documented evidence of the undesirable results of having such a toxic metal in the mouth.

Mercury toxicity is probably not a cause of ME/CFS, but it may contribute to immune dysfunction and to brain symptoms. In 1995 a study was carried out into immune abnormalities linked to mercury toxicity by Dr Don Henderson, immunologist at Charing Cross Hospital, London. Information on this research can be obtained by contacting:

The British Society for Mercury-free Dentistry
1 Welbeck House
62 Welbeck Street
London W1M 7HB
Please enclose a stamped addressed envelope.

SHOULD FILLINGS BE REMOVED?

Should people with ME/CFS who are not recovering, or are getting worse, and have a number of old mercury fillings get them removed and replaced with non-toxic fillings?

There are some problems to consider:

- the replacement is not available on the NHS, and will therefore be costly
- you need to have evidence first that the amalgam is causing trouble. There are tests which show if mercury is leaking, and if you are allergic to it, but not every dentist can do these tests
- the process of removing amalgam causes release of mercury, and may induce a severe relapse
- the removal needs to be done by a dentist who is aware of the hazards, with special precautions taken to minimize swallowing

or inhaling the amalgam. The fillings should be removed in a particular sequence, depending on which ones are causing the greatest reaction.

- some of the replacement materials may cause problems, and the patient should be tested for sensitivities to replacement fillings first
- because it is a procedure which causes worsening of symptoms, it is essential to take extra immune-boosting supplements (vitamins A and C, zinc and calcium pantothenate) before and for several weeks afterwards.

There is an urgent need for more research into the connections between mercury amalgam fillings and immune functioning, the nervous system, and indeed the whole physiology of the body. There are no figures to show whether the percentage of people with amalgam fillings is significantly different between people with ME/CFS and patients with other conditions.

In the mean time, the general advice of dentists and the ME Association is: *Do not rush into having your amalgam fillings removed*, especially if you are really ill. If you start to get better and feel you would like advice about it, contact the Dental Society for Clinical Nutrition (*see Appendix A*).

IMMUNIZATIONS

An immunization (sometimes called vaccination) is a procedure in which the body's immune system is stimulated to produce an antibody to a specific infection; so that if the virus or bacteria causing the infection enters the body at a later date, the white blood cells will recognize it and produce lots more antibodies very quickly. The antigen which stimulates antibody production is usually a form of the virus or bacteria which has been modified to make it harmless. When smallpox vaccine was developed, a modified relative, called cowpox, was used.

People with ME/CFS may need immunizations in these circumstances:

- before foreign travel – e.g. a typhoid, cholera, yellow fever, or polio booster
- to start or boost protection against tetanus, for going abroad, for gardeners and agricultural workers, or when there is a penetrating wound
- children with ME who would normally be at the age to have BCG (for TB), rubella (only girls need this), mumps and measles immunization, or any booster vaccine.

Practically every adult with ME/CFS will have had childhood immunizations to protect against tetanus, diphtheria, polio, smallpox, tuberculosis and possibly measles, mumps and rubella. If tetanus protection is advised because of a wound that carries a risk for tetanus, this must be done, because tetanus is lethal. Tetanus toxoid is not derived from live germs, and therefore may be less likely to produce a reaction.

The main occasion when you may consider having an immunization is before going abroad. Unless it is obligatory before entering the foreign country, the advice to ME/CFS patients is *don't have immunizations*.

Typhoid and cholera (commonly given together as TAB/cho) immunizations cause some reaction in all healthy people, and may lead to a severe reaction, a relapse, or possibly to no reaction at all, in someone with ME/CFS. It is better not to go to countries where there is a high risk of contracting enteric diseases; if you go, though, be scrupulously careful about hygiene: boil water before you drink or cook with it, and do not eat uncooked food in cafés. Anyway, typhoid and cholera injections do not protect against dysentery, hepatitis or *Guardia*, which are just as easily picked up in many countries.

Immunizations are intended to stir up the immune system, but if the immune system is not functioning normally one can end up with hypersensitive reactions, or incomplete immunity.

Hepatitis B Immunization

Cases of ME/CFS that developed following hepatitis B immunization are being reported more frequently. Protection against hepatitis B is routinely given to health workers, particularly nurses and doctors or anyone in close contact with patients. If you have had ME/CFS and have recovered enough to return to health work, you need to weigh up the potential risks of being immunized against hepatitis B. If on testing there is already adequate antibody to hepatitis B, then it will not be necessary. It is important to discuss this first with the Occupational Health doctor of the hospital or area.

Some Useful Drugs

Although there is no drug treatment to cure ME/CFS, certain medicines can be used to treat symptoms and make life more comfortable. It is important to treat pain, sleep disturbance and depression or anxiety if these develop. It is essential to address sleep disturbance and secondary psychological illness before a patient can start to recover.

A great deal of the skill of living with ME, CFS or any chronic illness is to be able to compromise and prioritize. This also applies to taking drugs and therapies. I do not agree with purists who say that all conventional drugs are wrong; nor with narrow-minded doctors who prescribe drugs with possible side-effects while condemning all 'alternative treatments' (usually through ignorance) which in general are safer and gentler than drugs. The rigidly obsessive ME/CFS patient whose life is dominated by strict rules is not going to be open to trying various therapies, nor to be aware of what suits him or her.

SLEEPING PILLS

If these are needed and other measures don't help, then one of the short-acting hypnotics is best, such as temazepam or triazolam, starting with a small dose. Some people worry about dependence on them, but using them to achieve healing sleep is more sensible than nights of wakefulness followed by days of feeling exhausted. As you get better you can do without them. A newer hypnotic, zopiclone, works in a different way from the benzodiazepines (temazepam, Valium, etc.), and is not so addictive. But sleeping pills may be less effective than tricyclics (*see below*).

MELATONIN

This product, based on naturally occurring melatonin produced by the brain, is no longer licensed to buy in the UK. It is said to be useful for resetting the 'biological clock' that controls sleep and wakefulness, and is used (where available) to help prevent jet-lag by long-distance air travellers. Some people with ME/CFS have found it helpful to improve sleep disturbances, especially sleep reversal – being awake most of the night then sleepy during the day – though others say it has no effect.

ANTIHISTAMINES

In small doses, an antihistamine such as *Piriton* (chlorpheniramine) can be very helpful if there are many allergic symptoms, particularly the chronic explosive sneezing and streaming nose experienced by some sufferers. It causes a little sedation, but if taken at night this is no disadvantage. Some newer antihistamines are non-sedative.

PAINKILLERS

Avoid aspirin and compounds containing aspirin. Many people are sensitive to salicylates, and aspirin is now known to cause allergic reactions and may be implicated in a hypersensitivity illness in children called Reye's syndrome. It is also irritating to the stomach. All the non-steroid anti-inflammatory drugs (such as ibuprofen) have the potential for stomach irritation, and should be taken with food.

Paracetamol has fewer side-effects than aspirin. Again, a small dose should be tried, such as $\frac{1}{2}$ or 1 tablet, instead of 2 tablets. A good remedy for pain is vitamin C, 500 mg every hour. It has anti-prostaglandin effects similar to those of aspirin and anti-inflammatory drugs, and is much safer. Stronger painkillers include co-codamol (a combination of codeine with paracetamol) and distalgesic (a combination that has opiate sedative properties and is only obtainable on prescription).

Ibuprofen (Brufen) is an anti-inflammatory that can be used for headaches, joint pain and period pain. Other non-steroidal anti-inflammatory drugs for more severe joint pains include Voltarol. These must all be taken with or just after food, as they can lead to gastrointestinal bleeding and stomach ulcers if taken on their own.

Migraines are a particular problem for many people with ME/CFS. In some people migraine may be triggered by particular foods. It is worth keeping a food diary to see if anything is regular trigger. In some women, migraines happen either just before or after a period, and are hormonally relat-ed. The severe headaches experienced by some ME/CFS patients may not be migraine, but could be due to fluid retention in the brain.

A specific anti-migraine drug is *Imigran*, which promotes serotonin (an important neurotransmitter that is faulty in migraine attacks) in the brain. It is expensive, however, and your GP may only prescribe it after other drugs have failed. If the migraine hits suddenly without warning, and the sufferer has vomiting, Imigran can be self-administrated by subcutaneous (under the skin) injection.

In some cases, the incidence and severity of migraines can be reduced by taking one of the SSRI (selective serotonin reuptake inhibitors) class of anti-depressants *(see page 186)*, which also promote serotonin levels. For example, I know of two women with ME who had severe intractable migraines, who have found an improvement from taking a small dose of *Sertraline* once or twice daily.

ANTIDEPRESSANTS

Tricyclic antidepressants are closely related (chemically) to antihistamines. The main benefit is improving the quality of sleep and a reduction of pain, probably by correcting the disturbance in non-REM sleep.

A dose that is much less than that used to treat severe depression seems to help not only sleep, but also other brain functions – cognition, concentration, memory; muscle power (reduces muscle spasms); emotional lability – amitriptyline is especially good for relieving anxiety; and allergic reactions such as asthma, sneezing. In fact, tricyclics were originally developed in a search for effective treatments for allergies, and have a chemical structure very similar to antihistamines.

These drugs do not suit everyone with ME/CFS, nor cure the underlying illness in most cases. Even in low doses, patients may complain of intolerable side-effects, and in a few, the effects on the brain are opposite to what is intended – maybe causing insomnia, anxiety or panic attacks, and a racing heart. Many patients do not tolerate tricyclics because the initial dose prescribed is too high. A tricyclic that has been tested on patients with fibromyalgia syndrome is amitriptyline. When prescribed at only 10 or 20 mg nightly, it improves sleep and muscle pain and tenderness in fibromyalgia syndrome.

Other antidepressants prescribed for ME/CFS are the SSRIs, such as Prozac or Lustral.

The only published controlled drug trial of antidepressants was one from Holland.[2] In this study the researchers concluded that:

'Fluoxetine [Prozac] in a daily dose of 20 mg does not have a beneficial effect on any characteristic of CFS. The lack of effect of fluoxetine on depressive symptoms in CFS suggests that processes underlying depressive symptoms in CFS may differ from those in patients with major depression.'

There is more about antidepressants in Chapter 9.

DRUGS ACTING ON THE GUT

The gut gives problems in many patients – alternating diarrhoea and constipation, distension, pain, poor digestion, malabsorbtion and absence of peristalsis (poor bowel control), to name the most common. These gut dysfunctions are probably secondary to hypothalamic malfunction.

Irritable Bowel Syndrome (IBS)

This is not a disease, but a collection of symptoms, and its cause is not understood. It appears to be more common in people with ME/CFS than the general population. Food intolerances probably play a part, and wheat and wheat bran may be culprits. Although we are being urged quite correctly to increase fibre intake, it is better to do this by having many more vegetables and fruit, and other sources of fibre such as oats, seeds and potatoes. *Fybogel* is a bulking agent that can be prescribed. It is also important to drink plenty of water if spasms and constipation are troublesome.

Certain drugs may sometimes be prescribed for symptoms of IBS, such as antispasmodics such as mebevarine (Colofac), or merbentyl. Some herbs are also worth trying, such as peppermint oil.

If diarrhoea with pain is a feature, other problems in the gut must be excluded, especially if blood is present in the faeces. Codeine phosphate or Immodium may be prescribed for this.

Nausea

This is common in ME/CFS, but probably arises from the brain, rather than from the stomach. In many patients it is a symptom of relapse, associated with others such as muscle pain, sweating, exhaustion and general malaise. There are various antinausea drugs available. One of the best is Stugeron, which also help dizziness and vertigo.

Tested Treatments

ESSENTIAL FATTY ACIDS

A trial in Glasgow[3] found that essential fatty acids have beneficial effects (*see page 216*). Blood levels of EFAs, which were abnormal at the start of the trial, returned to near normal after three months. EFAs have been shown to inhibit the production of cytokines and replication of viruses, and are essential for the integrity of cell membranes. The authors of the trial noted that no patients were cured, but that they could increase their activities and felt better.

IMMUNOGLOBULIN THERAPY

Two trials in Australia and the US (1990)[4,5] showed conflicting results on the benefits of immunoglobulin injections. This may sometimes be helpful for patients with ME/CFS who have low levels of IgG found on blood tests, and who are in the early stage of the illness. Patients in the Australian study who improved had abnormal cell-mediated hypersensitivity tests which returned to normal after treatment.

Other Treatments Being Tested

CALCIUM CHANNEL BLOCKERS

This treatment, used in the US but not generally in the UK, uses a calcium channel blocker such as *nifedipine* to treat angina, high blood-pressure and migraine. When used to treat CFS, calcium channel blockers may improve blood perfusion in the brain, and thus have a beneficial effect on cognitive function.

AMPLIGEN

Ampligen is double-stranded RNA which mimics the RNA in the immune system. It has both antiviral and immune-modifying effects, and may remove a block in the immune system which prevents it from recognizing virus.

A controlled trial of Ampligen, using 200 patients, was completed in July 1991. It showed that Ampligen was an effective treatment for the severely debilitating form of chronic fatigue syndrome, improving both the physical debility and the cognitive dysfunctions. There was no significant toxicity from Ampligen.

A further report[6] found long-term benefits in patients with poor function (Karnofsky scores of 20–60), who received Ampligen intravenously for 12 to 48 weeks. After 24 weeks there were improvements in cognitive function, exercise tolerance and oxygen uptake.

Ampligen is also being tested in Belgium, but despite these promising trials it is not yet a licensed drug in the US nor available in the UK.

GALANTHAMINE HYDROBROMIDE

This a selective anticholinesterase inhibitor, based on an extract from snowdrop bulbs (*Galanthus* is the botanical name for snowdrop!). The results of the first trial[7] were promising, and found a significant improvement in CFS patients in fatigue, myalgia and especially sleep, compared to those who received placebo. Unfortunately galanthamine gave some side-effects, commonly nausea. Further trials of galanthamine are at present underway the UK, and it will be interesting to see if the benefits are replicated. The study supports the probability that there is a malfunction in acetylcholine neurotransmission (*see page 76*) in ME/CFS.

At present, research into abnormalities in acetylcholine neurotransmission are at an early stage, and it is not known at what level (brain or periphery) the abnormality lies, nor whether it is a problem with acetylcholine receptors (which are hypersensitive) or transmission between cells. It may well be that galanthamine is only helpful for some ME/CFS patients, and further trials are needed to show whether the benefits outweigh possible side-effects.

REPLACEMENT OF ADRENAL AND THYROID HORMONES

A study in the US looked at the possibility that *hydrocortisone* in low doses could be beneficial for people with ME/CFS, because some patients have symptoms similar to hypoadrenalism. However, the researcher (Dr Strauss) found that any possible benefits, which were few, were outweighed by the suppression of natural adrenal function. Therefore cortisone therapy is not recommended at present.

There has been a lot of publicity of late about thyroid dysfunction, and taking lose dosages of thyroid hormone. There has been no research yet on the use of thyroid hormone in people with ME/CFS who have normal thyroid function tests. There may be a few patients who have low or borderline thyroid function tests, who find benefit from a very low doses of *thyroxine*. However, if someone who has normal thyroid function takes thyroxine, even in a small amount, there is the risk of side-effects such as fast or irregular heartbeat, mental disturbances and weight loss, plus suppression of natural thyroid output.

Until good research has been carried out to see if there is a subgroup of ME/CFS patients with reduced thyroid function, and also to find more sensitive tests of thyroid function, people with ME/CFS are advised *not to take thyroxine*, unless they have evidence of poor thyroid function and are under the close supervision of a doctor who specializes in endocrinology.

The search for a cure for ME/CFS continues. The fact that not all cases are the same will inevitably mean that even a therapy that has very good results in a properly conducted trial may not be appropriate for all patients. Members of the ME Association in the UK will find that all new findings about useful treatments are reported in the magazine *Perspectives*, which is published four times a year. 'Watch this space!'

Chapter 11

Good Nutrition for ME/CFS

Why is good nutrition so important for someone with ME/CFS?

- Deficiencies of essential nutrients may have developed before the onset of the illness.
- Digestion and absorption of food may be impaired. This can result from damage to the lining of the small intestine, or pancreatic involvement from an intestinal infection.
- The brain and the immune system need a good supply of protein, essential fats, minerals and vitamins in order to function efficiently.

Guidelines for Basic Healthy Eating

- Eat regular meals. Do not miss breakfast or lunch.
- Use fresh, unprocessed foods as far as possible. Avoid dried, packaged, dehydrated or canned food.
- Reduce intake of refined carbohydrates – sugar (brown or white), white flour, cakes, sweets.
- Avoid alcohol, and cut down on coffee and tea.
- Have more unsaturated fats (such as vegetable oils, fish oils)

and fewer saturated animal fats (fat in meat and dairy produce).

- Have good-quality protein at least once a day.
- Eat plenty of fresh fruit and vegetables.

Try to have some raw vegetable as salad every day. Cooked vegetables (but not potatoes or beans) should be done lightly in a little water or steamed, to conserve vitamins and minerals. Peel or wash fruit with skins and wash all vegetables thoroughly, unless you know they are organically grown. Use them as fresh as possible.

Be more adventurous with salads, using sprouted legumes, grated carrot, grated beetroot or shredded cabbage in winter when traditional salad foods are out of season. If you already possess a food processor you should make full use of it to prepare finely chopped salads and thick vegetable soups.

Vegetables and fruit are important, not only to supply a good daily level of vitamin C, but minerals and enzymes. Some raw food should be eaten daily, as vitamins and enzymes are partially destroyed by cooking. Irradiated foods, which may appear fresh because they do not go mouldy and have a longer shelf life, are dead foods because their enzymes have been destroyed.

Protein

Protein is made up of amino acids, the building blocks used for the repair and replacement of all body cells. They are also essential for making antibodies, neurotransmitters, hormones and the chemicals (lymphokines, or cytokines) produced by the immune system. Some amino acids can be made in our bodies; others must be supplied in food: these are called *essential amino acids.* For any diet to be adequate in its protein supply, it must supply all of the 12 essential amino acids.

So-called 'first-class' proteins contain all the essential amino acids in the right balance. These proteins are derived from animal sources: meats, fish, eggs and milk products.

'Second-class' proteins are deficient in one or more of the essential amino acids, and come from plants. However, by combining plant proteins properly (for example rice with lentils, wheat with beans) all the amino acids are supplied. This principle is used by vegans to construct an adequate diet.

Although meat is a good protein food, it can be high in saturated fat, and non-organic meat may contain traces of hormones and antibiotics which are added to animal feeds.

The best meats are poultry, especially if organic, game such as venison, rabbit or pheasant, and lamb.

Fish is an excellent food; it is a complete protein, easily digested, and contains fish oils which supply unsaturated fats. Both meat and fish are good sources of zinc, and fish also provides iodine. Try and have fish at least twice a week.

Eggs are an excellent food, because even though an average egg contains only 7–8 grams (g) of protein, it is a complete protein and easily digested. They are also a good source of cholesterol, B vitamins, vitamins A and E, and zinc. Eggs from free-ranging chickens are additive-free, and better for flavour and nutrient content.

If you are not allergic to milk, then dairy products are a good source of protein and also calcium. Skimmed milk has less fat than full-cream milk, and more protein and calcium per volume. The best cheeses are low-fat cheeses with no added yellow colour, or mould. Plain, 'live' yoghurt (containing *Lactobacillus* and other gut-friendly bacteria) is an excellent source of protein and calcium, and the bacteria help to maintain colon health. Some people who are intolerant of cow's milk can tolerate yoghurt, goat's or sheep's milk.

As in most illnesses, it is important to have a good intake of all essential amino acids for recovery to take place. Some people find it helpful to take supplements of amino acids, especially if they have frequent digestive and bowel problems. Bear in mind that meat is more digestible if cooked long and slowly, as in a casserole.

Some people may ask if a vegetarian diet is suitable. It depends on what you are used to, and how you feel on a high-meat diet. It is possible to have enough high-quality protein as a lactovegetarian (i.e. someone who eats vegetables and dairy products), but a vegan diet relies solely on protein from grains, pulses and nuts. This may be fine for those in perfect digestive health, but many people with ME/CFS are intolerant of wheat, and also have problems digesting pulses. A vegan diet can also lead to deficiencies of essential amino acids, vitamins B_{12} and D, zinc, iron and calcium. Soya products contain calcium and protein, however intolerance to soya develops easily in anyone with a tendency to allergies. So for these reasons, *a vegan diet is not recommended* for people with ME/CFS.

It is not a good idea to change suddenly from being a vegetarian to a flesh eater, or vice versa, while you are ill. The digestive system may be slow to adapt, so any diet changes should be made gradually.

Carbohydrates

These provide the main fuel for energy supply. Someone doing hard exercise daily, such as a labourer or athlete, needs plenty of carbohydrate to burn. An ill or sedentary person will need much less.

Refined carbohydrates are pure starch or sugar, from which the husk and germ have been largely removed by refining, providing calories but no other nutrients. Valuable B vitamins, protein, minerals, vegetable oils and fibre are removed in the milling process. Refined carbohydrates are quickly digested and absorbed, but may lead to low blood sugar in susceptible people.

Complex carbohydrates have starch together with the husk and seed-germ; as in wholewheat, unrefined oats, brown rice, other wholegrains and potatoes with their skins. They are more slowly digested, leading to a gradual rise in blood glucose. With complex carbohydrates you have to eat more in volume to give the same amount of energy as refined carbohydrate.

Sugar is a relatively recent addition to the human diet. The high consumption of sugar in sweets, cakes, breakfast cereals and canned drinks is responsible not only for tooth decay, but for poor blood sugar control, obesity, diabetes, heart disease and many other disorders. Honey is still a sugar, but marginally better as it contains minute amounts of minerals and vitamins.

Fats

We are being urged to reduce our fat consumption as part of a healthier diet. What is more important is to change the *balance* of fats we consume: to have more 'essential fats' and fewer saturated fats, which are mostly of animal source.

ESSENTIAL FATTY ACIDS (EFAS)

These are found in good-quality polyunsaturated vegetable oils and margarines, nuts and seeds, most vegetables and in fish, especially oily fish. They are essential for life and cannot be manufactured in the body so have to come from the diet. Apart from needing fat as a store of available energy and for insulation, we need essential fatty acids because they form the main structure of cell membranes and walls in every body cell; they are also needed to make highly active substances which are vital for all body functions. Eighty per cent of the white matter of the brain is made from essential fatty acids; nerves have an insulating coat, called the *myelin sheath*, also composed of the same fatty acids. (Hence the old saying 'fish is brain food.')

Fatty acids are divided broadly into two groups: *saturated* and *unsaturated*.

Saturated fats tend to be hard, and are found in meat, lard, cheese, butter, hardened margarines and overheated oils.

Unsaturated fats tend to be liquid or soft at normal temperatures. When unsaturated vegetable oils are overheated, as in deep frying, they take on hydrogen atoms and become saturated, hence losing their value.

It is the imbalance of too much saturated fat in relation to unsaturated that can lead to conditions such as heart disease, blood pressure and strokes. Eskimos living on their natural diet, which is very high in fish oil, are renowned for their lack of the diseases of Western societies, in spite of a high level of total fats in their diet.

Processed vegetable oils and hardened margarines are actually worse for you than butter or cream, because they contain types of saturated fatty acids which block the body's utilization of the good essential fats. The important *essential fatty acids* (EFAs) are linoleic acid, linolenic acid and those derived from fish oils.

WHY ARE EFAS IMPORTANT IN ME/CFS?

Essential fatty acids are needed to make, among other things, *prostaglandins*, which have very important functions in regulating the biochemistry and enzyme activities of all cells. Prostaglandins are very short-lived. One important prostaglandin is called *PGE1*, derived from linoleic acid, an essential fat present in vegetable oils.

Functions of PGE1

- Improves circulation of blood.
- Lowers blood pressure.
- Restores normal shape and movement of red blood cells.
- Inhibits inflammation.
- Activates T lymphocytes in the immune system.
- Has effects on transmission at nerve endings and nerve conduction.

Levels of PGE1 are found to be low in people with diabetes, hardening of the arteries, some psychiatric disorders, and allergies. Synthesis of PGE1 from linoleic acid can be blocked by deficiencies of zinc, magnesium, biotin, or vitamin B_6. Also by alcohol, chemicals, diabetes, and *viral infections*.

The blockage in the making of PGE1 from linoleic acid can be bypassed if *Gamma Linolenic Acid – GLA* (a substance needed in the pathway) is supplied directly in the diet. GLA occurs naturally in many seeds. The main sources of commercially-prepared GLA are seeds of the evening primrose, starflower and blackcurrant plants.

Another prostaglandin is *PGE2*, which is also derived from linoleic acid via *arachidonic acid*, which also occurs in meat. The PG2 series have different actions to PGE1 – they promote narrowing of blood vessels, clotting in the blood, inflammation and swelling. So if a diet is high in arachidonic acid (*meat*) but low in linoleic acid (*vegetables*) there will tend to be greater production of the pro-inflammatory PG2 series and reduced production of the anti-inflammatory PG1 series.

A diet with more vegetables and fish, and less meat will produce relatively more of the PGE1 prostaglandins, hence less inflammation, allergies or thrombosis.

Prostaglandin 3 series and related substances are derived from alpha-linolenic acid, found in beans, wheat and spinach, and from eicosapentanoeic acid (*EPA*), found mainly in fish oils. The PG3 series are important in preventing thrombosis, so eating plenty of oily fish is thought to help prevent heart disease.

It is currently thought that a combination of essential fatty acids from vegetable oils, nuts, seeds and fish oils is best for health. This can be achieved by:

- eating generous amounts of a wide range of vegetables
- at least 4 teaspoons daily of an unrefined vegetable oil (cold pressed olive oil is best) on salads in dressing
- using good-quality unsaturated margarine, or butter
- avoiding deep frying (which saturates the oil)
- using a little olive oil for frying, as this type of oil is not altered by heat
- eating fish two or three times a week. The best are herring, mackerel, sardine, tuna, whitebait, shellfish and roe.

Some people may need supplements of EFAs. It is best to take both Gamma Linoleic Acid (GLA), as *evening primrose oil* or blackcurrant seed oil, and EPA, as *fish oils*. This is recommended for people with ME/CFS, especially if they have developed allergies. A treatment trial of essential fatty acids[1] found that at least 3 g per day is needed for any benefit. A combination with higher amounts of marine oil relative to GLA is proving helpful in brain disorders including schizophrenia and MS.

Fluids

It is really important to drink plenty of water. Many people drink only tea, coffee and canned drinks, but these contain caffeine and sugar. Water tastes better if it is spring water, or is filtered. An average person should drink at least 2 pints (1 litre) of water a day in addition to tea or coffee, and more in hot weather or if ill or feverish.

Many people with ME/CFS have digestive problems. If you drink fluids with, or just after, a meal, the digestive juices are diluted and digestion is weakened, so it is better to drink fluids between main meals.

Fibre

Fibre is the indigestible residue from plant foods, which passes right through the intestines and forms part of the faeces. It has no nutritional value of itself, but it is essential to provide bulk in the large intestine (colon). Its chief property is in absorption of water, making a bulky stool which passes more quickly and smoothly through the colon to the rectum for evacuation.

Lack of fibre may result in:

• constipation, which contributes to piles, varicose veins and retention of food residues in the colon, leading to fermentation, absorption of toxins, etc.
• alteration in the balance of bacteria in the colon, which may favour the overgrowth of undesirable bugs. This imbalance is called *dysbiosis*, and may be implicated in many illnesses.
• diverticulitis, gallstones, risk of cancer of the colon, raised blood cholesterol.

Wheat bran is *not* the best source of fibre. It may cause problems – bloating, gas, pain, spastic colon – in people who are wheat intolerant, which may include some people with ME/CFS. The best sources of fibre are fruits and vegetables, wholegrains (including oats and unrefined rice) and some pulses, in generous amounts.

(Advice is given in later chapters about diets for Candida overgrowth and food allergies.)

Nutritional Supplements

This is a controversial subject. Some argue that if you eat a well-balanced diet of good, fresh foods, then it should not be necessary to take extra vitamins or minerals. For someone in perfect health, this is probably true.

However, the Recommended Daily Allowance (RDA) for each nutrient is calculated for a healthy person of average weight, and is often the amount which is just sufficient to prevent deficiency disease. The RDA may be much less than what is needed for optimum health. In disease states, the body's requirements may increase dramatically to a level which cannot be obtained from a normal diet, particularly if there is reduced appetite or digestive problems.

Many ME/CFS patients have problems with digestion and absorption of food. This is indicated by:

- weight loss in spite of good food intake
- stools containing undigested food
- stools that float, difficult to flush away
- diarrhoea, distension, abdominal pains.

If you have these symptoms, especially weight loss in spite of a good appetite, assume that you are not getting the full value from what you eat. As well as losing protein and fats, you may be losing calcium, iron, zinc, folic acid, vitamin B_{12} and the fat-soluble vitamins A, E and D.

Poor appetite or nausea will also lead to inadequate nutrition. Even when there is fluctuating weight gain, sudden weight gain in ME/CFS is usually due to fluid retention.

Poor absorption of food may be due to:

- virus infections, which may cause flattening of the micro-villi (tiny projections) on the surface of cells lining the small intestine, hence loss of absorptive surface
- if the pancreas has been involved in a present or earlier virus infection, there may be reduction of pancreatic diges-tive enzymes
- there may be increased gut motility, causing food to be rushed through the small bowel too quickly for efficient digestion and absorption. This overactivity may be due to disorder of the autonomic nervous system (*see page 69*).

There may be excess cytokine production during relapse in ME/CFS. This is known to block vitamin utilization, so extra vitamins may be needed to overcome this defect. Nutritional supplements may be needed for proper function of the body's immune system, nervous system and endocrine glands.

A problem for many ill people who are considering supple-ments is the cost. A few (such as evening primrose oil) may be obtained on prescription, if your doctor is willing to consider it. Otherwise, it is useful to work out how much the supple-ments are going to cost per day, then to see what could be giv-en up to pay for this, for example the price of a newspaper!

Like many decisions you have to take, it is a matter of knowing the priorities.

DIGESTIVE ENZYMES

These may be indicated for a few people who have evidence of impaired digestion of meat and/or fats. They are obtainable on prescription and are derived from pancreatic extract (their trade names include Pancrex, Nutrizyme). The preparation should be taken just before or with a meal.

VITAMIN C

This essential vitamin is not stored in the body, and is needed daily in food.

What Does Vitamin C Do?

- Vitamin C (ascorbic acid) is vital for the continuous repair of body tissues.
- It is used by the adrenal gland to make the hormones noradrenaline and cortisol.
- Vitamin C is a powerful anti-oxidant, mopping up free radicals of oxygen which are released in various biochemical reactions, and which may cause cell damage.
- Vitamin C has important effects on the immune system, promoting white cell production and mobility, destroying bacteria and dead cells, and making antibodies.
- In high doses (5 g per day) it acts as an antiviral agent, activates T lymphocytes, and increases interferon production.[2]
- Vitamin C inhibits the synthesis of chemicals that cause inflammation (PGE2 prostaglandins), therefore reducing pain and swelling.

Much valuable work on the use of high-dose vitamin C to treat infections, cancer and many immune disorders such as rheumatoid arthritis was done by Dr Linus Pauling. While many sceptics have dismissed his work, Pauling argued that in tests where people took vitamin C and no benefit was found, they did not take a large enough dose. The RDA of vitamin C in Britain is 30 milligrams (equivalent to one small orange!). A more realistic minimum for good health would be 100 milligrams (mg) daily.

Dr Pauling argued for a greater need of vitamin C from his calculations of the amounts of various nutrients in the diet of our ancestors. As humans evolved they became unable to make vitamin C in the body, unlike most other mammals, so they would only have survived by having enough in daily food. Early humans' diets had a much greater ratio of raw fruits, vegetables, nuts and berries than that of a 20th-century Western diet, although the total calorie intake was poor by our standards.

Someone with an infection, undergoing major surgery, or in emotional shock needs far more vitamin C than 100 mg a day. It is used up by the adrenal glands in response to stress; wound-healing requires extra vitamin C, and it is used by the immune system to fight infection. Vitamin C cannot be stored in the body; any that is not used is excreted in the urine. The main side-effect from taking more than is needed is diarrhoea.

If you decide to take vitamin C, it is best to take it morning and evening, but not to exceed 3 g per day except at times of great stress, such as severe infection or prior to undergoing surgery. People at risk of kidney stones should take no more than 1 g daily.

VITAMIN B6 – PYRIDOXINE
Vitamin B6 is important in many chemical processes, including those of brain chemicals which affect mood and behaviour. It is

also involved in the pathways of essential fatty acids (EFAs), which are needed for the immune system. B₆ is also needed for some minerals to work, especially magnesium.

Signs suggestive of deficiency are depression, irritability and red, greasy, scaly skin on the face. However, a lack of vitamin B₆ alone is unusual; usually there will be a lack of all B vitamins. The suggested supplement level is about 20 mg daily, as part of a B-complex preparation. Women with premenstrual syndrome may benefit from 50 mg daily during the week before their period is due.

VITAMIN B₁₂

The daily requirement of this nutrient is low, about 1 microgram (mcg). It is found in meat, fish and eggs, which is why vegans can be at risk of B₁₂ deficiency. As it is absorbed in the small intestine and needs a substance secreted by the stomach to combine with before absorption, people with deficient stomach juice or malabsorption in the small intestine are also at risk of B₁₂ deficiency. It is essential for red cell production and nervous system functions. B₁₂ deficiency may cause anaemia, fatigue, pins and needles in the feet, a stumbling gait and mental confusion.

It is useful for people who have had ME/CFS for more than two years to get their blood B₁₂ level checked, especially if they have these neurological symptoms, if there are digestive/absorption problems, and if they are middle-aged or elderly. There may well be people who think they have ME/CFS, especially in the older age group, who in fact have a lack of vitamin B₁₂, which is easily treatable.

Some ME/CFS sufferers do report an improvement in energy level and in neurological symptoms from B₁₂ injections, although no clinical trials have yet been done. Dr Paul Cheney of Charlotte North Carolina in the US uses vitamin B_{12} as part of his treatment regime, especially for treating fatigue. He recommends a trial dose of 3 mg twice a week (by injection). If there is a response, patients usually report improvement after two weeks, then can continue self-injecting 2–3 mg weekly. Dr Cheney says:

We do not understand exactly why B_{12} works in CFS ... an effect lasting only a few days does not fit in with normal B_{12} pharmokinetics. High-dose B_{12} must trigger some other effect, that lasts longer than the B_{12} itself. [3]

The best sources of B_{12} (providing it is being absorbed) from food are liver, other organ meats, and brewer's yeast.

A good vitamin B complex should be yeast-free and contain all the B vitamins, as follows:

Thiamine B_1	Niacin B_3
Riboflavin B_2	Pantothenate B_5
Pyridoxine B_6	Cyanocobalamin B_{12}
(about 10–20 mg	Folic Acid
of each of these)	Para Amino Benzoic Acid (PABA)
	Biotin

Information about the functions of other B vitamins, which are all needed as they are interdependent, can be found in books about nutrition.

VITAMIN A
Vitamin A itself occurs in animal produce; the best sources are animal and fish livers, kidneys, eggs and milk products. Beta-carotene, a precursor of vitamin A, is obtained from

vegetables, particularly carrots, and other green-, yellow- or orange-coloured plants. Vitamin A is needed for maintaining mucous membranes, skin, and cell membranes, and is important in resisting infections. It is one of the 'anti-oxidants' (along with vitamins C and E and the mineral selenium), and therefore prevents damage to cell membranes and has an important role in cancer prevention.

Vitamin A deficiency is one of the most common causes of blindness in poor countries.

As it is fat-soluble, and stored in the body, very high doses can accumulate, causing toxicity. The daily amount should not exceed 20,000 international units (IU); 7,000–10,000 IU are sufficient unless there are particular indications of deficiency.

The best way to supplement vitamin A is as part of a balanced multivitamin preparation, or in fish liver oil capsules, which also provide essential fatty acids.

PANTOTHENIC ACID (VITAMIN B₅)
This little-known vitamin is one of the B family and is essential for the proper function of adrenal glands, for making antibodies and fighting infection and allergies. It is present in most B-complex preparations. It seems to be helpful in high doses in stress-related diseases and conditions where the immune system is not working properly, as in the case of allergies or rheumatoid arthritis. It is recommended for ME/CFS, and can be taken as calcium pantothenate in doses of 300–1,000 mg.

VITAMIN E
This is another fat-soluble vitamin, and most important for its anti-oxidant properties. It occurs in vegetables, nuts and eggs. The recommended supplement is 100–200 IU daily. It is essential for proper wound-healing.

WHAT DO ANTI-OXIDANTS DO?

Oxygen is essential for cells to live. However, in certain circumstances toxic oxygen derivatives (known as 'free radicals') can combine with other molecules and cause damage to cells, including to the fatty acid part of cell walls, and alter the function of cells or cause them to become cancerous, or to die. These nasty free radicals are mopped up and made safe by anti-oxidants. Anti-oxidants are vitamins A, C and E, and various enzymes which contain trace elements such as selenium, zinc, manganese and copper.

Free radicals have multiple sources, including chemicals in air pollution and food, and cigarette smoke. They are also produced by lymphocytes in inflammation – that is, when the lymphocytes kill virus-infected cells. Some doctors have used the term 'sick cell syndrome' about ME/CFS. It is sensible for anyone with ME/CFS or multiple allergies, living in a polluted environment, to have a good intake of the nutrients needed for a good anti-oxidant system.

ZINC

Zinc is a trace element which is necessary for a wide range of chemical reactions in the body. Studies of zinc and its many roles have begun relatively recently, and there is still much to discover. Some results of zinc deficiency are impaired wound-healing, loss of sense of taste or smell, slow growth, infertility, hair loss, skin problems (including acne), allergies, poor resistance to infection, depression and other mental disturbances, and white spots on the nails.

Risk factors for zinc deficiency:

• those with a poor intake of zinc – those who are following a vegan diet, are slimming, on a strict allergy diet; those with

a poor appetite; the elderly; alcoholics; those being fed intravenously
- those who suffer poor absorption – for example due to a high-fibre diet with lots of bran, low stomach acid, lack of pancreatic enzymes, taking iron tablets, suffering from coeliac disease
- those with increased requirements – for example if pregnant, after suffering burns, major surgery, any severe stress.

The daily requirement is about 15 mg for a healthy adult; more in pregnancy; much more after major surgery, burns, or any severe stress.

It is prudent for people with ME/CFS to take extra zinc, especially if they are vegetarian, have poor food absorption, any immune dysfunction, or white spots on the nails. The absorption of zinc is inhibited by food, so it is best taken on an empty stomach. A preparation giving 20–50 mg elemental zinc, as zinc ororate, zinc sulphate or amino chelated zinc is suitable.

MAGNESIUM

Magnesium is absolutely vital for normal cell function. It is present inside every living cell as well as in teeth and bones. The correct balance of calcium and magnesium across cell membranes is essential for transmission of nerve impulses, and for muscle contraction and relaxation. Magnesium is also involved in many enzyme systems and chemical reactions in the body.

Magnesium occurs naturally in hard water, in whole grains, green vegetables, nuts and beans. A deficiency is most likely in someone on a poor diet, living in a soft water area, or with poor intestinal absorption.

Magnesium deficiency leads to:

- many neurological symptoms, tingling and numbness
- muscle weakness, muscle cramps or twitching
- heart rhythm abnormalities
- hyperactivity in children
- mental confusion
- depression
- anorexia
- nausea
- constipation.

In a well-publicized study of magnesium in CFS/ME,[4] the authors found low levels of magnesium in red blood cells of CFS. Twenty patients and 20 matched controls were used. Average red cell magnesium levels for patients were significantly lower than in controls. After a course of magnesium injections given by intramuscular injection weekly, 80 per cent of the CFS patients had significant improvement in energy, emotions and pain, compared with 18 per cent of the controls.

Unfortunately, the low levels of intracellular magnesium and clinical benefits of magnesium injections have not been replicated in any further study. The injections are painful, and anecdotal reports from patients who have tried this therapy since the trial suggest that while there is some benefit for a few weeks, the improvements do not last.

On the other hand, taking adequate amounts of magnesium by mouth does appear to help some people with muscle spasms, twitching, pain and insomnia. It also helps constipation, if this is a problem. Oral magnesium supplementation has not been subjected to any trials, however provided that the daily dose does not exceed 800 mg elemental magnesium, it is not toxic. The recommended amount is 300–500 mg a day. It is best to take a magnesium supplement twice daily, not with food, so morning and bedtime would be suitable. An amino chelated form is well absorbed. (*Details of reputable suppliers are in Appendix A.*)

Some doctors advise that calcium should be taken as well, as a separate supplement, about 500 mg a day.

SELENIUM

Selenium is important as an anti-oxidant, mopping up free radicals, and thus it helps to protect cells from damage, ageing and cancerous changes.

Selenium is usually taken as part of a high-potency multi-mineral supplement. It is toxic in high doses; the daily amount should not exceed 200 mcg.

ESSENTIAL FATTY ACID SUPPLEMENTS
(*See also page 216.*)

EFAs and their products are needed to make cell membranes, and are important constituents of white matter in nervous tissue.

What seems clear is that not only is EFA supplementation advisable for ME/CFS, but that high doses are needed – at least 3 g per day. Essential fatty acids in the body require adequate amounts of zinc, magnesium and vitamins B_6, C and E as co-factors, in order to be used properly.

AMINO ACIDS

Amino acids are the basic building blocks for the manufacture of all proteins in the body, including antibodies, all the lymphokines produced by white cells, digestive enzymes, neurotransmitters and hormones. Without these building blocks, taking vitamin and mineral supplements may be a waste of money. Certain amino acids are known to be needed for proper brain function – in conditions of famine or protein deprivation, psychological symptoms such as depression and confusion appear early.

Most people with ME/CFS do not need amino acid supplements. However, during severe relapse, if there is also reduced food intake and/or signs suggesting poor absorption, it may be helpful to take supplements containing all the essential amino acids for a short time. This helps improve brain function and may reduce depression and confusion (*see Appendix A for suppliers*).

Summary of Supplements

Ideally, someone considering taking nutritional supplements should consult a physician or biochemist who specializes in nutrition, and have his or her individual nutritional needs worked out. This is not usually possible due to distances and the cost of a consultation and tests. Failing the chance of such advice, then suitable supplements for someone with ME/CFS would be:

- a good-quality multi-vitamin and mineral tablet daily – ideally one which has high levels of B vitamins (10–20 mg of B_1, B_2, B_3, B_6 and B_{12}), and is yeast-free
- evening primrose oil or equivalent – 3 g daily. Plus fish oils, in combination or separately – e.g. cod liver oil capsules
- zinc – 20–50 mg at night
- magnesium – 300–500 mg daily
- selenium – 100 mcg daily (do not exceed 200 mcg daily)
- vitamin E – 100–200 I.U. daily
- calcium pantothenate (B_5) – 300 mg daily (up to 1,000 mg a day if very stressed or if severely allergic)
- vitamin C – 1 to 3 g a day; more if very unwell or exposed to infection.

Exceeding these amounts without medical supervision is potentially harmful, would bring no further benefits, and would be a waste of money.

Chapter 12

Alternative Therapies

If you suffer from an illness which goes on and on, for which conventional medicine has no answers, it is likely that you will look for help from the more traditional forms of healing. The art of healing is as old as humanity, and all ways of healing have one common precept: To heal is to make whole, and healing means *restoring wholeness*.

The word *health* comes from the word *hale*, meaning whole. Lack of health implies loss of balance of mental, spiritual and bodily functions. Symptoms are messages that things are not flowing smoothly within us. Many drugs just suppress these important messages, whereas most non-drug therapies seek to correct the underlying imbalance by helping the body to restore its own wholeness.

There is of course a lot of overlap between modern Western medicine and the so-called 'alternative' therapies. The visit to a doctor who also has a gift for healing (which is not given to all, in spite of degrees, diplomas and modern technology) is in itself therapeutic. You tell your complete story to someone who is prepared to listen. You receive words of explanation and comfort, and the touch of healing hands through a handshake or examination. You may be given a prescription for a medicine, and you are encouraged to *believe* that it will help you. The patient's belief that something will do good is an important part of any therapy, whether it is a bottle of pills, herbs, acupuncture or manipulation. This is called the *placebo effect*. It is natural and valid in all forms of healing, whether the healer is a witch-doctor, a famous professor, a family doctor or a herbalist.

The patient's belief in the possibility of improvement is a significant part of any healing therapy, because of the influence that mental attitude has over bodily recovery. It is known that, among people with a serious illness such as cancer, those who have an optimistic outlook and a reason for staying alive tend to do better than those who are pessimists and feel helpless.

People suffering from ME and other fatigue syndromes who improve report a great range of reasons for their recovery. In all survey questionnaires asking 'What things have helped you?', top of the league is *rest*. A variety of other therapies are mentioned, including changing diet, gentle exercise, homoeopathy, evening primrose oil, painkillers and anti-depressants. A few have recovered after the laying-on of hands in Christian healing. So far there is no single treatment that cures ME/CFS, whether it be a drug, diet or a complementary therapy.

It cannot be repeated too often that **you need to have enough rest, and to pace yourself during activity**, whatever else you undertake in the search for healing. The energy expenditure involved in travelling long distances to find a therapist who will cure you may undo the benefits of the treatment.

These days there are many different therapies available outside of conventional medicine. Ill people searching for a cure can be bewildered by the choice. Sadly, only a few types of therapy have stood the test of time, or have been subjected to careful scientific scrutiny in the form of published studies. There are various 'miracle cures' around that cost a great deal of money, and there are any number of unqualified therapists who are happy to give you something of doubtful efficacy or safety, and relieve you of your savings. People with poorly understood chronic conditions such as ME/CFS, multiple sclerosis and even AIDS are easy prey to such unprincipled charlatans.

Having issued this warning, I can endorse some therapies which have been found to be helpful and whose practitioners are trained and have to be registered with a professional organization: homoeopathy, acupuncture, osteopathy, herbalism, naturopathy and aromatherapy.

In this chapter I discuss some of these therapies, as well as healing, and light and oxygen therapy.

Homoeopathy

The word *homeopathy* comes from two Greek words, *homois* and *pathos*, meaning *similar* and *suffering* respectively.

A homoeopathic remedy is a highly diluted preparation of a substance which, when taken by a healthy person, produces a symptom picture that is similar to that of the patient. Homoeopathy follows the principle of 'like treats like,' unlike allopathic, Western medicine.

An example of homoeopathic medicine which was actually used as a conventional drug is quinine. This is derived from the bark of a tree and, when taken, produces symptoms of shivering, sweating and fever. A weaker extract of this tree bark is prepared as the drug quinine, and was used to treat malaria.

A homoeopathic remedy is prepared by diluting the constituent many times, in a process of serial dilutions called 'potentization'. In the resulting dilution there may be few or no molecules of the original substance left; however, during the dilution process the mixture is shaken very vigorously at each stage, and it is thought that some biologically-active property (perhaps an electrical one?) of the molecules of the original drug is imparted to the resulting potentized remedy, whether the dilution is effected with a liquid or a solid.

The greater the dilution of a remedy, the more highly potentized it is and the more powerful it is in its curative effect. This is one of the stumbling blocks for scientifically-minded doctors in accepting homoeopathy. The curative effect seems to arise as a result of stimulating the body to rid itself of whatever is causing the symptoms.

A homoeopathic remedy is selected after a careful history-taking, to establish not only all the patient's symptoms but other characteristics such as personality, seasonal influence, food habits and any other factors that influence symptoms.

Good homoeopathic prescribing requires skill and experience, and it is essential to consult a fully-trained practitioner. Homoeopathy is safe: even if the wrong remedy is prescribed, no harm results. However, when treating a chronic condition it is common to have temporary worsening of symptoms to start with.

Some remedies are used to treat symptoms only and are available over the counter in most pharmacies. These are in low potencies and are very useful for first-aid treatment of such things as headache, fever, stomach upsets, etc. For example, Arnica 6C is a remedy for bruising, sprains and muscle pain after exercise.

To treat a chronic condition a higher potency may be used, and fewer doses are taken. The deepest level of homoeopathic treatment for ME/CFS is based on identifying the infection which triggered the illness, and making a homoeopathic preparation of that infective agent. This type of remedy is called a *nosode*. Nosodes of chronic infections thought to be the past origins of ill-health have been used in homoeopathy for a long time – Tuberculinum is one example. It is possible to make a homoeopathic preparation of any infective agent.

There are two difficulties about treating ME/CFS in this way. The first is identifying the infective agent. The second is that if the correct nosode is taken, it is likely to induce a temporary revival of the symptoms of the past infection that initiated the illness. However, this worsening of symptoms normally only lasts a few days to a few weeks, and should be seen as a sign that the correct remedy has been chosen.

Some remedies which have been quoted as being helpful by people with ME/CFS include:

* *Aconite* – for fear and anxiety, especially at night, for the 'feeling of dying' with pressure on the chest, breathing difficulty, or palpitations
* *Sepia* – for dragging weariness, premenstrual symptoms, and loss of feeling for loved ones
* *Arnica* – for aching muscles and joints, exhaustion from overdoing things
* *Bryonia* – for arthritic pain, bursting headache, all pains that are better for pressure.

A British homoeopath, Robert Awdry, published results of a randomized double-blind trial of homeopathy treatment[1] using 64 patients who fulfilled the 'Oxford' criteria for chronic post-infectious fatigue syndrome (*see Chapter 3*). The final assessment showed that 33 per cent of the 32 patients who received homoeopathic treatment had improved after one year, compared to only 4 per cent of the group who received identical-looking but inert tablets. Awdry said '… these effects, however, are unpredictable and very variable … a wholly reliable outcome to the treatment of post-viral fatigue syndrome when using homoeopathic remedies is still far from certain.'

So it appears that while homoeopathy may improve symptoms, it does not guarantee a cure for ME/CFS. But neither, so far, does anything else, orthodox or alternative!

For further information about homoeopathy, you should read one of the many books on the subject, or consult a qualified practitioner.

Acupuncture

This healing art has been used by the Chinese for thousands of years, not only to treat pain and all kinds of illness, but also to maintain health.

A Chinese physician does not diagnose in the same way as a Western doctor. History and examination are carried out, but with particular attention to the appearance of the patient's face and tongue, and the quality of the pulse at both wrists. The practitioner is looking for signs of an imbalance of body energies, and of how the body functions are disturbed.

There is no such diagnosis as ME or CFS in Chinese medicine. A patient who presents with complaints of exhaustion, muscle weakness, feeling cold and insomnia would be diagnosed as suffering from deficient *Chi* (energy), and deficiency of Chi in various organs such as the heart, spleen and liver. Another patient may have a different diagnosis, but every patient with ME or chronic fatigue is lacking in body energy; this is reflected in poor function of the organs, and stagnation of Chi in energy pathways, leading to pain, poor digestion and absorption of food, or disturbed mental function.

Chinese medicine pays attention to the lifestyle of the patient, and advises on changing this where appropriate. ME/CFS would be regarded as conditions where the patient had depleted his or her energy and has no defence against bodily invasion of a pathogenic factor, which would go deep into the body and upset the workings of vital organs.

Acupuncture treatment for ME/CFS should be given in a way that does not drain energy from the patient, but rather supplies energy, or else balances the body's immune system. One technique that supplies energy uses a burning herb (*moxa*) placed either on the skin or on a needle at acupuncture points. The warmth enters the energy channels and disperses cold, invigorating body organs. The smouldering moxa does not burn the skin, it only creates a sensation of heat.

Chinese medicine uses both acupuncture and herbs, singly or together, although in China herbs are used much more than in Europe. There is no single prescription for treating ME/CFS. Each patient is assessed individually, and a diagnosis is formulated which may vary in different systems of Chinese teaching. It is important to consult a fully-trained practitioner, rather than someone who has done a weekend course and only knows how to treat pain. An unskilled acupuncturist could make ME/CFS worse. Treatment needs to be gentle, and to be given in a way that does *not remove energy*. Many people with ME/CFS are extremely sensitive to any treatment and also have heightened sensitivity to pain.

The insertion of an acupuncture needle is swift and virtually painless. However, acupuncture needling is not appropriate for someone in a severe stage of ME, nor for patients who have a lot of muscle pain. Moxa (heat) treatment is more acceptable in such cases. Some therapists now use a laser which stimulates the energy point below the skin, instead of needles. All registered practitioners are scrupulous about needle sterility, and most now use disposable needles. An alternative to acupuncture is *acupressure*, where fingertip pressure is used over acupuncture points. A variant of this is called *Shiatsu*.

Acupuncture can be helpful for insomnia, muscle and joint pain, depression, anxiety and digestive problems.

Osteopathy

Osteopathy is a system of physical manipulation that treats mechanical dysfunctions of the skeleton. It is thought by many to be similar to physiotherapy, but in fact has wider applications and can be used to treat illnesses as well as remedying physical abnormalities.

Its application for people with ME and chronic fatigue is based on the fact that the outflow of nerves of the autonomic nervous system (which controls all the unconscious functions in the body, and may be malfunctioning in CFS – *see page 69*) from the spinal cord in the thoracic region can be adversely affected by mechanical problems in the spine, and also by local congestion of lymphatic flow. A chance discovery in 1989 during conventional osteopathic practice by Raymond Perrin, an osteopath in Manchester, revealed a plausible correlation between a mechanical problem of the thoracic spine and the incidence of CFS. Promising results achieved by osteopathic treatment of patients diagnosed with ME or CFS have led to a hypothesis that one of the contributory causes of CFS/ME is a mechanical dysfunction affecting the upper back, which leads to a chronic disturbance of the sympathetic nervous system, and that this could be treated osteopathically.

The treatment includes manipulation of the joints in the thoracic spine, and massage of the surrounding soft tissues to relax the muscular tone, increase local blood supply and stimulate lymphatic drainage; also cranial manipulation (gentle pressure on the skull to improve free circulation of cerebro-spinal fluid) as appropriate for each patient.

A formal trial of this treatment has been carried out at the Department of Orthopaedic Mechanics, Salford University, over two years from July 1994, and the results are to be published in the spring of 1998. The objectives of this initial research were:

a) to determine the strength of correlation between mechanical dysfunction of the thoracic spine and the incidence of symptoms linked with CFS

b) to demonstrate and evaluate the effectiveness of osteopathy in the treatment of CFS by utilizing self-report questionnaires, clinical examination and objective muscle-fatigue tests.

The treatment group consisted of 33 patients with CFS/ME, who had no therapy for one year other than the osteopathic treatment. The control group had no physical therapy for one year.

Results have shown a 40 per cent mean improvement in all symptoms in the treatment group, of whom two were symptom-free by the end of the year. The control group's mean result was 1 per cent worse after a year without osteopathy, most of them showing little change overall in their symptoms. Exercise-induced muscle weakness was measured in all the treatment groups (using the quadriceps muscle) before and at the end of the year. These tests showed that at the end of the year of osteopathic treatment, there was a considerable improvement in resistance to fatigue in skeletal muscles, and this had been achieved solely by stabilizing the outflow of sympathetic nerves from the thoracic spine, which would improve the blood circulation to muscles.[2]

Herbalism

Plants with specific healing properties have been used for a very long time, throughout the world. Some of our modern drugs are derived from plant medicines – Digoxin, used for heart failure, is a synthetic form of digitalis, obtained from the leaves of the foxglove.

On the whole, herbal medicines are safer than modern, synthetic drugs, so long as they are taken in the prescribed way. A qualified medical herbalist does five years of training which includes anatomy, physiology and study of illness (pathology), as well as learning a vast amount about botany and the pharmacology of plants. For first-aid use at home, herbal remedies are available in herbalists, pharmacists and health food shops. They are all safe *if used correctly*.

For treatment of chronic ailments and deep-seated symptoms it is best to consult a qualified herbalist who will take a detailed history before prescribing a herb or, more usually, a combination of herbs, not just to suppress symptoms but to help correct the cause of illness. There are many similarities in diagnosis and prescription between Chinese herbal medicine and herbalism as taught in Europe.

The property of a plant for healing purposes is classified in terms of its functions of *heating or cooling*, *stimulating or sedating*, *antiseptic*, *blood-purifying*, etc. Some are particularly rich in essential minerals, which may be depleted in disease. Some of the most common herbs are found in our gardens and kitchens, such as onion, garlic, parsley, thyme and sage. Garlic is a powerful antiseptic and preventative against viral infections. Many familiar garden plants have medicinal properties, including nettles, dandelions and marigold.

Some herbal preparations have side-effects if used incorrectly or if the wrong part of a plant is used, but toxic side-effects are rare in comparison with side-effects from synthetic chemical drugs. Herbal teas can be used as alternatives to tea or coffee – peppermint aids digestion, and chamomile is a natural sedative.

A preparation of a plant, St John's Wort (botanical name *Hypericum*) has been found to help mood swings and mild depression, also insomnia. This may be useful for people with ME/CFS who sleep badly but cannot tolerate an antidepressant drug such as amitriptyline. It is available over the counter in chemists and health food shops, in a standardized tablet preparation called *Kira*. The dose is usually 1 tablet, 3 times a day. It can take anything from 1 to 4 weeks to start to feel any effects.

A word of caution about a remedy that is not strictly derived from plants, but is produced by bees from nectar and pollen. *Royal Jelly* is promoted as another 'wonder cure' for many ills. It is supposed to contain numerous goodies such as amino acids and minerals, but some people are allergic to the proteins in it (just as a few people have a major reaction to a bee sting), and cases have been reported of an anaphylactic asthma attack after taking Royal Jelly. A similar problem could arise from *Bee Propolis*, another product of bees manufactured by them to feed their larvae and queen bees in the hive.

BACH FLOWER REMEDIES

Bach Remedies are made from various plants, each of which has a specific effect on a disordered emotional state. They are very dilute preparations and work exclusively on the emotions rather than on other bodily symptoms. They appear to be safe, and even if a remedy is chosen which is inappropriate for the emotional state there is no harmful effect.

The most useful to keep at hand is Bach's Rescue Remedy, which is made from five specific plants and can be used in a situation of sudden mental shock or collapse. Another useful remedy is Olive, which helps a fatigued, exhausted mind. Bach Remedies have not been tested in clinical trials, but they do seem to work. The Faculty of Complementary Medicine at Exeter University is starting controlled trials to test Bach Flower Remedies.

Aromatherapy and Massage

Many people find massage helpful. If you cannot find a trained therapist locally, or cannot go out for treatment, look for a book which instructs simple massage techniques for a carer to learn. The massage needs to be extremely gentle, especially if the patient is very ill or has a lot of body pain. There is no place for the vigorous pummelling and rubbing traditionally thought of as massage.

Much of the benefit of massage comes from the physical touch of a caring person, just as a mother soothes a child by stroking him or her. The emphasis should be on comforting, soothing and relaxing rather than on trying to massage away muscle pain, and a much lighter touch is needed for ME/CFS than for a fit person.

Aromatherapy combines massage with essential oils on the skin. After an initial consultation, an aromatherapist may give you a supply of the oils for you to use at home, or to add to the bath. The prescription used will be individual to your needs, based on your symptoms. The oils are pure extracts from various plants which have healing properties. Minute amounts are absorbed through the skin, and the fragrance is inhaled to produce beneficial effects.

Different oils are used for different emotional and physical problems; some have stimulating properties (such as eucalyptus), others are relaxing and sedating (such as sandalwood), still others affect functions such as digestion and hormone levels. *Stimulating oils should not be used on people with ME/CFS.*

Those who have tried aromatherapy have found it very pleasant and comforting. Benefits include muscle relaxation, less muscle pain, better sleep and less anxiety. If a practitioner can be found who can visit you at home, so much the better.

Yoga and T'ai Chi

Yoga and T'ai Chi are therapies and also exercise. They are discussed in Chapter 7.

Healing

Healing by the laying on of hands, and through prayer, has been around for a long time. Some people are born with a special gift of healing. They can transmit healing energy to a sick person through their hands, and with the same hands can tell what parts of the body are not functioning properly. Some professional healers use purely physical healing energy; others use a spiritual approach as well as physical. The latter may have had teaching from the National Federation of Spiritual Healing (*address in Appendix A*). Most spiritual healers offer their services free, and accept whatever payment the patient wishes and is able to give.

I personally believe that regular prayer by a number of people does bring about healing in the sick person prayed for, even if the recipient does not profess any religious faith. Healing by prayer or by touch cannot be measured scientifically.

This is a good thing; we need to believe in miracles in our mechanized, material world. We also need to accept that there are many mysteries in life. Wisdom comes with acceptance of, and belief in, mystery and miracles as well as scientific facts.

Light

Natural daylight and sunshine are extremely important for health. The skin makes vitamin D in daylight, and full-spectrum light entering the eyes has a direct effect on health.

Light exerts a profound effect on plants and all animal life. We humans have largely overcome the lifestyle restrictions once enforced by darkness through the invention of electric light. With electric light, people can stay awake as late as they like, can work all day without daylight, sit up late watching TV, and play football at night. We have lost the habit of sleeping more in winter than in summer, and maybe this is why our energy levels and resistance to infection are depleted in late winter and early spring.

Dr Ott, an American scientist who studied the effects of natural light on humans, animals and plants, spoke of the loss of light as a result of air pollution in cities:

'... civilized man has cut himself off from more sunlight by living indoors behind walls and glass. Man has developed artificial sources of illumination that have almost no ultraviolet and distort the light spectrum of natural sunlight. More people wear glasses or contact lenses, which cut down ultraviolet light entering the eyes. To what extent is this polluted light environment affecting man's health and well-being?'

John Ott also recorded how he himself suffered badly from arthritis, at a time when he was spending a lot of time indoors. He accidentally broke his glasses and had as a result to spend some days outside in sunlight, being unable to drive or to work without them. To his surprise his arthritic pains improved dramatically, but worsened again if he had to spend time inside or behind glass. He had previously rested lying in sunlight, wearing sunglasses, with no benefit to the arthritis. He found that the pain only eased when he exposed his eyes, without spectacles, to daylight for several hours a day.

The effects of full-spectrum daylight on mood, health and animal fertility is not fully investigated. The influence of light depends largely on an adequate level of the ultraviolet part of visible light being received in the eyes. There are direct nerve connections between photo-receptive cells in the eye and the pineal gland, which is a small outgrowth of the brain situated behind the hypothalamus, deep within the brain.

Many people with ME and chronic fatigue deteriorate from November through till the spring. Maybe lack of light is responsible, as well as winter cold and damp, and increased indoor pollution. In tuberculosis hospitals (sanatoriums) before the development of TB drug treatment, ill patients on long-term rest were put outside on open verandas all the year round, so they could receive the benefits of both fresh air and sunlight.

I am not suggesting that people with ME/CFS, who are frequently light-sensitive, should sit outside and stare at the sun. But it does make sense to get outside each day if you are well enough; in strong sunlight rest in the shade, for there is still plenty of reflected full-spectrum light. Someone virtually bedridden should at least spend some time by a window; even though glass cuts out some light, it is better than nothing. If you wear glasses, leave them off while sitting or resting outside. If you cannot get outside much, get a full-spectrum light-bulb or light box and use it in the room where you spend most of your day. (*See Appendix A for suppliers.*)

Fresh Air and Oxygen

Unpolluted air is desirable for everyone. Oxygen is essential, but there are many pollutants in the air (especially from car exhausts) that damage lungs, affect children's brains and make chemically-sensitive people ill. In much of Europe the visible smoke from thousands of coal fires has been replaced by ever-increasing pollution from petrol and diesel fumes, as more and more people use cars instead of their feet or public transport. It is just as bad inside many buildings, because of the increased use of plastic and foam furnishings and equipment, air-conditioning which circulates dust and germs, and aerosol sprays.

The oxygen supply to some areas of the body in ME/CFS seems to be poor, especially during a relapse. Whatever the mechanisms of poor oxygen supply, it makes sense to try and improve the quality of the air you breathe in, and also to increase the depth and quality of your breathing.

Even someone who is housebound can do some deep breathing daily beside an open window. The correct way to breathe can be learned from relaxation tapes or from Yoga teaching. Many people breathe shallowly, using their chest muscles, and do not fully expel the air when they exhale. The main breathing muscle is the diaphragm, which when used pushes out your tummy; expansion of the chest is secondary.

In modern centrally-heated double-glazed homes, ventilation is often poor, allowing a build-up of moulds and dust. Each room should be properly aired each day by opening a window for a time. This is healthier than using 'fresh-air' chemical sprays.

HYPERBARIC OXYGEN (HBO) THERAPY

This treatment has been in use for some years for people with multiple sclerosis, and some people with ME/CFS have tried it in the past 10 years or so. The treatment involves breathing oxygen under pressure, sitting in a large chamber alongside other patients. This results in an increased level of oxygen in the blood, with improved delivery of oxygen to all tissues.

A small study reported symptomatic improvement in 28 out of 36 patients with ME attending an HBO therapy centre,[3] however it is not known how they were diagnosed, nor for how long the apparent improvement lasted. The few people I have talked to who have tried HBO treatment reported very mixed effects. So, at present, not enough is known for this therapy to be recommended.

There are some alternative treatments that are potentially hazardous and have not been properly studied. These include:[4]

Infusions of hydrogen peroxide
Germanium
Mushroom or fungus teas
Colonic irrigation
Sygnalysis
Some Chinese herbs
Royal Jelly.

For information about Registers of trained and qualified practitioners of alternative treatments, see Appendix A.

Chapter 13

Candida Infection and Dysbiosis

The possible association between a yeast called Candida albicans and ME/CFS is a controversial subject, and there are widely differing opinions on this subject within both orthodox and alternative medical professions.

Candida albicans is one of the many micro-organisms to be found living in and on all of us. It is a fungus, one of the yeast family of organisms, and is best known for causing thrush in babies' mouths, and vaginal thrush in women. It can also cause nappy rash, and soreness and itching around the anus and genitals in adults. This skin infection from Candida is more common in hot, humid conditions, and used to be called 'dhobie itch'.

Candida albicans lives in small numbers in the gut and on the skin of healthy people, and normally causes no harm. It is so prevalent that at least 90 per cent of children have had exposure to it by the time they are 6 months old. There are some circumstances, particularly of compromised immunity, that allow Candida to multiply and cause symptoms. The most extreme cases of Candida infection, with systemic involvement of the bloodstream, lungs or brain, occur in ill people with severe immune deficiency, for example people on immuno-suppressive therapy or those suffering from leukaemia or AIDS.

People suffering from ME or CFS may also, as a secondary complication, sometimes develop an overgrowth of Candida infection in the gut, in addition to thrush or skin infections. However, there has been no evidence to suggest that the yeast infects the bloodstream or internal organs.

Candida is only one of a huge variety of yeasts, viruses and bacteria which live on or in human bodies. The large bowel contains several pounds in weight of bacteria plus some yeasts, most of which are essential for fermenting undigested food, manufacturing some vitamins, and breaking down mucous. These micro-organisms stay in their place because of the colon lining and the body's efficient immune-surveillance system.

There are certain factors that tend to allow an overgrowth of both Candida albicans and other organisms in the large bowel (such an imbalance of bugs in the bowel is called *dysbiosis*):

- warmth and moisture (skin fungal infections)
- sugar – too much in the diet, or too much in the blood as in diabetes
- other gut infections – *Guardia*, dysentery, food poisoning, enteroviruses
- weakened immunity
- change in hormones – as during pregnancy, or when taking steroid drugs or the contraceptive pill
- stress
- broad-spectrum antibiotics.

Although unknown by many doctors, dysbiosis in animals has been recognized by veterinary surgeons for many years, and they routinely prescribe *probiotics*, which replenish levels of friendly bugs in the gut, to farm livestock and other animals.

Yeast infection many contribute to many common symptoms and medical conditions, including infections of the bladder and prostate, vaginal discharge, premenstrual tension, allergy to chemicals, athlete's foot, acne, abdominal bloating and fatigue. However, many of these symptoms may result from the person being hypersensitive to Candida, rather than just the infection. Many symptoms experienced from yeast problems overlap with those of ME/CFS and chronic fatigue.

There is no one reliable test that tells you if a yeast sensitivity or infection is causing your problems, however the following symptoms are suggestive:

- history of taking long-term antibiotics (e.g. for acne)
- recurrent cystitis and or vaginal thrush
- fungal infection of skin or nails
- new chemical allergies
- symptoms much worse in damp weather or in a musty smelling house
- bloating after food; alternating diarrhoea with constipation
- symptoms worse after alcohol or eating sweets
- itching or burning sensation round the anus
- craving for sweet things, cheese or alcohol.

If you have been diagnosed ME or CFS and believe that your illness may be related to, or caused by a yeast infection and/or dysbiosis in the gut, you can find much more detailed information in specialist books on the subject. But it is important to bear in mind that:

Not every person with ME/CFS has a yeast problem.

Treating a yeast problem or dysbiosis may improve many of the symptoms and clear up chemical allergies, but this will not necessarily cure the underlying illness, although removing one of the stresses on the body may help with long-term recovery from ME/CFS.

If you decide to embark on a treatment programme for Candida or dysbiosis, do it seriously for at least three months.

Treatment of dysbiosis or yeast overgrowth has three parts:

1. **modifying the diet** to starve the yeast of sugar and provide good nutrition
2. **strengthening the resistance** of the body and gut
3. taking specific **anti-yeast medication**.

1) An Anti-Candida Diet

Any ill person who is already seriously underweight should not embark on any further food restrictions without medical supervision. The point of modifying the diet is to deprive yeasts of their nourishment, which is sugar, to avoid consuming foods containing fungi or yeasts, and to eat very nutritiously to strengthen natural immunity to Candida. A strict anti-Candida diet forbids bread, cheese, milk products and fruit. A sensible compromise restricts fruit to one piece a day, avoiding those high in sugar or with yeasty skin, and allows a little non-blue cheese.

Foods to avoid
- Sugar of all kinds, including honey and molasses.
- Alcohol in all forms – it makes most people with ME/CFS feel ill anyway.
- Anything fermented – vinegar, soy sauce, tofu, most cheeses.
- Dried fruit and shelled nuts, especially if old.
- Melon and grapes.

- Mushrooms and truffles.
- Fruit juices in cartons.
- Any food which is mouldy.

Foods allowed

- Potatoes, rice, oats, sugar-free breakfast cereals, oatcakes, pasta, buckwheat.
- Fresh vegetables of all kinds. Garlic, onions, and members of the cabbage family are especially valuable.
- Pure vegetable oils.
- Meats, fish, eggs.
- Pulses – but these must be properly cooked or they produce wind.
- Water, tea, coffee, freshly-squeezed fruit juices, sugar-free bottled or canned drinks.

Foods allowed in moderation:

- Bread, preferably yeast-free (e.g. soda bread).
- Milk, non-blue cheese, sugar-free 'live' yoghurt (containing *Lactobacillus acidophilus*).
- Fresh fruit.

2) Supplements

PROBIOTICS

Unlike antibiotics, probiotics replenish the families of friendly bugs living in the large bowel, and therefore help restore normal balance and displace the unwanted bugs.

There are various preparations available, but it is important to obtain only those that are made by reputable companies. The usual preparations contain a mixture of *Lactobacillus acidophilus* and *Bifidobacteria*. These are also found in live yoghurt; pasteurized commercial yoghurt has no value as a source of probiotics.

People who have an intolerance to lactose in cow's milk can sometimes cope with live yoghurt, because the probiotics consume the lactose (milk sugar). The longest-living peoples of the world, found residing in areas around the Black Sea, reputedly eat a lot of yoghurt.

OTHER SUPPLEMENTS

Good-quality yeast-free vitamin and mineral supplements (*see Chapter 11*):

- magnesium, at least 300 mg of elemental magnesium per day. Magnesium tends to be low in people with dysbiosis.
- biotin, 300 mcg a day (also found in many multivitamin preparations)
- garlic, fresh, as much as you can stand. Use the flesh and juice immediately after crushing, on salads or with any food. Or use several uncrushed cloves in casseroles – or, if you cannot stomach so much, take it as freeze-dried enteric-coated capsules. Garlic is the best natural antiseptic plant there is; people who eat a lot of garlic do not get many infections or catch many colds!
- cold-pressed olive oil, at least 1 tablespoon per day. Oleic acid has natural antifungal properties. It is no mystery that Mediterranean peoples eating a local native diet, with plenty of olive oil, garlic, unrefined bread, and relatively little animal fat, do not on the whole suffer from allergies or high blood pressure, in comparison with people who have a more 'western' way of eating.

3) Antifungal Agents

Until a few years ago, *Nystatin* was the most common anti-fungal treatment prescribed. Nystatin is still used in suspension to treat thrush in the mouth. It is also available in tablet and powder form. However, there is little point taking treatment with Nystatin without also altering the diet, because if the conditions that allowed yeast overgrowth in the first place are not changed, then the problem will just keep recurring.

For treating general symptoms due to Candida overgrowth, the powder preparation seems to work best.

Because the start of treatment frequently brings on more severe symptoms, due to a 'die-off' reaction to dying yeasts, it is *essential to start with small doses*. It is also best to 'prepare the ground' first by having at least 2 weeks on an anti-Candida diet, probiotics and supplements before starting any prescribed antifungal agent.

Fungilin (Amphotericin B)

This can be prescribed in lozenge form, to suck or chew to clear fungal infection from the mouth or throat. However, for intestinal infection it is more effective taken as 100-mg tablets, 4 times a day. Similar 'die-off' reactions may occur as with Nystatin, and mean that the treatment must be continued.

Fungilin is thought to penetrate the bowel wall more effectively that Nystatin, however both are well tolerated, are not toxic nor absorbed from the gut, and are effective against Candida. Nystatin can cause side-effects such as nausea after a week or so.

Ketoconazole (Nizoral)

This antifungal agent is absorbed into the bloodstream and is very effective.[1] However it may be toxic to the liver, so it is usually only prescribed for systemic and severe yeast infections.

A research study in the US in 1990[2] monitored 1,200 patients over five years for their response to antifungal Ketoconazole treatment. The results 'suggest that colonization of yeast may play a role in [the] aetiology [cause] of chronic fatigue syndrome, and also suggests that patients may benefit from systemic anti-yeast therapy and a decrease of sugar in the diet'. It was noted that 85 per cent of the patients in the trial had been treated with the broad-spectrum antibiotic tetracycline for two or more years in the past.

Fluconazole (Diflucan)

This is a relatively new drug, is absorbed into the bloodstream, treats fungal infections at a mucosal level (mouth, vagina and intestines) and also systemically (throughout the body). It is safer than Ketoconazole, but is expensive and only obtainable on prescription.

It may be necessary to treat Candida yeast infections in other situations with different preparations: Nystatin and Fungilin lozenges for the mouth throat and gullet, pessaries to treat vaginal infections, and creams or ointments for the skin.

It is essential to continue with a low-sugar anti-yeast diet, and to take probiotics while taking any antifungal drugs. Treatment may have to be continued for several months, and even when the drug treatment is cut down or stopped, vigilance needs to be maintained with eating habits, otherwise the symptoms of yeast infection will return!

CAPRISTATIN

Some fatty acids have been shown to destroy fungi. One example is caprylic acid, derived from coconuts. It is effective if taken as a slow-release preparation, capristatin, which reaches the large bowel before it is absorbed. Capristatin may be useful for someone who cannot tolerate Nystatin or Fungilin, but is not available on prescription.

ANTIFUNGAL FOODS

As previously mentioned, garlic, onion and brassicas (cabbage family) all have antifungal qualities due to the sulphur-derived compounds they contain. They should all be eaten liberally, as well as olive oil.

HERBS

A tea made from a particular tree bark, *Pau d'Arco*, has antifungal and immune-enhancing properties.

Aloe vera is a plant with antifungal properties. It is available both for external use and as preparation to drink. Aloe vera has achieved publicity as a cure for ME/CFS, but has not been subjected to any trials, and can be expensive. It is more likely that people who feel better from Aloe Vera have symptoms mainly due to yeast/dysbiosis, rather than ME/CFS.

If you decide that a yeast infection could be contributing to your ill-health and wish to treat it yourself, it is important to decide on a programme of diet, probiotics supplements and possibly antifungal agents. If there is a definite improvement in your symptoms after 1 month, then keep on with the programme for a further 5 months. If after 2 months or so you find that there is honestly no improvement, then at least you will know that you have given it a fair trial; then leave it. Many people who believe that treating Candida did not help them have not carried out a programme consistently or for long enough.

RECOMMENDED READING

Candida Albicans by Gill Jacobs (Optima)

Candida Albicans by Leon Chaitow (Thorsons)

Chapter 14

Food and Chemical Sensitivities

The word *allergy* comes from two Greek words, *allos* meaning other, *ergon* meaning energy. An allergy is an altered reaction to some outside stimulus. Something that provokes such an altered reaction is called an *allergen*.

Another word for an allergic reaction could be hypersensitivity. An allergic response is one that is different from the response of the majority of people. Most people can breathe grass pollens; only a minority develop hay fever. Most people can happily eat oranges; a few people react to them. The allergies that are easily recognized are: hay fever, asthma, eczema, migraine, skin reactions such as nettle rash, and collapse after bee stings.

Hypersensitive reactions also occur to inhaled chemicals, to traces of chemicals in food and water, or even to apparently harmless common foods. The understanding of different types of allergy has broadened considerably in the last 40 years, the pioneers of observation and research of food and chemical allergies being Dr Albert Rowe in the 1920s, and Dr Theron G Randolph and his colleagues in the US in the 1950s.

Estimates of the numbers of people with ME/CFS who have allergies vary from 20 to 70 per cent. One explanation is that the immune system's defences initially act against infection, but stay switched on instead of subsiding when the infection has been overcome. The body's immune system may become overreactive to other foreign substances as well as to the initiating virus.

There is a difference between *food allergy* and *food intolerance*. A true food allergy is usually fixed, and may be inherited. The reaction happens very quickly, and involves an immunoglobulin called IgE. Even the tiniest amount of the food may provoke a severe response. Symptoms of IgE-mediated allergy include hay fever, asthma, swelling of the face, nettle rash, vomiting or, in severe cases, total collapse – called anaphylactic shock. Such allergies are usually fixed for life, and in some cases prevention depends on expert vaccination (e.g. hay fever shots).

Food intolerance is less easy to diagnose, as symptoms may not develop for up to 24 hours after the culprit food has been eaten, and a reaction may depend on the amount eaten. Intolerance to commonly eaten foods may come and go, and if a culprit food is avoided for some weeks, the intolerance may disappear. In general terms, a rapid-onset food allergy results from one kind of immune reaction called Type-1 sensitivity, in which IgE immunoglobulins are involved. A delayed reaction to food probably results from Type-IV hypersensitivity, in which IgG immunoglobulins are involved.

Most apparent food 'allergy' in ME/CFS is in fact food intolerance; however, since food allergy is the recognized word it will be used in this chapter. Not everyone who has multiple allergies has ME/CFS, but in many there may be an underlying Candida yeast overgrowth or hypersensitivity (*see Chapter 13*).

Three types of allergens may cause trouble:

1. those ingested – foods, liquids, chemicals in food
2. those inhaled – pollen, house dust mite, moulds, animal fur, chemicals (formaldehyde, petrol, alcohol, aerosols, smoke)
3. those that come in contact with the skin – metals (nickel in bra and suspenders), rings, watches; dyes; various chemicals.

Research by Dr Hunter at Cambridge[1] has suggested that many cases of food intolerance may be due to the presence of abnormal gut flora plus a lower activity of certain gut enzymes. 'Specific food residues are broken down by colonic microflora with the production of chemicals, which in susceptible people with low concentrations of liver enzymes, pass into the circulation to produce distant symptoms.' This finding is supported by the presence of abnormal colonic bacteria in other diseases – such as rheumatoid arthritis and Irritable Bowel Syndrome.

The successful management of allergies requires not only the removal of the allergens, but measures to improve immune function. Practical problems arise when a patient is found to be reacting badly to so many things that avoiding them all causes malnutrition, and necessitates total isolation from the world. For this reason, very restricted diets in ME/CFS may do more harm than good.

Many symptoms of ME/CFS are the same as those resulting from allergic reactions. Signs suggestive of intolerance/allergies are:

• symptoms that develop after eating, such as rapid pulse, wheezing, abdominal pains, bloating, headache, joint pain, sudden mood change, sweating
• symptoms that improve on fasting
• feeling worse when in traffic jams, in city centres, on exposure to aerosol spray, fresh paint, etc., suggesting chemical allergies

- feeling better for being outside in the fresh air, maybe because of indoor air pollution
- sneezing and itchy eyes, hay fever symptoms improving on change of location.

Allergic symptoms are so numerous that there is no point making a list of them. It is the variability of symptoms on exposure to different foods and chemicals that is typical of allergy. If you suspect that food allergies are causing some of your problems, then adding details of what you eat and drink to your diary, or keeping a separate food diary, may help to pinpoint culprit foods.

However, there may be foods which you eat every day that are making you ill. Instead of an acute reaction to something rarely eaten, such as swelling and itching after strawberries, you can be chronically unwell by eating something so regularly that it never gets cleared from your system. This is called a *masked allergy*, and is also a form of addiction.

What happens is that repeated exposure to the food leads to general ill-health due to the constant stress on the immune system (*see Chapter 8*). Avoidance of the allergen for 24 hours or more may lead to withdrawal symptoms, as happens when an alcoholic dries out or a cigarette smoker stops smoking. These withdrawal symptoms settle down in a few days, but then the subject becomes extra-sensitive to the allergen, and re-exposure causes more dramatic symptoms than when it was being taken every day, when the reaction was being *masked* through partial adaptation to the substance.

The elimination and provocation-testing method of food-allergy detection is based on understanding this masked allergy phenomenon. If you avoid the suspect allergen, allow it to disappear from your gut (which takes up to five days), and then eat it again, it will cause the symptoms to reappear more strongly. If there are no ill-effects, then it is regarded as safe.

The same principle applies to a chemical masked allergy. For example, a woman with chronic headaches, depression and fatigue went on holiday to a small Mediterranean island, and after three days she felt wonderful. On returning home to her kitchen, which had a gas cooker, she felt absolutely dreadful; her depression and headache returned with a vengeance within a few hours of entering the house. Fortunately, the departure to a place of clean air had also sharpened her senses, so that on entering the kitchen she detected a slight smell of gas. After the gas appliance had been removed, her symptoms cleared up.

The mechanism causing symptoms from exposure to allergens is complex. Frequently it is several allergens combined, plus other stresses, the total overload producing symptoms.

A good model for understanding this phenomenon is to think of a barrel of water. If the level of water is too high it overflows, just as, if the level of the sum total of stresses is too high, one further exposure to an allergen produces a reaction. The final drop of water into the barrel is like the last straw that broke the camel's back. It is the sum total of all stresses that causes symptoms. So if the basic level of water in the barrel can be lowered, for example by reducing stress, or chemical exposure, then a further stress may be less likely to cause symptoms.

Often the last straw is not an allergen, but a psychological stress. For example, a child with eczema possibly has a cow's milk intolerance, masked because it is drunk daily; the child drinks the milk every day and is chronically miserable and itching. When the child goes to a new school, or has a row in the classroom, the eczema flares up very badly. Is the mental stress to blame, or the cow's milk? The answer is both, of course. But if the cow's milk is removed, probably the school stress will have less of an effect on the eczema.

It is unrealistic for people with ME/CFS to try to succeed in avoiding every single thing they react to, and there is some cause for concern if someone who is already ill starves him- or herself on a strict elimination diet. Therefore, much of the management of allergies may rest in compromise.

Let us look at the various stresses and allergens that may be filling up the water barrel:

- too much physical exercise
- mental and emotional stress
- airborne allergens – house dust mite, pet hairs, pollens
- electromagnetic stress – TV, VDUs, electric cables
- chemical allergens – traffic fumes, aerosols, gas leaks, fresh paint, perfumes
- new carpets, printing ink, etc.
- food intolerances
- some ongoing infection.

Some of these things you cannot do anything about. What you *should* do is avoid as many of them as you can.

Detecting Allergies

None of the methods of testing is 100 per cent and, in a very sensitive person, allergies can change from day to day. However, the most important sensitivities come up repeatedly on subsequent testing, and these are the ones that the allergic person needs to avoid. The best – also the cheapest – way to test for foods that cause problems is by using an *elimination diet*.

THE ELIMINATION, UNMASKING AND CHALLENGE DIET

The elimination, unmasking and challenge diet is the simplest and probably most accurate method of diagnosing food allergy. The disadvantage is that it is time-consuming. *It should not be undertaken without medical supervision by any child, nor by any patient suffering from depression, epilepsy or asthma*, because of the possibly dangerous consequence of a severe reaction to food-testing after avoidance.

The patient fasts for five days, drinking only spring water, or else eating a few foods which are rarely eaten. Two foods are usually used, for example lamb and pears, or cod and broccoli. During the fast any symptoms are noted, as well as any cravings for particular foods. If it is not a complete fast it should be continued for at least a week, to allow symptoms time to clear up. If all the pre-fast symptoms are still there after a week, either food allergy was not responsible or one of the few foods taken used was not safe.

Foods are then reintroduced one at a time, one each day, the less commonly eaten foods first. If there is a reaction to the new food, it usually happens within 24 hours, although it may be delayed for 48 hours. All symptoms are noted, including the resting pulse rate before and 1 hour after a test food is eaten. A food that produces no reaction can be reintroduced, and as testing proceeds the patient hopefully develops a gradually wider range of safe foodstuffs.

However, this method requires strong motivation and meticulousness on the part of the patient, and sometimes a delayed reaction – the symptoms not appearing until 48 hours later – may confuse the picture.

THE STONE AGE DIET

This is a modified elimination diet. It was first used in Britain for allergy testing and treatment by Dr Richard Mackarness, a psychiatrist at Basingstoke. Why is it suitable?

Our hunter-gatherer ancestors ate a wide range of raw plants, plus a great variety of animal food which included shellfish, birds, rodents and molluscs. The introduction of cereal crops, milk, sugar, tea and coffee, and the pollution of foods by agro-chemicals and food additives, are all relatively recent changes in our diet. The human metabolism and digestion have adapted to these changes with time, but logically the foods that are most likely to give trouble if the adaptation breaks down are those most recently introduced to our diet.

Wild animals, unlike intensively-reared ones, have little saturated fats, and no chemical residues. And because the hunter-gatherer ate a wide variety of things according to the seasons, he or she did not eat the same few things every day throughout the year, as we now tend to do. So the modern version of the Stone Age Diet cuts out the foods likely to cause trouble:

Allowed

- All meats and fish (fresh or frozen).
- Fruit.
- Vegetables (fresh).
- Potatoes.
- Fresh shelled nuts.
- Pulses.
- Spring water.
- Pure vegetable oil.
- Salt.
- Milk-free margarine.

Not Allowed

- Grains (wheat, oats, rye, corn, rice, barley).
- Sugar – all kinds.
- Milk and milk products; butter and margarine.
- Tea, coffee, alcohol.
- Anything tinned, smoked or processed.
- Eggs.
- Dried fruit.
- Tap water.

This system works well if you are not allergic to any of the foods on the 'allowed' list. It is quite possible to follow the Stone Age Diet for months and have complete nutrition. The main things to test, if two weeks or longer on the Stone Age Diet have improved your symptoms, are eggs, milk and its products, tap water, and some grains. A good grain to test early is rice, as it is less likely to cause symptoms than wheat or rye and, if safe, provides another carbohydrate. Eggs are important to test early, as they are an excellent food.

Of the grains, wheat (in the UK) and corn (in the US) are most likely to cause problems. You may be sensitive to the gluten, which is protein, or intolerant of the husk or bran. Some people with wheat intolerance can manage one slice of unprocessed white bread a day or twice a week, but get symptoms if they go back to wholemeal bread. Oats have less gluten, and if tolerated are a better source of fibre than wheat. Rice is rarely allergenic, perhaps because it is not part of our staple diet, and is low in gluten. Unrefined rice is a good substitute for wheat as a starch. There are also less common gluten-free grains, for example tapioca, buckwheat and millet, which can be substituted for wheat.

CYTOTOXIC TESTING

This method uses the observed reaction of white blood cells to various foods. A sample of blood is sent to a specialist laboratory. The white cells are separated and exposed to a range of foods and chemicals, and their reaction is examined under a microscope.

The cell reactions are graded: No reaction; a mild reaction (the cells change shape); severe reaction (the cells die).

The correlation between the test results and clinical allergies is fairly good (about 85 per cent), but the test is expensive and is only available in a few places in the UK.

The patient is advised to avoid completely foods which give a severe reaction; to restrict, or rotate, those producing a mild reaction; and to eat freely of foods that produced no reaction.

One centre that carries out cyotoxic allergy testing is York Nutritional Laboratory, which also does IgG testing, which is more accurate but also more expensive (*see Appendix A for the address*).

INTRADERMAL TESTING AND NEUTRALIZATION TECHNIQUE

This procedure is used by several clinical ecologists. It is expensive and time-consuming, and patients can have bad reactions to the tests, which may last for hours and confuse subsequent tests. However it does have an advantage for the few severely allergic people, in that neutralizing drops, in the correct dilution, can be prepared specifically for the patient, and taking these drops may enable someone who is severely multi-allergic to survive without fasting. The disadvantages are:

- the time needed for tests – maybe a whole morning to reach one end-point

- the neutralization levels may change after a few weeks, and the desensitizing drops may have to be worked out over and over again.

APPLIED KINESIOLOGY (MUSCLE WEAKNESS TEST)

This test requires no sophisticated equipment, and depends on muscle reactions to contact with the test substance. The test substance itself, or a vial containing a solution of it, is placed over the centre of the abdomen. The patient lies down, relaxed, and the strength of one or more arm muscles is assessed, to begin with, then again after contact with the test item. Only very small movements are assessed and, if the patient reacts to an item, there is an immediate perceptible muscle weakness. This method is fairly accurate *with a skilled tester*, but not everyone can use this test. It has the advantage of being non-invasive, quick, and does not produce symptoms. With a skilled practitioner, applied kinesiology is almost 100 per cent reproducible if the same patient is tested on consecutive days. The patient should not know be told which substance is being tested each time, as this could affect his or her response to it.

Treating Food and Chemical Allergies

- Avoid allergens where possible.
- Correct nutrient deficiencies, and take supplements to help restore normal immune function.
- Desensitize, if severely affected, by using neutralizing drops or injections, or enzyme-potentiated desensitization (EPD – *see below*).

AVOIDANCE

For the majority of allergic people, avoiding the main foods that cause problems and cleaning up the chemical environment as far as possible, combined with nutritional measures, is best. If a major food allergen, such as wheat, is avoided for 6 months or so, the patient may become less sensitive and may be able to tolerate it if eaten in small amounts once or twice a week. If it is eaten daily and in increasing amounts, then a masked allergy may develop again.

Some allergies are fixed for life, and a long spell of avoidance does not change the sensitivity. There is often some enzyme deficiency associated with these allergies. Most patients soon find out if they have a lifelong allergy to something eaten rarely such as strawberries or shellfish.

Milk allergy is commonly caused by a deficiency of lactase, the enzyme needed to digest lactose (milk sugar). This is usually lifelong, is very common in Asian and African peoples, and occurs in about 30 per cent of Europeans. Lactose intolerance sometimes develops following some gastro-intestinal infection, such as by a parasite called *Giardia lamblia* (commonly picked up overseas), and also enteroviruses.

Some milk-sensitive people can tolerate milk if it has been treated with a lactose-reducing enzyme. Other milk sensitivities may be reactions to cow's milk protein, in which case goat's or sheep's milk may be tolerated. If you are allergic to cow's milk, it is worth asking for separate tests for milk protein and lactose when undergoing allergy tests.

Often, avoidance of one or two foods will reduce the overall 'load' and allow you to eat other things to which you are less sensitive. If the foods you are less sensitive to are eaten no more than once every four days, or perhaps twice a week, there is less chance of a masked allergy developing. This is the principle of the Rotation Diet, which can be used both for managing and diagnosing allergies.

The Rotation Diet means you allow four days in between eating foods from the same food family. For example, if you eat chicken, neither chicken nor eggs should be eaten for the next four days. This way of eating can be interesting on paper, using columns for food groups for each day, but in practice it can be tedious. It can even be unworkable if you have to cater for the rest of the family, and makes dining out difficult.

ENZYME POTENTIATED DESENSITIZATION (EPD)

This technique was developed by Dr Len McEwan, lately at St Mary's Hospital, London.

A mixture of minute doses of highly purified antigens is combined with an enzyme called Beta-glucuronidase. This solution is placed in contact with the skin on the patient's inner forearm in a small cup, the skin surface having been scratched to break the superficial layers. The solution of antigens and enzyme is left in contact with the skin for 24 hours, or less if a severe reaction develops. Many antigens can be included in the mixture – maybe 70 or more – so it is not necessary to have established the patient's sensitivities beforehand.

EPD is repeated at monthly intervals for 3 to 4 months, but the benefits (increasing tolerance to foods) do not develop for 6 to 12 months after starting treatment. EPD is expensive, however, and the results are not instant; nor is it available at many centres, and few of these in the NHS. However, those who complete the course report good results, though the improvement is not permanent in everyone.

SODIUM CROMYGLYCATE (NALCROM)

This drug is better known for prevention of allergic asthma attacks. It works by blocking the reaction of mast cells to the antigen, thus preventing the release of chemical substances (including histamine) which cause the allergic effects.

Mast cells are scattered in the membranes lining the nose, throat, airways, and also the gut. Nalcrom can be taken in capsules just before meals, and seems to be effective in aborting food allergy reactions in about two-thirds of the patients who try it. It is not a substitute for sensible avoidance of main food offenders, but could be useful to someone who is allergic to many foods; also if the allergic person copes well at home, but has problems when away from home. Nalcrom is only available on prescription in 100-mg capsules; the adult dose is 100–200 mg 3 times daily. It is safe, although occasionally causes side-effects such as nausea, joint pains or rashes.

Suggested Supplements for Allergic People

First, ensure that any supplements you obtain are free from gluten, sugar, yeast and colourings. The regime suggested for ME/CFS (*page 221*) is suitable.

The main deficiencies in very allergic people are of B vitamins, pantothenic acid, iron, zinc, magnesium and essential fatty acids.

Dealing with bowel dysbiosis and Candida infection (*see Chapter 13*) may improve food intolerances quite dramatically.

A Word of Caution

If you have lost weight or were underweight before becoming ill, or have severe symptoms, do not undertake elimination diets without specialized medical supervision. By further reducing your nutritional intake, you may become worse. If possible, seek advice from a medically-trained clinical ecologist, or a hospital specialist.

If you cannot find medical help, a suggested routine is:

1. follow the diet guidelines outlined in Chapter 11, avoid all chemicals in food, and take the suggested nutritional supplements. This may improve your symptoms after 2 months.
2. if you suspect food allergies, try either the Stone Age Diet, eating plenty of vegetables, meat, fish and fruit; or cut out either wheat, or cow's milk, one at a time, as these are the most common offenders
3. reduce your exposure to other possible allergens as much as possible, for example any chemicals around you.

Chemical Sensitivity

This problem seems to be increasing. You only have to consider the vast array of products made from petrochemicals (hydrocarbons) which have become part of 20th-century living, to see that we cannot possibly expect humans to have adapted to them in such a short time.

Rachel Carson's classic book *Silent Spring*, written in 1962, was a chilling forecast of the price we may have to pay for tampering with the environment. Talking about the effect of DDT and other pesticides on living creatures and food chains, she said, 'It looks as if we will go on swallowing these chemicals whether we like it or not and their real effect may not be seen for another twenty or thirty years.'

Many people with ME/CFS seem to have an increased degree of sensitivity to chemicals compared to when they were well. Some reactions are obvious – for example, someone who gets a headache and watering eyes when they open the morning newspaper is probably sensitive to printer's ink. However, there may be more insidious symptoms, harder to relate to the cause. Someone who is very sensitive may be unwell on days when the wind blows from the direction of some chemical factory 30 miles away. The presence of a smoker in the household may cause chronic worsening of symptoms in a susceptible non-smoker. A minute gas leak from an old cooker can make you ill.

Other than moving to a remote place by the sea, drinking spring water and growing your own food organically, you may feel that you have little control over your environment. You can, however, support pressure groups such as Friends of the Earth and Greenpeace, or write to your Member of Parliament about environmental issues. Nearer to home, there is a lot you can do to clean up your immediate environment.

CHEMICALS THAT FREQUENTLY CAUSE PROBLEMS

Hydrocarbons, or Fossil Fuels
- Petrol, diesel, oils.
- Paraffin (kerosene).
- Natural or calor gas.
- Coal, coke, anthracite.
- Wood, charcoal.

Hydrocarbon Derivatives
People who are sensitive to fuels are usually affected by hydrocarbon products:

- plastics – wrappings, bottles, cling film, food boxes, furnishings
- synthetic textiles – nylon, terylene, polyester (in clothing, carpets and upholstery)
- paints, especially gloss paint (water-based gloss is now available), varnish, solvents
- aerosol propellants – these are widespread, being found in hair spray, deodorants, air fresheners, etc.
- detergents, polishes and cleaning fluids
- cosmetics, perfumes, scented soaps and wax candles.

Phenol Products

- Carbolic acid – this is pure phenol.
- *Dettol* and other antiseptics.
- Many preservatives.
- Pesticides, herbicides.
- Polyurethane foam.
- Dyes, Bakelite and hard plastics.

Formaldehyde

- Widespread – in dyes, fabric finishes, textile proofings (if you feel ill in a large clothing store, it is usually 'outgassing' from the garments that is affecting you).
- Fertilizers, insecticides, foam rubber.

- Fabric conditioner.
- Paper manufacture, printing ink, photographic treatments.
- Most building materials, cavity wall insulation and many other products.

Gardening and Agricultural Chemicals

These are too numerous to list. Many are now banned, but can still be found lurking in garden sheds. Herbicides usually break down quickly, and fertilizers may be toxic while undiluted.

Pesticides are potentially the most harmful. DDT, although banned, builds up in food chains and has been detected even in the Arctic ice, it is now so widespread. But the most important insecticides relevant to people who develop ME or CFS are those in the Organophosphate group.

Organophosphates kill insects by interfering with their nerve function. They were used in the Iraqi campaign of genocide against the Kurdish people. Some humans are very susceptible to even traces of organophosphates, and sheep farmers in particular are at risk from sheep dip. In the last year there has been much publicity in the UK over the high incidence of diagnosed ME/CFS among the population of the Outer Hebrides. In these remote islands, which lie to the northwest of mainland Scotland, crofting is a way of life. Instead of large flocks of sheep managed by a farmer, most families in these remote islands keep a few sheep and other animals.

At the annual 'dip', many crofters and families come together to use a communal dipping tank, and the liquid dip, which contains an organophosphate insecticide to kill the parasites that cause sheep scab, can splash onto the clothing of not only shepherds handling the animals, but helpers and other family members in the households where the contaminated clothes are washed. An estimated number of 80+ cases of diagnosed ME/CFS were identified in early 1997: in a population of 23,000, this would give an incidence of over 350 per 100,000 – well above the national average.

Symptoms of Low-dose Exposure Organophosphate Poisoning

The symptoms of chronic OP poisoning are:

Headaches, muscular weakness and exhaustion, post-exertional malaise, nausea, diarrhoea, sweating, loss of co-ordination. Later, depression and problems with memory and concentration develop. The clinical picture is identical to that of ME/CFS.

High-dose OP exposure results in muscle spasms followed by paralysis, salivation, slow heart rate, difficulty breathing and, possibly, death.

The main risk is thought to be from skin contact with sheep dip, and the UK Government Ministry of Agriculture Fisheries and Food (MAFF) now urge farmers to take precautions and stress the wearing of boots, rubber aprons and gloves. However, there is also commonly a risk of skin exposure and inhalation of droplets of dip in the air, produced from the splashing of wet sheep as they go through the tank.

Another risk to farmers is from treatment of cattle for warble fly; this used to be compulsory using OP-based pesticides.

Even exposure to minimum amounts of OPs can cause the subject to become sensitized, so that repeated exposure leads to more symptoms. For example, a sheep farmer who feels unwell, with flu-like symptoms, pins and needles in his limbs and fatigue, for a week or so following dipping, may recover, but be more severely affected after the next dip a year later. Another consequence of exposure to a moderate or low level of OPs seems to be increased vulnerability to viral infection.

Apart from the risks to agricultural workers, ordinary people are at risk from household insect sprays, OPs in products against fleas in pets (including 'flea collars' for cats), or living or walking near crop fields that have just been sprayed. Shampoo used against head-lice, which is becoming a problem in school children nationwide, contains OPs as the active ingredient, and children could well be at risk from absorption of OPs through the scalp if their hair is washed with these shampoos several times.

Anyone who is inadvertently exposed to OPs and develops acute symptoms should seek medical help immediately. The first-aid treatment for OP poisoning is atropine given by injection. There are various anti-OP pressure groups (*see Appendix A*) who would like to see a total ban on the use of OPs in farming and domestic life. However, there is a significant problem in banning the use of OPs in pest control in the farming industry, because at present OP products are the most effective way of controlling sheep scab and cattle warble fly. What is urgently needed is the development of alternative, safer forms of pest control. The only way this will happen is for ordinary people to continue to put pressure on the Government by writing to and lobbying their representatives, and supporting environmental pressure groups.

FOOD COLOURINGS

Many artificial food colourings are now banned in many European countries. Some are quite safe, but others can produce allergic reactions. If in doubt, check the food labels.

COLOURINGS IN MEDICINES
Many medicines still contain synthetic tastes or colours. If in doubt, ask your pharmacist or write to the manufacturers.

CHEMICALS IN TOBACCO SMOKE
You need not be a smoker to be affected by the fumes from other people's cigarettes, pipes or cigars. This smoke contains many chemicals, and a sensitive person can be affected by traces lingering on clothes. If you or someone near you smokes, then avoiding all the other sources of chemical pollution may be a waste of time. You are entitled to a smoke-free place at work, and **you must make your home a smoke-free one if you are serious about improving your health**.

Minimizing Chemical Exposure

ON YOUR PERSON
Wear natural fibres if possible. Wash fabrics that have special finishes before wearing them, and thoroughly air clothes that have been dry-cleaned. Make sure clothes, once washed, are well rinsed. Avoid 'biological' washing powders. When buying clothes, look for cottons, pure wools or silk, and if a garment has any smell, wash it several times before wearing it. If you or someone in your house is chemically sensitive, avoid perfume, aftershave, perfumed deodorants, soaps or talcum power, and hair spray. Women wearing make-up should use scent-free products.

IN YOUR HOME
You and others around you must not smoke.
In the bathroom, remove air fresheners and toilet deodorizers,

and keep cleaning agents in a cupboard or elsewhere. It is a myth, fostered by advertising agencies, that artificial smells of pine or meadow freshness equal hygiene. Women brought up during a less chemically-inclined era will remember that bathrooms could be kept clean without all these smells.

Look under the kitchen sink and see what cleaning agents you can jettison. Those you decide to keep should be tightly sealed. Spray furniture polish, instant floor cleaners, insecticide sprays or fresh air sprays should all go out. The best air freshener is an open window. It is better to have a slightly grubby home than a shiny, scented house with ill occupants! Paints and solvents should be stored outside, in the shed or garage. Plans for redecorating should be postponed until you are feeling less ill or can go away while it is being done.

Wall-to-wall fitted carpets have become less fashionable. If you are chemically allergic it might be worth taking up such a carpet from your bedroom and keeping just the old linoleum that may be underneath, or having bare floorboards with rugs that can be shaken outside. Fitted carpets can never be thoroughly cleaned, and tend to harbour dust and house dust mites, a cause of asthma.

Very chemically-sensitive people may find benefit from creating one room in the house which is as chemical-free as possible – a 'safe haven' with cotton curtains, no plastics, no treated furniture, no foam and no fungicide-treated wallpaper.

One problem area is the bed. Should you have feather or foam-filled pillows? Good-quality feather pillows are better, provided you are not allergic to feathers. A lot of the allergic reactions to beds and bedding is due to the ubiquitous house dust mite, which establishes itself in all soft furnishings, so try to use washable bedding and pillows.

An undetected chemical culprit in your home could be a heating system that gives off minute quantities of gas or other fumes. Most homes in urban areas of the UK have gas central heating. It is essential to have all gas appliances checked and serviced regularly.

One way to test if gas is causing a problem is to go and stay somewhere with no gas at all and see if you improve. On returning, if you can smell any gas at all, you are probably sensitive to it.

Many people with ME/CFS seem to feel worse in winter. I believe that being indoors most of the time, with central heating and lack of ventilation, is probably as much to blame as is lack of natural daylight and sunshine. A lot of people never open any windows for fear of burglary or losing heat. However it is advisable to ventilate the house each day by opening some windows for a time. This also reduces damp and condensation.

Other sources of indoor pollution include **wood preservatives**, which can hang around for years after the wood has been treated and contain fungicides and/or pesticides; also cavity wall insulations (foam), tobacco smoke, damp and mould (adequate ventilation should prevent these), portable gas heaters, coal- or oil-fired stoves, and insecticides, as well as air-conditioning units and integrally-built garages.

Televisions and VDU screens, when in operation, may release formaldehyde from their plastic components. They also produce electromagnetic and other radiations which can affect some people. Many people with ME/CFS cannot tolerate watching TV for long.

One solution is to attach a special radiation-protective screen; having an ionizer in the room also seems to help.

A fairly drastic step is to move house, if there seems to be something harmful in your home or neighbourhood that cannot be corrected. Obviously there is no point in moving from a street with heavy traffic to a quiet country cottage surrounded by crop fields which are regularly sprayed! A person who is very sensitive to gas should look for a home which is all electric or has the gas boiler outside the main house.

Old houses may be unsafe because of treatment for timber and dry rot. Probably the best homes ecologically (in the UK) are those built between 1920 and 1960.

Combating an Acute Reaction

Drink a glass of water containing 1 g of vitamin C and 1 level teaspoon bicarbonate of soda. Repeat the vitamin C if necessary at hourly intervals, and continue to drink lots of fluids for the next 24 hours. This helps to neutralize the reaction, and gives a boost to the white cells and adrenals. Whatever the mechanism, this remedy does help, so keep vitamin C handy at home and if travelling. This mixture is useful to take on aeroplanes – air travel involves a lot of chemical exposure, both on the plane and in modern airport terminals.

If at home, change your clothes and have a shower to remove traces of the chemical from your clothes and skin. Go outside, or open a window and breathe deeply of clean air. If in a car, shut all windows and vents and try and get away from whatever it is – crop sprays, road works or a queue of buses. Bach Rescue Remedy drops (*see page 244*) are invaluable, and can be taken for any sort of collapse or shock, whether chemical, emotional or sheer physical exhaustion. Together with glucose sweets and some vitamin C and bicarb, a small bottle of Rescue Remedy should be part of every ME/CFS person's first-aid kit. I have found these things essential on occasions when travelling, when my expectation of what I can endure tends to exceed reality.

Desensitization

Some clinical ecologists treat very chemically-sensitive patients in a special ecologically safe unit, where everything is done to create a chemical-free environment. Patients often improve dramatically while in these surroundings, and can return home with a supply of desensitizing drops or injections. This is fine, so long as the patient also takes steps to clean up his or her home as much as possible, to deal with any likely Candida infection, and to correct any nutritional deficiencies.

Reducing exposure to chemical allergens, where possible, will help to reduce the overall stress on the body, and should be attempted by people diagnosed with ME or CFS as part of their self-help plan.

Chapter 15

ME/CFS in Children

Children and teenagers can and do develop ME/CFS. Children around the age of puberty seem most vulnerable (it is rarely found in children under the age of 5). Males and females are equally affected, up to puberty, then in the teens there is a preponderance of females. The most serious effect is the cognitive dysfunction, which causes loss of education at a critical age. Even if the child is well enough to attend school, his or her performance in class and at exams falls behind.

The most common, and serious, misdiagnosis is 'school phobia'. A physician who has made a particular study of childhood ME/CFS is Dr David S Bell, a paediatrician at Lyndonville, New York, where there was an outbreak in 1985: '104 patients were identified who retrospectively met criteria (for CFS). 44 patients were in the 6–7 year age group. All were followed up for at least two years, when only four children had made a complete recovery.'[1]

Children can also suffer from having a parent or sibling with ME/CFS. They may feel left out, neglected or unloved if more attention is given to a sick brother or sister, or if an ill parent hasn't got the energy for good parenting. A child may suffer anguish at seeing a parent devastated by the illness, and may demonstrate this by bad behaviour, depression or sleep disturbance. It is important to remember the silent suffering of a young child when another member of the family has a chronic illness.

The Onset of ME/CFS

This does not differ in a young person from that in an adult, although it is usually more acute and follows an infection which is frequently present among school classmates. Dr Bell has observed two patterns of onset: those aged under 10 are more likely to have a gradual onset, whereas adolescents tend to have an acute onset following a illness with clinical features suggesting glandular fever (but typically the tests for Epstein Barr are negative) or another flu-like illness, maybe with diarrhoea and vomiting. This makes diagnosis much more difficult in the younger age group.

Clinical Features and Symptoms

These are similar to those experienced by an adult, although some of the nervous system symptoms may not be so obvious because a child may find it more difficult to express problems with poor memory and concentration, or inability to learn or retain information, or stay alert for long in class. These symptoms manifest instead as poor school performance.

Symptoms that seem to be more common in children are:

Severe unremitting headaches, nausea and anorexia severe enough to cause weight loss, and abdominal pain. Ashen-grey pallor is commonly seen when the young person with ME feels ill.

Misdiagnoses

ME/CFS in children may be misdiagnosed as:

- migraine, abdominal pain syndrome
- atypical epilepsy ('petit-mal'-type seizures are more common in childhood ME than in adults with the illness) and some children have convulsions with loss of consciousness, or sometimes dystonic movements of limbs
- juvenile rheumatoid arthritis
- school phobia
- anorexia nervosa
- childhood depression, if there are few objective signs in a child with ME/CFS who withdraws from contact with family and friends.

Children tend to become ill rapidly if they develop an infection, and they will tend to have a higher temperature than would adults, and more severe symptoms. They react more rapidly than adults, but also recover more quickly from most acute infections. So it is really noticeable when a youngster who has been laid low with a feverish illness fails to make the expected recovery in a week or two.

Particular Problems of ME/CFS in Children and Young People

DIAGNOSIS
The agreed criteria for diagnosing ME/CFS include a length of illness of 6 months or more. Clearly, parents want to know what is wrong *before* their child has been ill for 6 months. Bearing

in mind that physical activity makes the condition worse, and that rest early on may encourage early recovery, it is obviously very important to get an assessment and provisional diagnosis when the child is not recovering as expected from an infection – this may be a diagnosis of post-viral fatigue to begin with.

Once this diagnosis has been reached, maybe as early as 6 or 8 weeks after the onset of illness, the child can be allowed to rest as needed, the school is informed, and pressure to go to school or do sports is removed. The diagnosis may become ME/CFS if the illness continues for 3 months or longer, with classical symptoms of muscle fatigue and brain disturbance.

Some GPs and school doctors are still reluctant to diagnose ME/CFS in a child. They may either still consider that ME/CFS is psychological, or believe that it is a condition mainly experienced by the over-twenties. Although ME/CFS is less common under age 20, many children suffer prolonged fatigue after an infection; some of these do continue to be unwell, or even deteriorate, and have the classic ME/CFS syndrome for a year or more. It is tragic for a child and his or her parents to have to battle with doctors and education authorities for months, while the child may try to attend school and live a normal life but keeps on relapsing and possibly deteriorates.

If your doctor is ignorant or unhelpful about ME/CFS and other post-viral syndromes, you can do several things:

a) contact one of the national ME support groups (*addresses in Appendix A*) and obtain information about ME/CFS to show your doctor
b) change to another GP
c) find out if there is a specialist in your area who understands ME/CFS and ask for a referral, or arrange for a private consultation. At the time of writing there appear to be few

paediatricians in the UK who believe that ME/CFS is an illness that can happen in childhood and that it is a neurological rather than mainly psychiatric condition.

Because there are often strange psychological symptoms, and easy fatiguability and other symptoms such as headache or nausea make the child unable or reluctant or to do school work, some doctors and education authorities find it easier to diagnose school phobia rather than suspect ME/CFS. They may also try to diagnose some family-behaviour problem to explain the child's change and inability to attend school.

Factors Which Help the Diagnosis of ME/CFS

- A child who was previously enjoying school and sports has changed since becoming ill — the psychological problems are new and out of character.
- The association of what was obviously an acute infection — in the child, or in the family — with the onset of the illness. The infection may have given few symptoms in the child, but others in the family may have had it more severely.
- No other precipitating factors in the family circumstances.
- Worsening of the child's symptoms after exercise or mental exertions — for example after sports or when studying intensively for exams.
- Fluctuating symptoms from week to week or day by day.
- Aches and pains quite unlike anything the child has had before.
- Symptoms not improved by going on holiday, or at weekends; in other words, normal family life and exercise out of school are just as bad as school activities. A child with school phobia would be expected to make a dramatic improvement during holidays.

Before the consultation with a GP or specialist, write down the history of the onset of the illness, and any of the above factors if they apply to your child.

Do not be fobbed off by a doctor if you think your child has ME. Insist that adequate tests are done to exclude other illnesses, and if there is no firm diagnosis, ask what is making your child ill.

If the doctor does not understand ME/CFS and finds no abnormal physical signs, and blood tests are normal, the next stage may well be a referral to a child psychologist or psychiatrist. This assessment can be quite exhausting for a child. However, many parents do agree to such an assessment because a properly-trained and skilled psychologist should be able to establish that the child has no psychological condition and is physically ill. The results of such an assessment may actually strengthen your case.

Management of Children with ME/CFS

Complete physical and mental rest should be encouraged at first, but not total bed rest. For the first few weeks or months, general nursing care, as would be done for any ill child, is appropriate. The appetite may be poor, there may be nausea, constipation, diarrhoea, tummy pains or severe headache. Pain from severe headache may be a problem, and your doctor may be able to prescribe something for this, also for nausea if this persistent. Otherwise paracetamol, in a children's dose, can be tried. Constipation can be quite stubborn, so encourage plenty of fluids and as much vegetable and fruit intake as possible – a liquidizer for making vegetable soups is invaluable.

Try and avoid giving the young person drinks and foods that are high in sugar and fat. If milk is not tolerated, fruit yoghurts may be a good way to give protein and calcium. The diet guidelines in Chapter 11 also apply to children, and adequate protein intake is especially important for weight to be maintained and growth to continue. If there is loss of appetite and nausea, meals may have to small and frequent, and easy to swallow.

Problems arise when the child appears to make some recovery, and wants to do activities with friends, or to go to school and behave normally. You should not discourage an increase in activity, but should monitor the child for signs of collapse or an increase in symptoms. Trial and error will soon tell both child and parents what sort of activities and how much can be sustained without relapse.

Your child's friends may be unsympathetic, or even cruel when they see their pal going to school for half a morning, looking quite normal, then having to go home to rest for the remainder of the day. Keeping up with the peer group is very important for children and teenagers, and the loss of friends and activities shared with them can be as damaging psychologically as the pain and other symptoms. This is where support groups for young people with ME can play a valuable role – see the end of this chapter.

When the child is getting better enough to want to do things, then a diary is a good idea, as it may show improvement, and also what things could bring on symptoms.

A plan of rest and activity for the child can be discussed among the whole family, so that he or she is involved to some extent with managing the illness. Brothers and sisters and friends should be encouraged to include the child in any discussion of what is going on in school and in their activities.

EDUCATION

Hopefully, once you have a diagnosis the school authorities will be understanding and co-operative about restricted ability to attend school. Many schools and Education Authorities are more educated about ME/CFS in their pupils than are doctors. Sometimes it is a teacher who spots the typical symptoms in a pupil – falling behind with work, frequent days off with 'a virus', collapsing after gym or sports, falling asleep or looking grey-white halfway through a lesson – and can alert the parents or get a referral to the school doctor.

Some children are too ill to go to school at all, and even if they want to go for a short time, the effort of getting there, walking about carrying a sack of books, then sitting up in a chair and trying to concentrate for an hour, together with the general noise and sensory input in a crowded classroom, may all be too much and result in worsening of symptoms with no learning taking place. In this case trying to get the child back to school will be a waste of time and energy.

Some professionals argue that attending school is paramount and is the goal to be aimed at by rehabilitation, but learning can take place at home, with the teaching from a part-time home tutor, and/or using distance-learning with material supplied through the post, or on video, or through the Internet. Sometimes a teacher from the child's school will be able to teach at home for a few sessions a week, and this has the advantage of the pupil being kept in touch with the class. In some areas there may be enough young people with ME/CFS to get together so that affected children and adolescents can meet and receive home tuition as a group.

Social contact with friends and peer groups is also recommended by well-meaning professionals, but conversations with more than one friend can be exhausting. Moreover, the majority of children with ME/CFS soon try and catch up with both learning and social activities once they are well enough. While still ill, contact with peers can be achieved instead through ME support networks. It is enormously helpful for an affected youngster to have friends who have the same problems, even if the communication is by post. This sort of contact helps to relieve the isolation and loss of friendships that can seriously undermine a young person's confidence.

The disruption to schooling and social development which results from getting this illness as a child or adolescent is potentially serious. The average length of the illness is about 4 years; sometimes a seriously affected child can develop ME aged 10 and still be unwell aged 18. At an age when things move on quickly, to have to drop out of life for a year or more can have long-lasting consequences. The pressures on youngsters to succeed – at sports, with classwork, in national exams and at university – are great, reflecting the intense competition for jobs that awaits school-leavers and university graduates.

Avoiding sports such as gymnastics, team games and athletics is mandatory until it is clear that improvement is virtually permanent. As with adults, children and students who have ME/CFS will find that if they do less physical activity, they will have more energy available for the brain. Some learning may be possible so long as physical exertion is strictly limited.

In all discussions between the child, parents and professionals, it is really important that the health of the sick child comes first, with such learning as is possible taking second place to the child's physical and emotional well-being. Regimes of 'rehabilitation' whose only goal is to get the child back to 'normal functioning' (i.e. attending school and behaving like other children) without consideration of the reality and the severity of the illness nor the child's intellectual capabilities, will fail, and can lead to greater psychological problems, such as the child feeling a failure because he or she cannot seem to achieve the intended goal of 'wellness'.

Parents, educational services and health professionals should help children with ME/CFS to feel good about themselves. For young people suffering with this debilitating and often painful illness, it is bad enough having the ongoing symptoms and missing out on normal life for months or years, without having other people setting goals which the child is not capable of achieving. Failure to please the child psychologist, teacher or parent can further damage a child emotionally and shatter his or her self-esteem.

Thanks to the work of the ME Association, Education Directors and their Special Needs Advisors have all been sent information about ME. Information has also been sent to the Association of Clinical Psychologists and to the Advisory Centre for Education (ACE) in the UK.

A survey of some schools in the UK, showing the impact of ME/CFS on teachers and pupils, was published in May 1997.[2] A striking finding was that ME is the most common reason for long-term absence (over 3 months) among pupils from school, being more significant than any other illness – the next most common being childhood leukaemia. This study also showed that teachers are vulnerable to the illness, the average rate among teachers being 5 per 1,000 in the schools surveyed.

The Task Force for CFS/ME (*see page 98*) has a Focus Group of doctors and education experts who are preparing a special report about children and young people with ME. It is expected that this report will be published in the spring of 1998. Copies of this report will be available from Westcare (*see Appendix A*).

Health professionals may exaggerate the secondary emotional problems of a child with ME/CFS if their belief is that this is primarily a psychological illness. The reality is that ME/CFS is a illness with a biological basis, as is juvenile rheumatoid arthritis or childhood leukaemia. Behavioural 'problems' such as depression, withdrawal, panic attacks or refusal to go to school can all happen in any child who is ill for a long time, and are even more likely if the child has an illness which is poorly understood, or one which creates conflict between parents and professionals.

It is really important as early as possible in the illness that a clear diagnosis of ME/CFS is made (or ruled out), and that it is made clear to the child and his or her family that this is a real illness and not a behaviour problem. Dr Nigel Speight, consultant paediatrician in Durham, has this advice to GPs and paediatricians: (from his talk at a conference on education of children with ME, Bristol, November 1997):

- use the term ME. 'Fatigue' is a pathetic description of what the child goes through.
- stress the potential severity and the absence (at present) of a cure
- get the rest of the family on the side of the child
- involve the GP, paediatrician, school doctor, head of school, etc.
- avoid referring the child and family to psychiatrists
- support applications for benefits such as DLA (Disability Living Allowance – *see Chapter 17*)
- encourage the family to be involved in joint parent-child support groups
- offer advice when asked
- keep seeing the child regularly
- cope with your own feelings of helplessness
- use whatever drugs might help.

What **not** to do:

- don't try to predict recovery
- don't make hasty, over-optimistic comments (e.g. 'you're looking much better today,' when the child feels ghastly)
- try to avoid admitting the child to hospital
- do not prescribe graded exercise or cognitive behaviour therapy
- do not discourage the family from exploring alternative therapies, provided they are not expensive or totally useless or harzardous

None of this should be beyond the capacity of the average paediatrician or GP. Looking after children who have ME very severely may involve the same principles as palliative care. Children with ME need to be given a full acceptance of their illness, that it is real and genuine. Principles of management are: **positive diagnosis, support, and protection**.

If your GP appears to be at a loss when dealing with you and your child, it may be helpful to pass on Dr Speight's guidelines for management (tactfully, of course!).

A request from young person with ME to the teacher/home tutor (also quoted from the Bristol conference):

- please speak slowly and be patient
- keep explanations simple
- pause and wait for my response
- don't speak while I'm thinking
- Mminimize processes needed to complete the work
- let me help control the pace of work
- let me stop the moment I need a break
- ask my energy level, not how I feel

- help me to make the best of life
- let me use energy-saving aids
- listen to me when I try to explain.

Case Study

This is John's story – a severe case of ME – told by his mother:

In May 1986, John fell ill after returning from a school trip; he was then 11 years old. His father and I both developed the same bug – swollen glands and nausea. Then in August we were on holiday by the sea. John was very sick and had diarrhoea for 24 hours, and was in bed for several days, as he began to feel achy and so tired. A trip to the zoo was a disaster, as the walk up the drive from the car park was just too much, he was exhausted and in tears with tiredness. He *never ever* got back to his real self; however, he did start his new school and seemed to settle in well.

September 1986 – He was ill at school, burning up, headache, sore tummy and his glands were still swollen. Teachers and other pupils were all ill with the same thing. John did not improve, he had bad headaches, sore throats, felt sick all the time, and sweated very heavily. He had very acidy-smelling breath, especially in the mornings, and poor appetite because of the nausea. Tests for glandular fever were negative. Later blood samples showed there had been a huge virus infection.

November 1986 – We saw a paediatrician for the first time at the hospital. John had been ill now for six months. He had a brain scan, which was normal, and more blood tests.

Christmas, 1986 – He began to lose his balance and started to drag his right leg. His legs seemed to be getting very weak, he still had nausea, and could not sleep.

February 1987 – John was no better, and his legs were weaker. As we live in a remote area, we had to fly down to the hospital, where he'd been referred for a second opinion. We had a wheelchair and lift on and off the plane. He was examined and had blood tests, X-rays, brain scan, EEG, etc. These were all clear, and when we saw the specialist, he said John had Post-viral Fatigue Syndrome, and although this could be worse than the actual virus, he felt sure John would make a good recovery.

Back home, John was prescribed Optimax (which we found out was for depression, and was not recommended for children), also Motillium for nausea, but he had so many side-effects from these two drugs that we stopped them.

April 1987 – John had all the same symptoms, but was getting worse. The paediatrician suggested we see a psychiatrist, to help keep his spirits up. John has never been depressed.

Our GP suggested some very gentle leg exercises to try and keep the muscles going for when he started to feel better. We only went to physiotherapy once, as John found it so exhausting. We carried on with some of the exercises at home, but it made him feel more sick, tired and sore, and the bad breath came back.

May 1987 – we took John to see a psychiatrist. He said that the virus which had affected John could be Coxsackie B, as this can cause disability like polio, but that you can get better from it. He also said that only complete and utter rest could cure it, and that this could take up to two years.

July 1987 – we went to the main hospital again for tests to be repeated. No tests were carried out, only an examination, and one of the staff told John there was 'nothing wrong' with him and he would be walking in two weeks. The neurologist we saw there felt it was a psychiatric problem, and that John would be better in a psychiatric ward, removed from the environment in which he had become ill. However we did not accept the psychiatric treatment offered, and took him home. Back at home John was admitted to our local hospital to have the tests we had expected in the main hospital. The only test carried out was a lumbar puncture, the result of which was normal.

They started giving him physiotherapy, which made him feel really ill, the pain brought tears to his eyes, but he was told 'not to be a baby'. John couldn't grip a spoon or a fork any more, and could hardly lift his arms. He was encouraged to feed himself – this would take him ages, and his food would go cold. His voice was now getting weaker and it was often too tiring for him to repeat something. He would tell us he couldn't put up with much more. It seemed other people could not believe how ill he really felt.

Soon after this, we were given an article from a magazine called 'What is this scourge called ME?' There in black and white were all the symptoms our son had – mental confusion, headaches, sore threats, sickness, vivid dreams, heightened sensitivity to light and sound. Here at last was the answer; we now felt we had found out what was wrong.

August 1987 – We went to see a neurology specialist at a famous hospital for Nervous Diseases, where after an hour's consultation and an examination he said John was a severe case of ME or Post-viral Fatigue Syndrome. We were pleased to have a diagnosis. He said it could be years before John was really better, that school was out for the foreseeable future, and physiotherapy was wrong until he started to show an improvement; he said that he would write this in his letters to the doctors at home.

September 1987 – John needed to have laxatives every fourth night. He also started to cough when he came into contact with smoke, or car fumes, especially diesel from buses and lorries if they passed us on our walks in his wheelchair. Grass-cuttings, perfumes and washing powders would all make him sneeze, and set his body shaking as though his balance had gone. His voice became so weak that it was just too exhausting for him to repeat anything. His fingers were now curled into a fist, and it was too painful to ease them out. We came to feel that the psychiatrist was trying to get a response to his questions that would show that it was something in John's mind that was making him ill. We have always believed, and still do, that our son is physically ill, it is not in his mind, and we will go on and on fighting for him.

October 1987 – John had huge ulcers on his lips. He got confused if too many questions were asked at once. TV and flashing lights hurt his eyes, he had to wear dark glasses.

We decided to take John privately to see the neurologist again in the Nervous Diseases Hospital, as since August John's voice had gone altogether, and he could no longer open his fingers.

Blood tests, brain scans, X-rays, EEG were carried out, and all were fine. They fitted splints to his fingers to open them. All the doctors there said he had a physical illness, and always said he had ME.

(John's mother recounted all this to me in 1990).

The above story illustrates a typical onset and symptoms of a child of 11 who developed severe ME. However, it is not the whole story, because the parents were eventually advised that their son needed admission to a psychiatric unit. Both John and his parents went to visit the psychiatric ward he would go to, but found it was a locked ward, full of disturbed youngsters. They knew instinctively that this was not the place for him, declined this treatment, and took him back home. Shortly after they got home, out of the blue came an ambulance with a Care Order to remove John from his home, on the grounds that he was a seriously ill child and 'the parents had refused treatment.' John's life was never in danger, and no one from the local Social Services had even visited the home to investigate whether his life could be at risk.

After some months in hospital, where at first his parents were not allowed to visit him and efforts to get him to walk and talk failed, on representations from a legal team he was allowed home. While 'in care' in hospital, he was given physiotherapy which made him ill, was put in a pool to see if he would swim (he couldn't), and generally treated as though he was not really ill but was faking all his symptoms.

Once at home, John had gentle physiotherapy, good diet, evening primrose oil and magnesium supplements. He did eventually recover completely, 5 years after becoming ill. His story highlights the difficulties faced by families with a child who develops severe ME/CFS, and whose illness is believed to be purely psychological by professionals. Several decades ago, people with leg weakness caused by polio used to be given harsh regimes of physiotherapy in the belief that exercise could restore paralysed or weakened muscles to normal strength. It usually made the patients much worse, and could convert weakness of a limb into outright paralysis. The same misconceptions still, in 1997, cause some children with muscle weakness, loss of voice or difficulty swallowing to be similarly abused. Whilst psychological support, possibly low-dose antidepressants, and very gentle physiotherapy are certainly helpful in many cases, hospital admission is not usually appropriate. Children with ME/CFS are acutely noise-sensitive, and deteriorate in the face of any stress, so a quiet home environment with familiar faces is usually the best place for recovery.

Fortunately, although children may have the illness more

severely than adults, their chances of complete recovery are much better, provided they are free from stress and that they are not pushed into exercise or school attendance before they are ready, and that 'disturbed family dynamics' (to use the jargon) do not create secondary psychological problems for the child.

Resources for Children with ME/CFS

SUPPORT GROUPS
The Association of Youth with ME (AYME)
AYME throws a lifeline to its members through its bi-monthly magazine called *CHEERS*, where children and young people write their own articles: personal, humorous, useful tips, letter pages, etc., boosting their self-confidence.

In addition, an organized, matched pen-pal/tape/e-mail service is offered with smaller membership services such as a Chat-Line, birthday cards and a postal library which are serviced by the Young People's Committee.

A two-day conference is organized annually for social contact, mutual support and information for the young people and their families. Those who are unable to get to the conference are all contacted by phone or letter from the hotel.

The voices of the members are heard through a pyramid structure of Young People's Advisory groups. This organization empowers young people and breaks through their isolation.

AYME has available a short information video, entitled 'What Do You Know About ME?', in which young members of the Association, two doctors and a youth therapist answer questions put to them by teenagers.

Leaflets: 'ME in young people' and 'How to manage ME' have been written by the young members of AYME. For these, and other information about AYME, contact:

AYME
Sunbow House, 5 Medland
Woughton Park
Milton Keynes MK6 3BH
Tel/Fax 01908 691635
e-mail ayme@powernet.com
AYME is also online! Website:
http://www.btinternet.com/-ayme

The ME Association Young Persons Group (MEAYPG)
c/o ME Association
4 Corringham Road
Stanford-le-Hope
Essex SS17 0AH

TYMES (The Young ME Sufferer)
9 Patching Hall Lane
Chelmsford
Essex CM1 4DH
Tel 01245 263482

TYMES was established to help combat the isolation of ME, and was the first group to produce a regular newsletter for young people with ME.

Action for ME/CFS
A national support organization, which has information about ME/CFS in children. They provide:
    Children's Information Pack, containing: Medical factsheet about ME/CFS in children, also Guidelines for Schools. Price £2.50 including p+p.

Education Pack, for educational professionals. Free.
Both are available from:

Action for ME/CFS
PO Box 1302
Wells BA5 1YE
Tel 01749 670799

EDUCATION

The Advisory Centre for Education is a national independent education advice service for parents of children in state schools. They can give advice about legal rights, the roles and powers of Local Education Authorities and, where necessary, support for legal actions.

ACE (Advisory Centre for Education)
18 Victoria Park Square
London E2 9PB
Tel 0171 354 8321

Gridlink (a new online education system)
Frensham House
New Street
Honiton
Devon EX14 8BZ
Tel/Fax 01404 42445
e-mail gridlink@clara.net
Website http://www.gridlink.clara.net

ME-IT

(ME Information Technology), offers monthly updates on ME news, therapies, and campaigning news. Contact:

ME-IT
497 Lanark Road West
Balerno
Edinburgh EH14 7AL
Tel/Fax 0131 449 2725
e-mail 101501.365@compuserve.com

National Association for Education of Sick Children, (NAESC)

NAESC was set up in 1993 to ensure that all children and young people get the education they need when sick.

NAESC
St Margaret's House
17 Old Ford Road
Bethnal Green
London E2 9PL
Tel 0181 980 8523
Fax 0181 980 3447
e-mail naesc@ednsick.demon.co.uk

BOOKS ABOUT ME IN YOUNG PEOPLE

ME – The New Plague by Jane Colby, published by First and Best in Education Ltd, 34 Nene Valley Business Park, Oundle, Peterborough PE8 4HL. Also available from Action for ME trading – Tel 01749 670799 to order.

Somebody Help ME by Jill Moss, available from Sunbow Books, PO Box 605, Milton Keynes, MK6 3BH. Price £15 (inc p+p).

Chapter 16

Women with ME/CFS

Women seem to be affected by ME or CFS about three times as often as men in the age group 20–50, the years of both employment and fertility. Of course, in institutions where outbreaks occur, for example an army camp or a nurses' residential home, there may be 100 per cent of the men or women affected. Yet, because the illness appears to be more common in women, some doctors wrongly conclude that hysteria and neurosis contribute to the disease. This is inaccurate, speculative and scientifically unproven rubbish, and is insulting to women. This attitude continues to prevail, however, mainly among paternalistic older male doctors.

In fact, the reasons for the female/male ratio in ME/CFS are simple, knowing as we do that the illness is most commonly triggered by a virus, in people who are stressed or exhausted: Who are the people most exposed to viruses, particularly enteroviruses? Who are the people most likely to have to carry on working even when they are ill with a virus infection, or to have to return to work before properly recovered?

The high-risk occupations for contact with viruses are:

- teachers, especially of primary school
- mothers, many of whom hold two jobs – homemaker plus outside paid work
- nurses and those in other health care jobs
- agricultural and sewage workers (yes, these are usually men)
- to some extent, all jobs with high levels of public contact expose the employees to more viruses.

Of these, the people least likely to be able to rest enough from a viral infection are mothers of young children, teachers, and all health care workers, particularly nurses. A man with an office job who can sign off work for a week and be cared for at home if he gets flu is probably at lower risk of developing ME/CFS. This is not sexist propaganda, just commonsense observation!

There may also be a hormonal link with the conditions in the body that are right for ME/CFS to develop, but the mechanisms of this are not established.[1] It may just be coincidence that the child-bearing years (18–40) are also the years of when the most demands are made in work in the high-risk jobs listed above.

Possible Problems for Women with ME/CFS

- Menstrual periods – painful, irregular, heavy or disappearing altogether.
- Endometriosis.
- Premenstrual syndrome (often called PMT), which may become worse with ME.
- Pregnancy – to be or not? Will the baby be affected?
- Contraception – is the Pill OK?
- Menopause plus ME – may make each other worse.

- Cystitis.
- Vaginal infections.
- Relationships and sex.

PERIODS

In some women, their cycle may become longer, shorter or irregular. The flow may be lighter or heavier than before, or even disappear during severe illness. These changes may happen with any long-term illness, and also with chronic stress. Reduced thyroid function (hypothyroidism) is an uncommon secondary feature of ME/CFS, secondary to hypothalamic disturbance, and this may result in prolonged or heavier periods.

Whatever the cause, if you develop very heavy flow, you must see your GP and have a blood test to check for anaemia. Getting extra iron and vitamin C (in the diet or with supplements) is then a good idea.

Periods may become light, scanty or disappear altogether. Some women with ME/CFS have an early menopause. Blood tests from your doctor can determine if you have a low level of oestrogen. Oestrogen therapy is sometimes prescribed, and many women have reported an improvement in symptoms of fatigue and depression if low oestrogen is treated.

Two gynaecologists in London measured levels of oestradiol and follicle stimulating hormone (FSH) in 28 premenopausal women who were all diagnosed ME/CFS, and had severe symptoms of PMS (*see below*).[2] They found that five women had a marked degree of oestrogen deficiency, and also reduced bone density in their spine and hip. These women with proven oestrogen deficiency were treated with replacement oestrogen, and most of them improved.

PREMENSTRUAL SYNDROME

Also commonly known as PMT – premenstrual tension, though tension is not the only symptom, but is the one most obvious to other people! Premenstrual syndrome means that symptoms appear only during the 10 days before a period and are relieved when the period starts. Common symptoms are:

- weight gain
- bloating
- tender, swollen breasts
- irritability
- irrational behaviour
- depression and weeping
- mood swings
- insomnia
- food cravings (usually for sugar and chocolate)
- headaches.

Many of these symptoms are due to fluid retention, and may overlap with a yeast problem (which may contribute to PMS). If the condition has been experienced before developing ME/CFS, then it may become worse once you have the illness.

Measures to Improve PMS

Avoid blood-sugar swings by having small, frequent meals of complex carbohydrates regularly. Reduce your intake of sugar, red meats, coffee and tea.

The following supplements are of proven value:

Gamma linoleic acid as evening primrose oil (EPO)	At least 2 g daily. If EPO is being taken for ME/CFS it is a good idea to increase the dose during the premenstrual time.

Magnesium	250–500 mg a day
Vitamin B₆	20 mg a day in addition to B vitamins taken as part of a good multivitamin preparation.
The homoeopathic remedy Sepia	Useful for symptoms of exhaustion, weariness, and depression.

It is also important to be aware of any reduced mental function or lack of emotional control at this time, and to avoid tasks involving important decisions, or situations where you could be at risk, for example driving.

If the PMS is severe and the woman over 30, it may be worth asking for hormone assessment from a doctor. It is important to remember that other treatable medical conditions, in this case menopausal premenstrual depression (which can be devastating in ME/CFS), may need to be diagnosed and treated with conventional treatment.

Many of the symptoms of PMS are probably due to water retention. This mechanism also happens in ME/CFS, and contributes to weight gain, headaches and other brain symptoms.

ENDOMETRIOSIS

There are a significant number of women of child-bearing age, with or without ME/CFS, who suffer from an unpleasant gynaecological condition called endometriosis. In endometriosis, tiny pieces of endometrium (the lining of the womb, which is shed with every period) grow outside the womb. These abnormally situated endometrial tissues can be found anywhere, mostly lying on the outer surface of the womb, on the bladder, on the large bowel, or on the ovaries and their supporting tissues. These 'seeded' tissues grow and then bleed at each period, and cause a lot of pain, and also scar tissue.

Typical symptoms are:

* severe period pain
* deep pelvic pain during and after intercourse
* unexplained lower abdominal and pelvic pain, any time in the cycle
* infertility
* irregular bleeding or bleeding from other sites, such as the bladder or rectum.

The condition can only be diagnosed with certainty by surgery or laparoscopy (a narrow telescopic tube is inserted into the abdomen through a tiny incision, usually with the patient under anaesthetic).

The cause of endometriosis is not understood. It can affect women at any age from puberty up till the onset of the menopause. There appears to be an association with yeast infection, and current research is finding abnormal immune functions similar to those in ME/CFS. It is possible that a common mechanism predisposes a woman to having both endometriosis and ME/CFS.

Current treatment for endometriosis is either hormonal – something to suppress oestrogen levels – or surgical. The latter involves removing affected tissues, often including the ovary and Fallopian tube, or a hysterectomy. For a lot of women with this condition, a big problem is getting their doctor to recognize it; he or she may instead dismiss their increasingly severe menstrual and pelvic pain as psychological, and refuse to refer for a specialist opinion.

Management

High-dose essential fatty acids (such as evening primrose oil, 3–4 g per day), B vitamins, magnesium, and vitamin E may be worth trying before agreeing to more drastic treatment.

Some women with may attribute symptoms of pain and abnormal bleeding to ME/CFS, and not seek help and further diagnosis – another reminder that when you have one illness, you must not assume all new symptoms are caused by it, especially pain, which may be due to something else and may be treatable.

PREGNANCY

Many women who have ME/CFS have successful pregnancies. No one denies that there will be extra fatigue during the early years of caring for babies and young children. However, a woman with ME/CFS who is considering pregnancy may want to know:

Can my illness be passed on to the baby, either in the womb or thereafter?
Will my partner and I be able to cope with the extra demands of pregnancy, labour and lack of sleep?
Can we afford to pay for extra help?
How will pregnancy and labour be affected?

There are no simple answers to these questions. Early research has found a small but definite number of ME/CFS pregnancies that have not progressed normally, but this seems to be more likely if the mother has signs suggesting active infection during the early stages of pregnancy. Any virus, if active during early pregnancy, may occasionally cause miscarriage, or abnormalities in the newborn. Rubella (German measles virus) and cytomegalovirus, for example, are well-known culprits.

There is also the probability that there is some inherited factor which may make the child more susceptible to developing ME/CFS, in the same way that a tendency to allergies is inherited.

Some women with ME/CFS feel better throughout pregnancy (which is a natural immune suppressant), but relapse after an exhausting birth, or with the postnatal drop in hormones. Some are ill throughout pregnancy. The consensus of advice from doctors, and from mothers who have experience of ME/CFS, is to put off pregnancy until the illness has stabilized and signs suggesting infection (e.g. fevers, diarrhoea, lymph glands, throat infections) are settled. Then only consider it if the mum-to-be can rest well during pregnancy, and if plenty of domestic help is planned (and budgeted for – more important than fancy frills for the baby) after the birth.

There is no evidence that suggests that breastfeeding could transmit ME/CFS to an infant. Breastmilk provides the best protection against other infection, and is also the best source of natural GLA (an essential fatty acid) which if deficient can lead to allergies.

Obviously, good nutrition is supremely important during pregnancy and while breastfeeding. A useful source of information on nutrition for pregnancy, especially for women with allergies, chronic infections or a history of pregnancy problems of any kind, is the organization called Foresight. Another useful source of advice is the National Childbirth Trust (*addresses in Appendix A*).

Even the strongest of new mothers can suffer from the results of lack of sleep, exhaustion, and postnatal depression. Having ME or CFS will not exempt you from these tribulations! However, the joy of a new child may well outweigh the problems, and ultimately a decision about embarking on a pregnancy must be for you and your partner.

Childbirth

The question of drugs during labour, such as painkillers, gas and air, or an epidural, is one to discuss beforehand with your obstetrician and midwife. Many women with ME/CFS do cope quite well with labour, however exhaustion in the second stage may set in earlier than normal, so there may be a greater likelihood of needing help (e.g. forceps) with delivery. It is essential to let the health workers concerned with your pregnancy and delivery know in advance about your illness and how it affects you, emphasizing the nature of the muscle fatiguability.

CONTRACEPTION

This is obviously important if pregnancy is thought to be a potential hazard, and should be discussed with your GP or a planning clinic. The Pill has many drawbacks even for healthy women:

* reduces the available levels of vitamin B_6
* interferes with carbohydrate metabolism
* increases the likelihood of depression
* Zinc deficiency is associated with taking the Pill.
* The Pill has been shown to affect the function of the immune system, and increases any tendency to getting yeast infections.
* Women who have taken the Pill for some years have increased incidence of allergies and immune dysfunction diseases.

It is probably safer to avoid the contraceptive pill if you have ME/CFS, for all the above reasons. However, effective hormonal contraceptives now have much lower levels of synthetic oestrogens and fewer side-effects than they did 15 years ago.

Intrauterine devices – coils – can lead to infection in the womb and heavy periods, complications anyone would wish to avoid. This leaves the safest and most non-invasive birth control methods: a diaphragm or cervical cap plus spermicidal cream, or the combination of a condom plus spermicidal cream.

The alternative, if you and your partner are sure you do not want any children in the future, is sterilization. This means tubal ligation in the woman or vasectomy for the man. Sterilization is virtually 100 per cent effective for birth control, but is irreversible, and couples need careful counselling before making this decision.

MENOPAUSE AND HRT

In many women this time is passed uneventfully, but others experience distressing symptoms, which may be confused with chronic fatigue syndrome. These are:

- abnormal fatigue
- mood swings
- depression
- sweating
- hot flushes.

Anyone familiar with the true features of ME/CFS will be able to distinguish them from menopausal symptoms, as the former include the particular muscle fatiguability, and symptoms made worse by exercise – not the same as the general weariness and slowing down of a woman during the menopause. Menopausal women with severe symptoms of fatigue and depression may wrongly fear that they have ME or CFS. This makes diagnosis and exclusion of other conditions especially important for the self-diagnosed sufferer of this age. If ME/CFS is already diagnosed, the onset of the menopause may exacerbate some symptoms. Many women with ME/CFS experience an early menopause, or a drop in natural oestrogen levels, maybe while still in their thirties.

Hormone Replacement Therapy (HRT)

Some women with ME/CFS are worried about taking HRT. But the hormones used in HRT are natural ones, unlike the synthetic ones used in the contraceptive pill. In fact it is even more important to consider HRT if you have ME/CFS, because the relative lack of exercise poses a greater risk of developing osteoporosis (loss of calcium from the bones) and increased fractures in later life.[3]

You should ask your GP for a blood test of hormone levels. This will show if you have started the menopause or are well into it. The simplest type of HRT is replacement of some of the oestrogen, levels of which drop as the menopause progresses. The easiest way, with fewest side-effects, is to use oestrogen skin patches, from which a steady dose of oestrogen is absorbed through the skin. Patches start at 25 mcg, then can be increased to 50 or 75 mcg. The more complex form, recommended once the periods have completely stopped, is to take tablets or have patches of oestrogen and also take a progesterone-type pill for one week every month. This results in artificial, light periods and is important to prevent the slightly increased risk of cancer of the womb posed by oestrogen-only HRT. The progesterone is not necessary if you have had a hysterectomy.

Most women I have spoken to have found they feel better on HRT, and if it is prescribed before the periods finally stop, HRT can significantly reduce premenstrual depression and mood swings. It is also advisable to take extra calcium, especially if you are avoiding dairy produce in the diet (*see Appendix A for sources of supplements, and the address of the Osteoporosis Society*).

It is quite common for any woman to experience depression around the menopause. For some, going on to HRT and getting advice or support from other women can be as effective as taking antidepressant drugs.

Nutritional Supplements Useful for the Menopause

Vitamin E	200–600 IU per day, the anti-ageing vitamin, helps dry skin and loss of elasticity
Calcium	In an absorbable form; 1–1.5 g per day
Zinc	20–30 mg per day
Evening primrose oil	2–3 g per day
Vitamin B complex	Or as part of a good multivitamin pill

A nutritious, balanced diet is also needed. Some weight gain is usual after the menopause, but should be less pronounced if you are on HRT. It is obviously important to exercise if possible; regular walking and/or swimming are best if you are able to exercise at all. It is the lack of exercise that increases the likelihood of osteoporosis.

CYSTITIS
This bladder problem is more common with women, because the urethra (the outflow tube from the bladder) is much shorter than in men and can more easily become contaminated by micro-organisms from outside, especially from the bowel.

Symptoms
- Frequency of micturition (passing urine).
- Urgency, discomfort or burning.
- Maybe visible blood in urine (if severe).
- Lower abdominal pain, possibly fever.

Self-management

Drink masses of water, rest completely, and see your doctor as soon as possible so that a urine specimen can be collected in a special bottle for bacteriological testing. A simple remedy, obtainable from any pharmacy, is potassium citrate (Mist Pot Cit), which makes urine more alkaline and reduces the burning.

If the symptoms are not severe, it is better to wait until results of the urine culture before starting antibiotics, because sometimes symptoms of cystitis can arise with no bacterial infection, and also because if an infection is present it is very important to have the correct antibiotic.

The reason I have included something about cystitis in this chapter is to emphasize that, although antibiotics should be avoided unless really necessary if you have ME/CFS, *bacterial infections of the urinary tract must be treated seriously*. Long-term damage to the kidneys may result if an untreated bladder infection turns into pyelonephritis (infection of the kidneys). A course of antibiotics prescribed for bacterial cystitis must be completed, and a further urine specimen should be tested to check that the infection has gone.

Sometimes in ME/CFS, symptoms of cystitis develop but nothing is grown on urine culture. It is possible in such cases that the infection is a yeast; food allergies are another possible culprit (*see Chapters 13 and 14*). Or there may even be a neurological disturbance of bladder sensation and bladder function, locally or maybe centrally in the brain.

Anyone who has repeated attacks of cystitis should make sure her nutrition is good and take extra supplements to boost resistance to infection.

The homoeopathic remedy for acute symptoms of cystitis is usually *Cantharis*.

VAGINAL INFECTIONS

Thrush, caused by the yeast Candida albicans, typically causes a white discharge, with intense itching around the vaginal entrance.

Recurrent thrush is a common female problem. However, any abnormal discharge should be investigated if it persists. It may indicate some other infection which needs treatment. If the discharge is yellow, offensive or blood-stained, you must see your doctor.

Thrush tends to flare up in conditions of poor health, stress, too much sugar in the diet, diabetes, taking birth control pills, local conditions of heat and humidity (e.g. wearing nylon tights and pants, or during hot humid weather) and poor hygeine.

It is possible now to buy a one-off drug treatment for thrush at a pharmacy, though it is expensive. It is a good idea to use anti-fungal vaginal pessaries and cream as well. Bear in mind, though, that anti-fungal drugs or local treatment will not clear up thrush for long if your diet is wrong.

As the bugs causing vaginal infections can be transmitted to and from a male partner it is best to abstain from sex while the infection lasts, and he should get treated as well.

Another common bug is *trichomonas*, which like Candida is widespread and easily transferred between partners.

The use of tampons during a period may increase the likelihood of vaginal infection, as they act as a reservoir of blood in which bugs multiply (especially if the tampon is not changed often enough). While the majority of healthy women can use tampons with no complications, I believe that if you have ME/CFS it is prudent to minimize the risk of infection anywhere in the body.

SEXUAL RELATIONSHIPS

The problems that sexual relationships (or rather, the lack of them!) cause with any chronic illness are discussed more fully in Chapter 19. Loss of interest in sex is a very common symptom for both men and women with any illness causing chronic fatigue. The body wishes to use available energy for what it considers more important activities. Loss of interest in sex is also common in depression, low thyroid function, and many other chronic illnesses.

Even if always exhausted, a wise woman will try and find times when sex is least stressful, to help maintain the bond with a caring partner. As with post-menopausal women, vaginal dryness and discomfort may be discouraging, but using *KY* lubricating jelly may help.

Loss of an adequate sex life (every couple has different needs) can be very detrimental to a relationship already rocked by the effects of illness on one and perhaps both partners. Sometimes there are psychological blocks as well as physical constraints, and some time with a skilled counsellor may help one or both partners. (The organization Sexual Problems of Disabled People – SPOD – may be helpful; *address in Appendix A*).

Chapter 17

Finance and Benefits

It is bad enough to have a disabling disease that causes pain and exhaustion, but many people with ME/CFS endure the added stress of financial hardship through being unable to work. In addition, people with ME/CFS who have paid regularly into an occupational pension scheme for several years may lose their jobs but then have to battle to get the ill-health retirement pensions they should be entitled to.

Since December 1996 in the UK a new *Disability Discrimination Act (DDA)* became law. The DDA makes it unlawful to discriminate against disabled people in relation to employment, provision of goods and services, or the sale/management of property. However, the Act does have loopholes – for example, employers with less than 20 employees are exempt from employment laws.

At present there is no Government Commission with powers to enforce the DDA. The Act effectively means that it is now illegal for an employer to dismiss an employee on the grounds of disability without looking at ways of changing the employment conditions to assist the employee to stay in work.

You can get an information pack about the DDA by phoning 0345 622 633. And the ME Association has an information sheet about the Disability Discrimination Act (*address in Appendix A*).

Fortunately, chronic fatigue syndrome (or ME) is becoming more generally accepted by employers and the Department of Social Security as a real disabling illness. However, because some people in authority still believe the syndrome is largely psychiatric in nature, this sometimes makes it more difficult to qualify for a pension, and ill employees may be requested to undergo psychiatric assessment and treatment before they can be accepted as having permanent disability.

For many conscientious, hard-working people who develop ME/CFS, loss of income may puts the brakes on recovery, because of the stress and anxiety that result from the inability to meet financial commitments such as mortgages, school fees or debts. Obtaining financial support from Incapacity Benefit, Disability Living Allowance or a pension can be the turning point for the start of recovery. Some pension schemes, for example in education, will grant short-term ill-health pension that can be reviewed after some time, to allow for a later return to work if the recipient recovers.

Employment and Social Security Benefits in the UK

When you first become ill you may be in an employed position, and therefore eligible for sick pay. If you are self-employed, you may be able to get Sickness Benefit. The real problems arise if you are still ill after 6 months (28 weeks), at which point you and everyone else start to wonder how long this is going to go on. If you are making some recovery it may be tempting to try returning to work. If the job is full-time, and physically and emotionally demanding – such as nursing, or teaching – the chances are that you quickly find out that you are *not* fully recovered, have to stop work again, and have a major relapse brought on by the exertion. No one can predict how long you will need to be off work.

Recovery from ME/CFS does happen, but you have to think in terms of months or years. It is often a gradual process, and the possibility of relapse is always around. Some people may be able to negotiate part-time work, with the flexibility of resting at the work place or going home should their energy run out. When considering a return to work, you need to consider whether the work itself will hinder further recovery or bring on a relapse, leading to stopping work permanently, or if you can manage to improve despite working.

It may possible to work *if other activities are given up*, and you have someone else to take care of domestic needs – shopping, meals, cleaning and laundry. Even if these have to be paid for, getting back to some sort of work could improve your quality of life and restore your self-esteem.

A lot will depend on whether you are self-employed and therefore your own boss or, if employed, on the attitude and sympathy of your employer. You should also consider whether you can really be effective in your job if you are still unwell. It may be that clients, pupils, patients or colleagues suffer on those days when you are struggling and mentally under par, even though *you* may believe you are doing a tremendous job.

If it seems unrealistic that you will be able to return to your former job in spite of partial recovery, then consider a change of direction to something that is maybe less demanding physically, but which can utilize your skills in a new way. Some people with life-changing illness manage to learn new skills, such as writing or after doing an Open University degree at home. I could not have predicted, 12 years ago, that in 1997 instead of being an eye specialist I would be working as medical adviser to the ME Association, giving talks, speaking on radio and TV, and writing – all these activities using communication skills I never knew I had!

It may be necessary to exist on State Benefits while you are retraining or studying, but this should be regarded as a temporary situation. Someone who qualifies for Benefits while unable to work due to illness, may be able to earn a little money which is counted as 'therapeutic earnings', while still officially too disabled or sick to do a full-time job.

So, in summary – if you consider returning to work:

- your health must be the first priority
- do not be too proud to claim any State Benefits you are entitled to
- accept that your presence at work is not essential
- remember there are thousands of other conscientious and skilled people who have had to give up working; you are not unique
- remember you will probably improve
- when well enough, explore the possibility of part-time work, with the flexibility to rest if you relapse
- do not squander energy on unnecessary activities outside of work
- remember the principle of *pacing* your energy. Planning for a rest during the day, should it be necessary, may allow you to stay in work.

Summary of State Benefits for People with Disabilities (as of November 1997)

1) INFORMATION

Booklet FB2 Which Benefit? is a guide to all Social Security benefits.

Booklet HB6 A practical guide for disabled people has information about benefits for sick or disabled people.

Both these booklets are available from Post Offices and Department of Social Security offices, and contain lists of other leaflets that cover more specific services.

The Benefit Enquiry Line 0800 88 22 00 is a confidential phone service for people with disabilities or their carers. They can advise you on what benefits you could apply for, and will arrange to send you application forms. People with *speech or hearing problems* using a textphone can dial *0800 24 33 55*.

The ME Association (address in Appendix A) has information for members on the Disability Discrimination Act, Incapacity Benefit (IB) and Disability Living Allowance (DLA). The information packs give useful advice on how to fill in the long application forms for IB and DLA.

Incapacity Action is a group which campaigns on behalf of disabled people who are trying to get a fair adjudication for their Incapacity Benefit. They cannot help individual cases, but are keen to hear about applicants' experiences and can send advice about IB. Write with an SAE to Incapacity Action, 65 Casimir Road, London E5 9NU.

2) SUMMARY OF BENEFITS

Given the ever-changing nature of the Government's plans to overhaul the Benefits system, it is best to contact one of the services listed above, and also to consult *Social Security booklet FB2*.

Statutory Sick Pay (SSP)

If you are employed and are sick for at least 4 days in a row, you can get SSP from your employer for up to 28 weeks. You will need to be in a job where National Insurance contributions have been paid. Leaflet NI 245 is the employee's guide to SSP.

Incapacity Benefit

If you are unable to work after 28 weeks, you will get short-term IB, payable from week 28 to 52 of your illness.

If you are still sick after a year, you will get long-term IB paid at the highest rate.

After 28 weeks, you will have to fill in a long questionnaire about your illness or disability. You may also be examined by a Benefits Agency doctor: this medical assessment is called the 'All Work Test'. For more information see leaflet IB202.

Income Support

If you are too ill to work, but have not paid enough National Insurance contributions, you can apply for Income Support.

The amount of Income Support is made up of:

- personal allowance
- – plus disability premium, if ill more than 28 weeks
- – plus premium payment (for people with special expenses)
- – plus possible housing costs payment.

Help with NHS charges is available for those on Income Support or a low income: Free prescriptions, free dental treatment, sight testing, and help towards the cost of glasses.

Severe Disablement Allowance

SDA is a tax-free benefit for people unable to work for at least 28 weeks, but who have not paid enough NI contributions to get Incapacity Benefit. The 'All Work Test' for Incapacity Benefit is used for assessment of SDA. You will need to be regarded as being 80 per cent disabled.

If you are unable to work, but cannot get a sick note to send to the local Social Security office for some reason (such as not having your illness diagnosed, or having a doctor who does not believe you are too ill to work – fortunately this is now uncommon) you may have to claim *Job Seekers Allowance* – this used to be called Unemployment Benefit – and report to your local Job Centre to register for work. If you are ill, this state of affairs is obviously not a good thing, so it is really important to have your illness named and validated (*see Chapter 3*).

The Social Fund

This helps with exceptional expenses.

Disability Living Allowance (DLA)

DLA is a tax-free and non-means-tested benefit for people with disabilities who are under 65.

DLA has two components:

1. *care component.* This is paid at 3 rates, and is for those who are so disabled physically or mentally that they need attention for a significant part of the day and/or night in connection with their 'bodily functions', and/or to remain safe from danger
2. *mobility component.* This is paid at two rates. To qualify for the higher rate the disabled person must be unable, or virtually unable, to walk, or the effort of walking must be considered likely to cause a significant deterioration to their health.

The lower rate is payable to those who can walk, but need supervision or help from another to walk outdoors. For example, someone who is visually impaired or at risk from epilepsy, or by reason of a mental health condition is unsafe outside alone.

For each component of DLA the need for help must have existed for at least 3 months.

If the applicant is over 65 when the needs for Care or Mobility arise, the benefit becomes Attendance Allowance. See also leaflet DS704.

A child with ME/CFS may be entitled to DLA, but the Mobility component is not awarded to children under 5. There is a special claim pack for DLA for a child.

MEDICAL ASSESSMENTS FOR IB, SDA, OR DLA

You may be asked to go to a Benefits Agency Centre where you will be seen by two doctors, or you may be visited at home. BA doctors carrying out these assessments are called Examining Medical Practitioners (EMPs). These doctors have different role from GPs; they are there to assess disabilities, to see how your condition affects aspects of daily life. They are not there to make diagnoses (although if they find or suspect something serious, they can contact the GP) or to prescribe treatment.

Always have someone with you for the assessment who knows you well. This could be your partner or a close friend or neighbour. This observer can make notes of what happens, such as activities the EMP asks you to do, or any prejudicial statements about ME/CFS he or she makes (hopefully these are now uncommon). If you are refused the benefit, you are entitled to see copies of the BA documents, including the notes on the medical examination.

Remember when filling in forms, or seeing the EMP, to say how you are affected when at your worst, and how the disabilities vary. Many people with ME/CFS, and indeed other disabling conditions, underestimate their inabilities and may feel 'inadequate' or stupid when describing some of the things they can't do.

Invalid Care Allowance

This is payable to those caring for people receiving the higher and middle (but *not* the lowest) rates of the Care component of the Disability Living Allowance (*see also page 328*).

Disability Working Allowance

DWA is a benefit for people who are working 16 hours or more a week, and have an illness that limits their earning ability. In practice this is a benefit that does not appear to apply to most people with ME/CFS.

APPEALS AGAINST DECISIONS ABOUT BENEFITS

Every applicant who wants to appeal against being turned down for benefits – in practice this seems to be the majority of people with ME/CFS who apply for Incapacity Benefit, and many who apply for DLA – has to fill in a special form in leaflet *NI246 How to Appeal*. If you disagree with a decision you should appeal as soon as possible. *It is essential to get advice when going for an appeal.* Sources of such advice and help could be someone in your local ME support group, or the ME Association (if you are a member), or a Citizens Advice Bureau, or a solicitor. If you cannot easily find a source of help, look in the Yellow Pages under 'Welfare Organizations', which will list organizations in your area. Or you can contact your Local Authority (e.g. City or District Council) and ask if they have a

Welfare Rights Adviser office. The local Benefits Agency may also point you to somewhere to get advice.

You may be able to get free legal advice if you are on a low income, or pay a fixed amount for a one-off consultation. People on a low income may be able to get more legal help if they are eligible for Legal Aid.

If the Appeal fails, you may wish to take your claim to a Disability Appeal Tribunal. Here it is essential to have a solicitor to represent you.

THE DISABILITY HANDBOOK

The Benefits Agency has a Disability Handbook, with input from the Disability Living Allowance Advisory Board. This Handbook gives information for the lay adjudicators who decide on entitlement to benefits, about all kinds of illnesses that could lead to disability.

The entry about 'chronic fatigue syndromes' has recently been revised, thanks to pressure from the national ME organizations, and now gives a more balanced picture of the needs of some people with ME/CFS. Here are some excerpts, which could be useful for any GPs with little understanding of the illness:

About muscle and mobility:

Severe fatigue in the absence of any objective evidence of muscle wasting or weakness does not necessarily imply a definite and exclusively psychological cause. Furthermore, in individual cases, causes for severe fatigue which have not yet been diagnosed may be present.

And on care needs:

It is necessary to discover what a person can do on a bad day as well as on a good day, and to establish how often each type of day occurs. A satisfactory level of physical and mental activity is one which can be sustained day after day without leading to a prolonged increase in symptoms, and not the amount managed only on a good [day].

This revised entry about CFS in the adjudicators' Handbook reflects the improved understanding in the Department of Social Security that ME/CFS has a range of severity, and that symptoms may fluctuate from day to day.

REGISTERING DISABLED

The Register of Disabled Persons was set up by the Manpower Services Commission (MSC) to help disabled people to get employment. You can apply for registration whether you are in employment or not. Registration is voluntary, but some facilities are only available to those who are registered.

Applicants will be asked to produce medical evidence to support their application, or to have a medical assessment.

Registering as disabled with the MSC is not the same as registering with the Social Services. You can get further information from your local Job Centre. Various benefits from registering disabled with the MSC can include adaptations to help with your work, help with public transport, parking, rehabilitation, and training schemes.

What if your work is unpaid, and is essential? I am of course referring to that underrated profession called 'housewife/ mother'. The reasons for stopping work and resting apply to you as well, but pacing and sticking to a daily routine is nearly impossible with young children. Paying for child-care may be an option, or enlisting support from a family member, neighbour or friend. If you have young children, and have no one to take them each day while you rest, Social Services may be able to arrange a child-minder for a few hours a day.

You can be assessed by someone from Social Services who will visit you at home. When you are being assessed and questions are being asked, remember how you are at your *worst*, even if the visit takes place on one of your better days. Be quite definite about how much disability the illness is causing. It is no good saying 'sometimes I can stand for long enough to cook a meal' if this is the exception rather than the rule. The problem with ME/CFS is in demonstrating that your energy runs out, and that it is difficult to sustain activity. You must describe yourself as you are at your worst, and not minimize or be apologetic about your disability. Most application forms for various types of Benefits now provide for being able to describe abilities as they vary, for example 'how many days a week do you need help with…?'

Local support services (mainly Social Service) can arrange occupational therapy, home helps, home visits by chiropodists, home aids, etc. The Social Service Transport Section organizes the Orange Badge Disabled parking scheme (*see below*).

The Citizens Advice Bureau can advise on these and other services, and if necessary will visit you at home.

MOBILITY
You can apply for an Orange Badge disabled car sticker if you cannot walk more than 50 yards. There may be occasional days when you can walk over 50 yards without detriment, but if the disability is the rule rather than the exception, apply for the

Badge. Application forms are supplied by your Local Council Transport Section, and will be posted to you in response to a phone call.

However, at the time of writing it is difficult to get disabled parking concessions (Orange Badge) unless you are getting DLA Mobility at the higher rate, although evidence from your GP or consultant may be enough for you to be granted an Orange Badge. Regulations have recently tightened up to prevent abuse of the scheme, and you now need to have a passport-size photo in your Orange Badge. You can use the badge even if you do not drive or have a car. The Badge is the property of the disabled person, and should be displayed in the car only when you are using the car (driving or as a passenger). It is a good idea to keep it with you and not leave it visible in the car.

If you do qualify for a Disabled Badge, use it when you cannot walk or have difficulty walking. If you luckily have a remission or some good days, do not abuse the Badge. Also you must not park anywhere that creates a hazard or obstructs traffic. Traffic wardens can be helpful when there is difficulty finding somewhere to park. It always pays to ask for help as politely as possible, and to explain your problem.

Having help for mobility can improve the quality of life enormously – visiting a bank, a hairdresser, the library and friends whose houses are near double yellow lines all become possible. There are usually parking places for disabled people at all supermarkets, libraries and rail stations.

Two useful leaflets are:

HB2, Equipment and Services for Disabled People
HB4, Help with Mobility

You do not have to be well enough to visit a Benefits Agency office to get Social Security information leaflets. Phone 0800 88 22 00, or write to:

The Stationary Office Ltd
The Causeway
Oldham Broadway Business Park
Chadderton
Oldham OL9 9XD

The Disability Rights Handbook is republished every April, and has information on allowances, legislation, the Benefits Agency, Council Tax and Housing Benefit.

In 1997 it cost £10.50, and is available or can be ordered at most booksellers.

Chapter 18

Practical Problems

Mobility

WHEELCHAIRS

You do not need to be totally unable to walk to consider getting a wheelchair. A wheelchair, plus someone to push it, can open up horizons for you if cannot walk very far. You can potter round a shopping centre, visit art galleries or stately homes, or go for an outing in your neighbourhood. Trips away, holidays, all sorts of journeys may now be possible with a wheelchair. For advice about NHS provision of wheelchairs and information about buying them privately, ask for the leaflet 'Guidance Notes' for the NHS Wheelchair service, from your GP, health centre or hospital clinic. You should be able to borrow a wheelchair from your local Social Services, or the Red Cross.

Caution – **do not wheel the chair yourself.**

ME/CFS affects the arms as well as the legs, and the wheelchair is meant to conserve your energy! The helper who pushes you will need a few practice sessions away from a busy road or pavement. A common mistake for the learner-pusher is to allow the chair to tip forward when going off a pavement, risking the occupant falling out. To negotiate pavements, steps or bumps, the chair must be tipped back so the weight is all on the main wheels. The other main rule in the 'wheelchair code' is **brakes on when parking**. Your pusher needs to be reasonably fit, as well as willing – wheelchairs can be hard work, especially on uneven ground.

Many moderately disabled people whose walking is quite limited shy away from the idea of a wheelchair, because they do not want to become, or be seen as, an invalid. Being an invalid is partly a state of mind and partly a way other people perceive you. Better to see the wheelchair as a useful tool to help you get out of the house and join in the rest of the world at times. When you have a remission or get better, you won't need it.

WALKING ASSISTANCE

The best aid, other than a wheelchair, is a folding stool-stick which can be used as a walking aid and then unfolded easily into a seat when needed. It is absolutely invaluable if you get collapsing, aching legs when having to stand for any time. If you are halfway round a supermarket and feel dreadful and shaky, you can park yourself on the stool for a few minutes – also at the checkout, in queues at the bank, at bus stops, railway stations, etc.

A stool-stick is *not* the same as a 'shooting stick', which has a pointed tip to push into the earth and a very small seat (devised to sit on while you watch others shoot game birds). These are quite unsuitable, as the sharp point will not stay put on a floor or pavement. The best stool-stick is sturdy, with four non-slip rubberized feet and a strong canvas seat, and is made in different heights.

Stool-sticks are obtainable from various retail outlets, including National Trust Centres, and shops for country sports (the address of one supplier is given in Appendix A).

TRAVELLING
It is possible to go away on holiday with ME/CFS, but obviously not while acutely ill. For some, a change to sea or mountain air, the sun, and new horizons may be enjoyable and benefit the health. For others, especially those who get vertigo and visual problems from movement, the journey may be too uncomfortable and the need to adapt to new surroundings, a different bed and a new daily routine may be too much to cope with.

There are a few rules worth following, to make travel of all kinds less stressful:

- plan in advance, and try and travel away from peak times such as bank holidays, school holidays or half-terms
- if going on holiday, choose a location that is quiet and uncrowded, and avoid extremes of climate or areas that require vaccinations or are high-risk for diseases such as malaria
- allow plenty of time for packing and domestic arrangements, otherwise you will start the journey exhausted from last-minute panics
- make sure you have regular food on the journey
- if you get travel sick easily, eat small frequent carbohydrate meals and take an anti-nausea pill such as Stugeron before the journey
- if using public transport, travel light
- allow lots of time for connections between trains or at the airport
- allow for things to go wrong (they usually do!).

By Car
This is ideal if you can drive, or can afford a car, or have a partner/carer who drives you. However, if you are unwell or suffer

from back or neck pain, it is important to have a supportive seat and a properly adjusted headrest. If you are driving and have ME/CFS and if the illness affects your driving and has lasted more than 3 months, the law says you must inform the Drivers Medical Branch, DVLC, Swansea. You may also be asked to specify any long-term illness with your insurance company. If you do not and are involved in or are the cause of an accident, you may be breaking the law. Some insurance companies specialize in disabled clients. Their names can be obtained from RADAR (Royal Association for Disability and Rehabilitation – *address in Appendix A*).

Most people recovering from ME/CFS are safe to drive, but it is important to have frequent stops, eat regularly, and to stop before sudden exhaustion or brain fog comes on. Some sufferers may be unsafe because of poor concentration, delayed reactions or variable vision, depending on whether they are unwell on the day. It is really essential to be aware of these possibilities and to be able to say 'no' to driving at such times. If you are unsure about being safe enough to keep a car and drive it, discuss this with your GP or Occupational Therapist.

There are special centres for assessment of disabled drivers. The main one is in Surrey (*address in Appendix A*). They can also give advice about any special adaptations needed for the car. Examples of useful extras are:

- a padded steering wheel cover to help with grip
- supportive headrest and moulded backrest
- two properly adjusted side mirrors
- power steering, and/or an automatic gear box.

For peace of mind in the event of breakdowns or emergencies, especially if you travel alone, it is worth joining one of the main motoring organizations (e.g. the AA or RAC), who offer special Breakdown and Recovery services for disabled drivers and will also advise about buying a suitable car. And, if you can afford it, a 'low-call' mobile cellphone gives you extra security.

As a passenger, if you are one of those who gets vertigo and visual problems from looking out of a moving vehicle, you may be less uncomfortable travelling in the back seat, or even lying down. If the driver is someone who does not know you, he or she may want to be sociable and talk a lot during the journey, which may be too tiring for a passenger who is ill and already stressed from the effort of travelling. Here again, the back seat may be more peaceful.

Public Transport

If you do not drive, or have chosen not to, then using public transport may end up as a cheaper option than the cost of running a car. Some cities have a special reduced rate scheme for disabled people, such as Taxicards or bus passes. It may be worth enquiring at your local council's Transport Department.

By Air

This may seem quick and simple, but in practice can turn out to be quite stressful. If you decide to go for a holiday by air, it is wise to choose a time of year out of season, and to avoid those airports that are notorious for congestion or delays. It may actually be worth paying extra and travelling on a scheduled instead of a charter flight.

Distances on foot may be 400 yards or more at air terminals, so if your walking is restricted ask the travel agent or airline representative to arrange a wheelchair or buggy. This facility should be organized in advance, and will then be available from the check-in desk at the airport. To avoid standing in long queues at the check-in desk, or at Immigration at the destination airport, take a stool-stick to sit on. One advantage of asking for official assistance is that you are taken straight through security and immigration lines of people!

The other disadvantage of air travel, apart from the stress and noise, is the level of chemicals in aircraft and terminals. If you are chemically sensitive then you may feel quite unwell for a day or two after the flight. Some sufferers are adversely affected by the drop in pressure in the aircraft (this may particularly affect those with breathing difficulties and/or poor brain function), however this is temporary, and if you feel unwell in the aircraft the cabin crew may be able to find you somewhere to lie down.

A reaction to chemicals by air travel, or indeed any travel where increased exposure to chemicals and stress occurs, can be helped by taking extra vitamin C (1–3 g) before and during the journey, and by drinking plenty of water.

Railway Travel

Travelling by train is in theory the least stressful way for long distances. British Rail has now been split up and privatised, and the various new Train Operating Companies, plus Railtrack which is responsible for tracks, signals and stations, are still in the process of re-organization. Railcards for Disabled Travellers are still in operation, however, and qualify the disabled person and one escort for a 30 per cent reduction on all rail tickets. Application forms can be obtained from most stations. Ask for the leaflet *Rail Travel for Disabled Passengers*, which includes an application form for the Disabled Railcard. You will have to provide proof of disability, such as DLA higher rate Mobility, or Severe Disablement Allowance.

If you need help on or off the train, request this if possible at least 48 hours before the journey. Since privatisation you need to telephone the relevant train company to arrange assistance. Give the time and date of your train, and the coach number of your reserved seat.

For a long journey it is worth travelling at weekends, when you can sit in First Class with a standard class ticket, on payment of a small supplement (£5 to £7, depending on the route). The seats in First Class are roomier and it is usually quieter than in Standard carriages.

Train timetable and fare information can be obtained by calling 0345 484950. Tickets and seats can be booked on 0345 000125.

If things go wrong and you want to complain or comment about the journey, you should ask staff for a form to fill in for the relevant Company.

A pocket guide, *High Speed Train and Sleeper Services* (formerly InterCity Services) has the timetables for all mainline routes, plus addresses of Train Companies. It is revised twice a year. To receive a regular (free) copy, write to:

Guide Mailing List
PO Box 208
Derby DE1 9BR

Something that *has* improved since privatisation is the attitude and helpfulness of staff on the trains and at stations. The Senior Conductor on board is the person responsible for the welfare of passengers – who are officially now called customers! If you need help with luggage getting off the train, with queries about reserved seats, or assistance making a connection, he or she is the person to ask. At every Mainline station there are Customer Care staff, to be found on the platforms wearing uniforms according to the Rail Company they represent. They are there to help with train time information, to sort out missed connections, help disabled people or families with luggage and children, etc.

Even if you can walk reasonably well, remember when you are packing that carrying your own luggage round rail stations can be exhausting. It is really useful to have a small case with wheels and a retractable handle, as this can be wheeled even up steps. As a regular traveller myself, I learned long ago the benefits from travelling very light, because although fellow passengers are happy to help if asked, luggage trolleys are not always at hand, nor porters.

If you do not drive, or cannot afford to run a car, and do not have a carer or relative to drive you, then rail transport for long journeys is relatively painless, provided you ask for assistance at least a day in advance. It is really important, though, to book seats in advance for any other than short journeys, and if possible you should plan to avoid travelling around bank holidays or half-terms, when the trains get very crowded. For journeys of more than 2 hours it is a good idea to take something to eat, especially if you have particular dietary needs. Food on train buffet-bars is based on bread, and anyway you may have to walk along a jolting train and stand in a queue for it!

The decision on whether or not to travel, and how, is a very individual matter. But the opportunity to travel and escape from four walls should not be dismissed out of hand. A journey will need much more planning and thought than it did when you were well, but is still possible. People with ME/CFS who can hardly walk can still have enjoyable trips abroad with the help of a wheelchair, other people, and schedules that allow plenty of rest.

Tripscope is a company founded by Claudia Flanders (wife of Michael Flanders, wheelchair user and famous for songs such as 'Mud, Mud, Glorious Mud' with Donald Swann) which can give information on sources of help for a range of travel needs, from holidays to going shopping. Their helpline numbers are in Appendix A.

Practical Help at Home

There are lots of ways of making home life easier. Most energy-saving ideas have come from fellow-sufferers, and in every copy of your local ME/CFS support group newsletter you will find many helpful ideas. In the house, to conserve energy, look at the layout of rooms and furniture:

Bed
Have the bed on the same floor as the bathroom if you are at present too ill to manage stairs safely. The bed should be firm and supportive, and easy to get at to change bedding.

Bathroom
If having a bath is difficult, consider a shower cabinet with a fold-down seat. If this is not practical or affordable, a board across the bath under a shower, or a bowl of warm water next to the bath and a large mug or scoop to slosh water over yourself – or for a carer to do so – is a good substitute. In countries with limited water or no plumbing, this is the normal way to have a shower!

A warm bath or shower is good for warming, also for improving circulation and lymph-fluid flow and for removing waste products that the body gets rid of through the skin via the sweat. Many people forget that the skin is an organ that eliminates toxins and body waste, so sweating a lot when you are ill is not a bad thing. It is also important to replace the sweat with plenty of fluids by mouth. The kidneys, skin, colon and lungs all get rid of waste, plus water, which needs to be replaced in ample amounts.

Although a daily warm bath or shower is advisable, a hot bath (over 99°F/37°C) is *not* recommended if you are ill, weak, or have any heart symptoms, because of the extra strain the excessive heat puts on the circulation. Unless specifically advised as treatment, bath water should not be greater than body temperature.

Part of the benefit of a bath or shower comes from a rub down all over when drying: this stimulates circulation of lymph, the fluid carrying the white cells. Drying yourself may be the most exhausting part of the washing process, and you may need to ask for help with this if there is much muscle pain and fatigue. It's better to forget modesty and have some help rather than forego a regular bathe, which does much good to morale and body.

You should always use a non-slip bath mat, and have grab-rails next to the bath or shower. A high stool may be useful for washing hair or teeth at the basin. The bathroom must be warm.

Kitchen

Do everything in the kitchen sitting down, if possible, by arranging a chair near the work surface for food preparation, and using a high stool at the sink for washing up, or raising the washing-up bowl to the same height. A dishwasher gets things really clean while eliminating the need to hold or scrub pans, though it's best to have one that goes on a work surface – having to bend down to load or empty a dishwasher can defeat its labour-saving purpose!

Collect everything in one container that you need for preparing a meal, e.g. washing-up bowl or basket, and take them to the work area before sitting down.

There are various gadgets that can make food preparation easier – for example, an electric tin opener is essential. An Occupational Therapist can give useful advice to an individual about what things might be useful, and where to get them. Large branches of Boots stock all sorts of home aids – you can telephone for a list. If you have to prepare meals, remember that these days frozen vegetables, while not quite as good as fresh ones, are ready-prepared and better for you than tinned ones. A microwave and freezer are indispensable for a disabled person living alone, so that nutritious meals can be frozen and heated easily when you haven't the energy to cook from scratch.

Iron sitting down, or don't iron at all; there are few clothes that really need ironing, or cannot be ironed by someone else.

Telephones

It is really worth getting a cordless type to take round the house. It is also important to have phones in the house that can be switched off during rest periods. A 'hands-free speakerphone' is a boon for someone whose arms or hands cannot hold a receiver for long, for occasions when a phone call may last more than a few minutes. Although for people on a low income being on a phone line may seem a luxury, being able to communicate with other people is a life-saver when you are housebound.

The Garden

In the garden, have a comfortable seat at hand, such as an adjustable sunbed, to lie or rest on. Doing gentle gardening can be very therapeutic to the soul if you are well enough, and it gets you out of the house into the fresh air and light, but there must be somewhere to rest at frequent intervals. A special gardening stool for disabled people is available from most garden centres, which one sits in while still being able to weed or use tools at ground level. Even in a wheelchair it is possible to work in raised beds and borders. Sowing and 'potting on' can be done in a greenhouse from a chair.

The main damaging action in the garden is bending over or crouching, which places great strain on your thigh and back muscles. Sitting on newspaper or other waterproof layers beside a section of plant bed is preferable.

KEEPING WARM

Keeping warm is very important. In ME/CFS the circulation is usually bad; the body's thermostat doesn't work properly and a lot of energy can be wasted in fighting the cold – energy that is needed for other vital functions. Nor is the problem confined to the winter months, at least not in the UK, where temperatures can drop low enough to require heating, hot water bottles and electric blankets even in June!

Remember to keep your feet warm at all times, and that 30 per cent of body heat is lost from the head. A woolly hat may be helpful, not only for outside,but in bed at night, or while indoors in cold weather. Several thin layers of clothes are always better insulation than a few thick ones, and extra layers should always be at hand to put on wherever you are, especially if away from the house. A sudden feeling of chilliness can strike at any time, regardless of the weather, often due to a drop in blood sugar or rapid exhaustion; your actual body temperature may bear no relation to whether you feel hot or cold. A sudden attack of iciness may mean you need to have something to eat, and to have a sleep.

Just because others in the household may be comfortable in shirtsleeves doesn't mean that it is warm enough for you. But rather than turning up the central heating (70°F/21°C is the maximum advisable) you should wear more clothes and pay attention to keeping your head, feet and neck warm. It is important to have some ventilation in the home, even in cold weather.

In cold weather it is sensible to have a stock pot of soup or a stew on the go. This supplies instant hot food with minimal time to be spent in a cold kitchen just before a meal. Certain foods have warming properties, such as ginger, most curry spices, peppers, garlic, and brown lentils. These foods will warm you whether they are taken hot or not, and are good to include in stews or soups.

Heated mini-blankets, or heat pads, are a good way to supply warmth to the back, chest or tummy as needed if you are cold and have stiff or painful muscles. An electric blanket is marvellous for providing instant warmth when you get into bed, all the year round. Do make sure it is safe, though, and do not leave it switched on if it is an underblanket.

WORKING IN THE HOME

'Work' can mean different things, but the basic principles of pacing work with breaks for rest apply, whether the work entails cooking, housework, or working at a computer.

Here is a quotation from a pamphlet written by an Occupational Therapist, advising on pacing for someone with painful arthritis. The principles are the same for ME/CFS:

Work Simplification

Carry out activities in the simplest, least tiring way so that more energy is available for more pleasurable activities.

Assess your daily routine.

Ask yourself:

1. purpose – is this task necessary?
2. place – is this best place for the task?
3. when – is this the best time to do the task?
4. who – am I the best person to do the task?
5. means – is this the best way to do the task?

Redesign areas to avoid unnecessary bending and stretching.

Use labour-saving equipment whenever possible.

Remember the 4 Ps – planning, pacing, priorities, and positioning:

Planning – plan your day. Organize each task. Combine errands with a trip to another part of the house. Avoid rushing and last-minute jobs.

Pacing – balance work with rest, e.g. alternate light and heavy tasks with rest.

Priorities – make sure an activity is really necessary before starting.

Positioning – stand well, lift correctly, sit well, take the weight off your feet.

Many additional helpful hints will come from people with ME/CFS whom you meet or telephone through local support groups. Only someone with the same problem as you can really advise you on how to solve it.

Useful addresses of organizations for disabled people can be found in Appendix A.

Chapter 19

Caring and Relationships

In writing about 'relationships' I am including those between friends, neighbours and other relatives as well as immediate family. By 'carer' I mean the person or persons most closely involved with providing practical and emotional support for the person who has ME/CFS, whether a parent, partner, friend or neighbour.

The illness of any member of a family, household or group inevitably adds to the strain on relationships. If someone has an acute illness, or an injury, or an operation, there is an expectation that he or she will get better after a predicted period of convalescence, and will return to more or less normal life. So the period of upheaval is seen as temporary, it has some sort of boundary; the illness or operation is usually definable and recognized, and the whole episode, including convalescence, can be coped with.

But if having ME/CFS is a sentence of unknown length with no remission for good behaviour for the sufferer, it may be an equally long sentence for the people closest to the patient.

A lot of the difficulties with ME/CFS result from having to make adjustments within the household or immediate community, rather than in hospital or in a nursing home. This applies to other chronic disabling conditions such as heart disease, multiple sclerosis, arthritis or after a stroke.

However, what makes ME/CFS different is the *variability* and *unpredictability* of both the patient's physical state and mood. As a carer, one day you may rejoice to see the patient happily doing a little gardening, yet the next day may find you helping with dressing and washing. One day there are hours of sobbing and anguish, the next there is a calm person who does not realize what a hard time he or she gave you yesterday. And sometimes, because there is still disagreement in the medical profession about the existence of ME/CFS, and doubts that it is a physical condition and not psychiatric, the patient and carers may have to cope without the support and backup of their GP.

The unpredictability of this illness makes it difficult to plan for the future. By the time the diagnosis is made, the patient has probably already been unwell for six months or more. Can you confidently go ahead with plans that affect the household, such as moving house, holidays, renovations or job changes?

Fear of the future may be worse than the reality of today. It is possibly better *not* to make long-term plans or predictions. While too much pessimism is bad for everyone, unrealistic optimism often leads to disappointment, so living from day to day and adapting to things as they are has to be the best way to cope.

In any close relationship there is a tendency for the emotional mood of one to have an effect on the other. If one person is sullen, withdrawn or depressed, the other thinks 'What have I done to upset him/her?' With the case of illness it is sometimes useful for a carer to remain detached. If you are a carer, try to remember that your patient's rapid emotional changes may be due to the illness, and may not always reflect changed feelings towards you, or a diminished need of you.

Because everyone's life can be disrupted, this may cause resentment on the part of the carer, and guilt for the sufferer. And both parties try very hard not to let these natural feelings show. Guilt on the part of the ill person, at being a nuisance or a burden, is common, and of course it just adds to the mental suffering already experienced. It helps if the apparently useless wreck can be encouraged to feel he or she is still loved, whatever the disabilities, or the demands on the carers.

The resentment felt by a carer at having his or her own life disrupted by this interminable illness is a natural feeling and should not be underestimated. He or she may then feel guilty about being resentful but cannot express it for fear of upsetting the patient, and so ends up irritable and moody. It is in this situation that a relationship that was once loving, accepting and open can deteriorate.

As a carer, you may experience anger, grief, resentment and frustration because:

the person you love is ill, and you don't know when he or she is going to get better
both of your lives are turned upside down
you may have had to sacrifice your job, social life, income and holidays for the patient.

These feelings are perfectly normal; you were not born to be a saint! What *is* wrong is to bottle everything up, which can lead to untold damage to yourself, the patient and other members of the household.

The ME Association in the UK provides valuable support for sufferers, through local groups and a 'Listening Ear' telephone service. But carers need support as well, and it may be helpful to talk to other carers, to people in your local support groups or to anyone offering a sympathetic ear if you feel you can't cope with the illness and the patient.

It is very important for the carer's sanity that she or he creates the time to maintain other friendships and interests outside the household or community, so that she or he has the opportunity to be somewhere both physically and emotionally away from the dynamics of invalid—carer. This valuable 'time out' may be away from the house, or could be in another room speaking on the telephone or with a visiting friend.

Sadly, a number of relationships do break down completely under the stresses created by ME/CFS, leading to separation, divorce, loss of a lover or close friend, or children leaving home. I do not have the skills necessary to advise on how to prevent these separations; they happen to many healthy couples, but are harder to bear if illness is the main reason for the split.

Sometimes a relationship has been going wrong anyway, before the illness developed, and in such cases a severance may *remove* a major stress, and allow the patient a better chance of recovery. On the other hand, sometimes the human resources of loving and understanding develop in two people as a result of one of them becoming ill, and a lukewarm relationship may then grow into a much deeper and warmer one.

Sex – Does It Have to Be Abandoned?

Possibly one of the most important aspects to suffer from chronic illness in a close relationship is the sexual bond. A lessening of sexual desire or ability is probably not confined to ME/CFS, but may happen with many chronic illnesses. After all, becoming ill is a sign that the whole body-mind complex is not functioning properly.

An animal or child that is ill will rest, following the body's need to conserve energy for healing. Sick adult humans should also stop expending energy on unnecessary activities. Sometimes there is not enough energy for digestion or for talking, so the body is certainly not going to give much priority to the act of lovemaking! In women who are ill, loss of interest in sex may be a subconscious protective mechanism against becoming pregnant while unable to cope with it.

The loss of sexual desire is a common symptom with ME/CFS, but is not something that people find easy to discuss with their family doctor. There are, of course, other ways of expressing affection, completely outside of sex. Some couples may succeed through compromise, such as finding occasions when the fatigue is not so great; using different techniques or positions; or perhaps by accepting that this is one aspect of the relationship that may have to be put aside for some time. Mutual understanding of why the problem arises, and accepting it as just another activity to forego for a while – just as one has to postpone long walks, late nights or socializing – are ways of coping with this problem.

Practical ways of compromising about sex may include:

- if you are the ill partner, don't look on sex as a chore or duty. Be honest with your partner, and discuss ways of finding a time of day or night when you can cope with sex, then make time and allow energy for it, just as you would for any other activity, as part of pacing your energy.
- it is better to make love infrequently and to enjoy it as a special occasion, than to push yourself into trying more often than your body can cope with
- if lovemaking leaves you drained and muscle-achey afterwards, try taking painkillers and *Arnica* (*see page 238*) before

and afterwards, and maybe have a warm bath before to relax the back and limb muscles
- experiment with positions that allow the ill person to remain lying down
- remember than mutual touch, caressing and masturbation are ways of expressing love; satisfying lovemaking does not depend on full penetration in the missionary position
- if things don't always go as you expect, laugh about it, it's not a contest!
- if you are the relatively healthy partner, reassure the one who is ill or weak that if he or she cannot 'perform' you still love him or her
- remember the big Hs for loving – HUGS and HOLDING – especially when the ill one is really hurting emotionally.

It is enormously helpful for the person with ME/CFS if the carer can demonstrate that he or she believes the patient has a genuine illness, and at the same time demonstrates a belief in possible recovery. It can be a bit difficult to draw the line between being supportive/helping every aspect of living when needed, and encouraging the patient to be an invalid.

There are times when the patient needs to be allowed to stretch his or her wings and to do a bit more, and times when the carer needs to be firm and say 'That's enough, you must rest.' Balancing the roles of protective nurse and occupational therapist can be tricky even when looking after someone whose illness is predictable. With ME/CFS, playing it just right is nearly impossible, when your patient is so unpredictably up then down.

Here is some advice from someone with long experience of caring for someone with ME/CFS:

The carer must have patience, compassion, resilience, and belief in ME as a mentally and physically crippling disease in varying degrees.

You have to learn not to mind when people say that you are being exploited by waiting hand and foot on someone who usually looks perfectly fit, e.g. in a wheelchair one week, and next week walking.

You need to be aware of the varying limitations of the patient and be ready to step in, such as rescuing a patient from long and exhausting telephone conversations.

Be prepared to help in all aspects of daily living, as required.

If the person with ME/CFS, in desperation, behaves out of character, do not take it to heart, and learn not to be thrown by wide mood swings.

Try to maintain the fine line between having a life of your own and yet still realizing the extent to which you are needed for moral as well as physical support.

In short – be a perfect person!

Carers often feel isolated, and need help and support. Most people do not know exactly how the Health and Social Services function; if you or the person you look after need outside help, you may not know how to go about asking. Remember that someone who stays at home to care for a person who is chronically sick or disabled may be entitled to Invalid Carers Allowance. ICA is a taxable weekly benefit for people of working age who are caring for a severely disabled person. To claim ICA you must be looking after someone who is getting DLA or Attendance Allowance at the middle or highest rate for personal care; be spending at least 35 hours a week as a carer; and not earning more than £50 pounds a week (after deducting allowable expenses). (*For more on Benefits see Chapter 17.*)

Sources of Help for a Carer

YOUR FAMILY DOCTOR

Do not neglect to tell your GP about your own health problems – a sick carer is entitled to medical help just as much as the patient. Ask about any help which may be needed with lifting, dressing or bathing the person you care for.

A district nurse may be asked to call round and give advice.

THE HOSPITAL

If the ME/CFS person has been to hospital or attends an outpatients clinic, ask the specialist to explain any disabilities. Also ask the doctor, ward staff or receptionist how to get an assessment from an Occupational Therapist, for aids in the home. The OT should be able to visit to carry out a home assessment.

Many people with ME/CFS prefer to avoid hospitals, as not all doctors and nursing staff understand what the illness is, and may want to institute rehabilitation regimes that are unsuitable or badly administered. Hospitals on the whole are not good environments as regards getting plenty of sleep and avoiding chemicals!

SOCIAL SERVICES

The phone book gives you the address and number of your local Social Services. You can ask for a visit to assess the patient's needs.

A free Caring for Carers' helpline – 0800 100 100 – gives information about entitlement to benefits and local support networks.

The Benefits Inquiry Line – 0800 88 22 00 – can answer questions about Benefits you or the sick person may be entitled to.

SUPPORT ORGANIZATIONS

There are many carers' groups in many areas. Your local ME support group may know of some, or else your local Social Services, Citizen's Advice Bureau, or local voluntary services may know of support for carers. (*See Appendix A.*)

Supportive breaks for carers can be provided by the Kiloran Trust, a charity that can provide residential supportive breaks for carers who are exhausted. Telephone 0171 602 7404.

Further useful addresses for carers are given in Appendix A.

This last case history is of someone I have met. She and her family have shown great courage and patience for the four-and-a-half years of her illness.

Clare's Story (told by her mother)

In December 1986, Clare was a second-year university student doing Psychology and English Literature. She lived in Halls of Residence, was generally fit, and enjoyed dancing and other active pursuits. On the morning of 6th December she woke with what seemed to be flu. She returned to our house, spent eight days in bed, and felt exhausted. However, she seemed to recover, did her end-of-term exams, and felt reasonably well over Christmas.

The flu returned in January 1987 and, because she felt so exhausted, she went to the doctor. The GP took a blood test which showed a high antibody titre to Coxsackie B virus. Clare then returned to Halls, feeling decidedly more tired and much slower in her actions, some nights having to go to bed after tea. Another visit to the doctor and another blood test – this time there was no high Coxsackie antibody. In the meantime I had read about ME and asked if this was a possibility. The GP totally rejected this, told Clare she had a post-viral condition, that she should continue with her studies, but not take any strenuous exercise ('Aerobics maybe, but squash no!').

During the period from February to the end of the second term, Clare's condition worsened, with only a few brief spells of remission. She had greatly slowed down, couldn't walk very far, and was generally behind with her studies. During the Easter holidays she decided that she could no longer continue as a student, and left the University in April.

Around this time her GP referred her to a consultant at Ruchill Hospital, who gave her a diagnosis of Post-viral Fatigue Syndrome or ME and estimated that it might take anything up to three years to get better.

Gradually Clare ceased to be able to get up for meals. She began to experience what she called 'a wobbly head' – a frightening feeling where her brain seemed to be losing contact with her eyes. As well as the intense fatigue, other symptoms appeared in the following months – cold (almost wet) feet, a sensitivity to light with after-images, and sensitivity to sound combined with a ringing in the ears, culminating in a severe and constant headache.

Any kind of stimulation seemed to produce pain for her. She was no longer able to tolerate visits from friends and could have only limited contact with her family. Having a bath or washing her hair was beyond her. She suffered intense malaise and often felt that she was dying. From this time on her mobility disappeared, and she had to be pulled to the bathroom on a chair with rollers. Some days she was unable to sit up for meals and had to be fed.

During this period Clare's father and I, in increasing desperation, sought help from various sources. A herbalist recommended an anti-Candida diet, which after five days made Clare feel very sick and caused vomiting. It also made her lose half a stone in weight, which, combined with the loss of muscle bulk, left her weight at 7 stone. She discontinued the diet as she felt unable to cope with the nausea and further weight-loss.

In July of 1987 a three-day stay in a homoeopathic hospital was equally unsuccessful. She returned home with a promise to the doctor-in-charge to continue on a wheat-free diet for some six weeks (which she did), and to try and sit on a chair for some 10 minutes per day, which she was unable to do. A physiotherapist was sent from the local hospital, but even sitting out on a chair for more than a few seconds caused Clare to break out in severe sweating, so this was discontinued.

Autumn 1987 came round and Clare's symptoms were at their worst. She lay all day every day in a room with the curtains drawn and with wax plugs in her ears. An eczema-type rash developed on her face and was only kept at bay by daily applications of cortisone cream. The encephalitic symptoms were predominant – constant severe head pain, a sense of unreality, and nightmares. Another homoeopathic doctor, whose speciality was 'psionic medicine', was contacted. In all telephone calls and letters he promised 'a significant return to health in the very near future'. After three months and no sign of recovery Clare's disillusionment was intense. Reflexology was equally futile.

In January 1988 Clare was able to have the curtains opened – an hour a day initially, then throughout all the short winter days. She also decided to dispense with all diets, keeping her food balanced and additive-free (and cut out all chocolate, which she found had a bad effect on her). There had been no proof that the diets had helped her, and she felt her life was restricted enough. During March/April her headaches were as bad as ever, although her sensitivity to noise had abated somewhat.

In April 1988 she heard that injections of Parentrovite [vitamin B complex] were being tried with some success by an immunologist in Belfast. With the agreement of her GP, Clare had six fortnightly injections which did seem to help her condition somewhat.

She could now watch television for short periods, listen to the radio, have a bath and wash her hair once a week. She no longer needed her ear-plugs, and could cope with much more family input. The headaches and the ringing in her ears were still there, but were more intermittent and not so severe. This improvement was not dramatic, and was in fact imperceptible on a day-to day basis.

She then began taking amitriptyline, one of the tricyclics, to combat panic attacks, as a *Horizon* TV programme suggested that it might be useful in some ME cases. Initially there were some side-effects, but these were outweighed by an overall improvement in her condition.

However, after a year and a half in bed Clare was still unable to walk more than five steps, and her full recovery seemed a long way off.

Postscript: 1991
The following two years saw Clare make some progress, to being able to get up a little each day, being less sound- and light-sensitive, and able to watch TV and speak on the phone. However, her muscles were very weak and she was still mostly bedridden, and an increasing feature was anxiety/depression. A weekly visit from a physiotherapist seemed to do more harm than good. In October 1990 Clare agreed to accept treatment in the Psychological Medicine Department of a local hospital. The doctor in charge took the view that ME is an organic illness, and was interested in alleviating symptoms.

Clare's mother again:

Clare stayed there five weeks, coming home two weekends. To begin with the staff didn't seem to do very much, and encouraged but didn't force any activity. They also changed her antidepressant to Clomiprimine. Despite the alien hospital conditions (patients smoking, lack of good sleep) we did notice a change in Clare over the time she was there. When she came home she began to try more things – going out in a wheelchair at first, then for short walks. She has gradually increased this activity and can go into town and for short trips in the car (she has given back the wheelchair). She still suffers from head pain and exhaustion, but nowhere near as severe or long-lasting as they once were. She also has big emotional troughs, and sometimes it seems harder for her to cope with the frustrations of being half-well than it was when she was completely incapacitated. She hopes to return part-time to university, but some days this seems unlikely.

I want to emphasize that she still has ME, but maybe there was, after four years, some psychological element that had to be overcome before she could continue her progress to recovery.

Conclusion

In this book I have given an overview of the illness that was once called epidemic neuromyesthenia, and today known as ME or chronic fatigue syndrome. Although many doctors still do not recognize the typical clinical picture in a patient, very few can now deny that ME or CFS exists.

I believe that if ongoing research looks at clearly defined subgroups of people with CFS, the causes will become clearer. Of course what patients want is a cure. But before knowing what is going in the brain, or – to be more accurate – what is happening at the level of the living cell and its metabolism, whether brain or muscle, it is unrealistic to expect research into effective drug treatment.

But the answer to the question 'Can anything be done to help ME/CFS people?' is *Yes!* Nearly every individual can do something to encourage some degree of recovery, however small. And for some, cognitive therapy or graded exercise may be extremely helpful. Because this is an illness with such variation in symptoms and severity, no two cases are the same, and most sufferers have to find out for themselves what works for them.

As with other chronic disabling illnesses, new information and ideas spread around over time, and it is important that people who have ME or CFS communicate with each other – 'network' in modern jargon – to keep up to date with new developments in research and treatment. This is where national and local support organizations are invaluable. Doctors do not all have the time to keep abreast of research into other conditions, let alone about ME/CFS, and often they learn from their patients. Most of the improvement in awareness about ME/CFS, in the medical profession, the general public, and Government agencies, has come about through the persistent work of the ME organizations. If you are newly diagnosed and think there is still a lot of ignorance about your illness, be glad it is 1998, not 1978 when very few doctors or lay people had heard of ME!

It's also worth remembering that people afflicted by multiple sclerosis, which everyone now knows something about, had to battle for years to have their condition accepted as being a serious neurological illness. Thirty years ago many MS patients were being dismissed as neurotic or hysterical.

Fortunately very few people die from ME/CFS, which ironically is perhaps why it is not yet taken seriously by the medical hierarchy, nor by politicians in most countries, although this is changing for the better in the US. No one would want to see a rising death rate from ME, but the fact is that the disease AIDS, which until recently had a high mortality rate, only began to be seriously researched when it became obvious that many people were dying from it.

There other examples of diseases that used to be misunderstood and stigmatized: leprosy being a good example. Most prejudice or abuse of ill people arises from fear of 'catching it' and a cultural dislike of anything mysterious that cannot be analysed.

Here is a quotation [edited] from a paper about sociocultural influences on CFS:

We have a cultural intolerance of the not yet known or the unknowable. A contributing factor has been the elevation of science/technology and quantitative systems of knowing, with the devaluation of qualitative systems of knowing. In this concept, all that is real or true is observable, measurable and ultimately knowable. So anything that does not yield to this criteria is suspect. This cultural elevation of the quantitative and measurable over the qualitative and unmeasurable, has contributed to the view that ambiguous problems are somehow dangerous and possibly immoral, and should be avoided. This is reflected in the economic and status rewards for people who choose professions that use technology-driven methods.

We do not like chronicity; it disrupts our action-orientated, achievement-orientated culture. We prefer illnesses that are acute, and disrupt our organised lives in a predictable manner. Heart disease, appendectomies and medicated depressions return us to the workplace in a timely manner. Illnesses that do not have a distinct beginning, middle and end, and are not easily treatable, upset a healthcare system view that any real illnesses have one cause and will respond to a 'magic bullet' approach. Illnesses like CFS, with unclear causes, course and outcome are frustrating, potentially expensive and consequentially devalued.[1]

In this book you will have noticed that I have not used the word 'cure'. Perhaps you are disappointed, having hoped to find the magic remedy that will make you feel fit and full of energy to live the life you used to enjoy. But there are many illnesses that do not have a total cure, and one of the great secrets of having a fulfilling life is actually getting on and living it. If you cannot live your life in same way you did before getting ME/CFS then that is tough, but so long as you can still think, feel and breathe, you have a life to be lived. The trick is to make the most of what you *can* do, even if it is very little, and to let go of the things you cannot do.

Developing any illness that lasts for some time can damage morale. It is useful for anyone who has a chronic illness to consider the two words **health** and *fitness*, because they can be mistaken as meaning the same thing. They are not!

Fitness is a state that is desired by athletes, and by people who want to be able to exert themselves without suffering ill-effects. The heart, lungs and muscles must be in perfect working order. And many people do feel better in themselves if they are physically fit and in perfect working order. However, physical fitness only applies to one part of a human being, and ignores the state of the mind and the soul. Someone can be apparently superbly fit for the task of running up mountains or having the endurance to run 25 miles, yet still develop a prolonged illness following a viral infection. In fact, too much exercise can lead to the 'overtraining syndrome' seen sometimes with athletes, whose immunity seems to drop so they are an easy target for a post-viral syndrome.

Health has a more subtle meaning. I understand it to mean being integrated, balanced in oneself, at peace with the world, and content. A state of perfect health – if it exists! – would mean the perfect functioning of body and mind, and a pure spirit. In a person who has ME/CFS the body certainly does not function properly, but I do believe that there is more to health and life than a super-fit (or even half-fit) body.

I know two people who demonstrate this difference (the descriptions are of real people, who of course actually do not have these extraordinary names!):

Mr Super-fit takes great care of his body; he runs or plays squash every day and goes skiing or rock climbing (both to top levels of endurance) at weekends and holidays. In his forties, he has the body of someone much younger. However, he is unhappy, tense, gets lots of headaches and vague symptoms, is antisocial, irritable, and sometimes depressed.

Mr Laid-back is also aged forty-something. He is a bit over-weight, as he enjoys his food and wine. He loves his job teaching young children, loves entertaining friends, is generous and always cheerful. Apart from walking and standing all day at school, and pottering in the garden, he takes no exercise whatsoever, and does not feel the need for it. He has not had a cold or a day off work for years, and has no bodily complaints.

Which of these men is healthiest? And which of them would cope best with getting ME or CFS?

Health means *wholeness*. The body that is stricken by ME/CFS may sometimes appear as though every part of it is broken down! But continually I am amazed at the wholeness of the spirit and personality of people I come across who are physically disabled in various ways.

I can still recall vividly a patient I knew when I was working in a cancer and chemotherapy unit. She was only 38, her children were still young; she had cancer that had spread throughout her body, and suffered constant severe pain. She had plenty to be resentful about, every reason to feel frightened. Yet, following some sessions of healing with her parish priest, and knowing that many people were praying for her, she announced one day that she was healed. Her body did not miraculously rid itself of the cancer overnight; to a casual observer she still seemed desperately ill. What had changed was that she had accepted her condition, stopped being afraid, and felt completely at peace with her family, friends, and her Maker. In her last few weeks of life she gave out so much love to those around her, that those of us caring for her felt enriched by her company. To my mind this lady was more healthy than most of us caring for her.

So I think that one of the keys to getting on with ME/CFS is acceptance of how you are. This is not the same as wallowing in self-pity and pessimism, or becoming a passive victim. No, it means saying something like:

This illness has come into my life, it is a fact of life. I am not to blame. I shall do what I can to improve the way I feel. I shall change my lifestyle, feed my body well, nourish my immune system, and give myself lots of tender loving care. I shall stop yearning for what I cannot have for the present, and count what blessings I have. If I listen to my body and look after myself I shall probably improve, but it will not happen overnight. I shall seek out whatever sources of support and practical help that seem appropriate, and when I have less pain I shall try out some new activities, very gradually, to see what my body can do. If I do not get back to how I used to be, I will nevertheless continue to be alive and able to appreciate many good things in life, by living from day to day, and looking for joy in little things.

Those who cope best with ME/CFS seem to be the people who try to go along with it, who adapt daily life round the limitations, rather than fighting it. Ironically, there are other conditions when 'fighting for life' is necessary – perhaps during a severe infection or after an accident. But with ME/CFS it is better to be less aggressive – although there is still a need for fortitude and resolution, and some discipline about not doing things.

And because nobody who has a chronic illness can foresee when improvement or recovery is going to happen, if at all, it is very important to be able to get on with some sort of life, even if it is only 50 per cent of the level living there was before.

And if certain tasks now take much longer to do, because of the limits of energy for the brain or muscles, never mind. Your value as a person is no longer dependent on how busy you are, or how much money you earn! So if it takes a week to write a letter, which used to take 20 minutes, that letter will still be special.

Living with ME/CFS is possible at all levels of disability. Remember that the majority of people with ME/CFS do improve, and some may recover enough to get back to work or education. Whether you believe in a spiritual life or not, you can appreciate this well-known prayer – it says, in a few words, what needs to be done:

God, grant me the serenity to accept the things I cannot change, Courage to change the things I can, and the wisdom to know the difference.

Appendix A

Sources of Help

THE ME ASSOCIATION
The ME Association was formed in 1976 by a small group of people with ME. It has now grown into a large and professionally organized charity with local groups all over the UK. Membership stands at about 9,500 as of August 1997.

The Association has three objectives:

1. to offer support to people with ME
2. to spread information about the illness
3. to promote medical research.

The Association acts as a lifeline for those who are isolated, despairing, confused and devastated by ME/CFS. For many people with these illnesses, the first positive development comes when they find they are not alone, that they do have a real illness (even if this is not recognized by their doctor), and that others have similar experience and are there to offer friendship, encouragement and hope.

A confidential telephone help line, Listening Ear, is manned by volunteer counsellors who are themselves sufferers.

A newsletter, *Perspectives*, is issued every quarter, and gives up-to-date information including current research, medical information, news nationally and from the local groups, and members' articles and letters.

The Association has helped to fund several research projects in different medical specialities. It gives very valuable support to people with ME/CFS through its central office and the activities of local groups.

The Association has actively campaigned for, and achieved, UK Government recognition of ME/CFS. In order to promote greater understanding in primary health care, it has undertaken the circulation of diagnostic information to all GPs. Information packs have been sent to a wide range of professional and voluntary agencies, with which sufferers may come into contact. These include Government departments, Directors of Education and Social Services, Disability groups, Trades Unions, professional associations, and information services.

The Association also gives individual support for those seeking benefits and services.

The ME Association has raised awareness of those with special needs, such as children with ME/CFS, and chronic severely affected patients. The ME Association's Young Persons Group (MEAYPG) offers support and friendship to children and young people with ME.

The address to write to – with SAE please – is:

ME Association
4 Corringham Road
Stanford-le-Hope
Essex SS17 0AH

ACTION FOR ME AND CHRONIC FATIGUE

The charity Action for ME is a national membership organization offering help, information and other services to people with ME. It also funds research and campaigns to bring about the full recognition of ME as a genuine physical illness as well as working for improved treatment, benefits and help for sufferers.

The hallmark of AfME is its acceptance of both orthodox and complementary medical approaches and its pro-active publicity and campaigning. Action for ME has a membership of 8,000 (1997) and is growing rapidly.

Action for ME was founded in 1987 by Sue Finlay, who was frustrated at the lack of support and information available to fellow sufferers. Novelist Clare Francis was the founding President – a role she was to hold for 10 years. Since 1987 its main achievements include the introduction of the first ME Patients' Bill in Parliament, a high-profile publicity campaign to highlight the plight of children with ME/CFS; the creation of its membership journal, *InterAction*; the development of a wide range of member services; and the funding of the first research in the UK of brain perfusion in ME.

Members of Action for ME receive 3 copies per year of *Interaction*, which contains up-to-date medical and therapy information and acts as a forum for the exchange of ideas amongst sufferers. Sufferers also benefit from a telephone therapy information helpline, counselling and welfare benefits advice, and can be put in touch with a network of local support groups.

Action for ME also produces a number of factsheets, including a Therapy Information Pack which summarizes information about the various therapies that people with ME have found helpful. Other literature includes factsheets for doctors, teachers, employers and carers.

Action for ME welcomes enquiries from sufferers, carers and professionals – as well as donations towards its work. Please send an SAE to the address below for a free enquiry leaflet:

Action for ME
PO Box 1302
Wells
BA5 1YE
Tel: 01749 670799

A 24-hour recorded information line operates on 0891 122976.

WESTCARE

Westcare is a registered charity which provides professional services relating to chronic fatigue syndrome (CFS) or ME. The main services are:

- an information service – leaflets and books
- a telephone advice and counselling service provided by a professional counsellor. Appointments are booked in advance.
- a counselling clinic in Bristol – individual consultations are provided by professional adviser/counsellors, who offer acceptance and reassurance, information about the illness and advice about management. No charges are made, but donations are requested.
- a home counselling service, available to people with ME/CFS in Bristol
- residential rehabilitation courses – week-long courses held at a comfortable venue near Bristol. Staff on these courses include a doctor, occupational therapist, nutritionist and counsellor. The aim of the courses is to help with self-management of the illness, and to assist improvement or recovery. Many participants are fully funded by the NHS.

- workshops for doctors and health care professionals – dealing with the practical management of ME/CFS
- co-ordination of the National Task Force on CFS/ME – an independant scientifically-based body which produced a landmark comprehensive report on CFS/ME in September 1994. The report is still available from Westcare (£9.95 inc p+p). Further reports are being prepared.

For further information please contact:

Westcare
155 Whiteladies Road
Bristol BS8 2RF
Tel 0117 923 9341
Fax 0117 923 9347

THE NATIONAL ME/CFS CENTRE

This is a registered charity which was established to provide facilities for both in-patient and out-patient care of patients with chronic fatigue syndromes of all types. It is independent, whilst based within a National Health Service Trust.

The Centre offers counselling (medical and non-medical) for patients with a firm diagnosis of CFS/ME. It is linked to both general medical and neurological clinics for appropriate diagnostic work-up of patients. It is also linked to the regional neurological unit at Oldchurch Hospital, Romford, which has facilities for in-patient assessment and rehabilitation for patients with CFS/ME.

For more information please contact:

The Administrator
National ME/CFS Centre
Disablement Services Centre
Harold Wood Hospital
Romford
Essex RM3 9AR
Tel 01708 378050

RESOURCES FOR CHILDREN AND YOUNG PEOPLE WITH ME/CFS:
Please see Chapter 15.

CHROME (CASE HISTORY RESEARCH ON ME)
CHROME is a registered charity set up in 1994 with the aim of identifying as many severely disabled ME sufferers as possible in the UK, and monitoring the course of their illness over a period of 10 years. From this study a body of statistical data will be collected and analysed which will supplement medical research in important ways.

So far, over 200 cases of severely affected people with ME have been identified. One important aspect of CHROME's work has been to draw the existence of such patients to the attention of researchers whose view of the illness has tended to be limited to those who are well enough to attend hospital out-patient clinics.

If you are housebound or bedbound, or know someone who is, please write to CHROME, with a brief account of your condition. You will be sent further information and, if appropriate, a questionnaire.

CHROME's first annual report, *The Story from Below*, is priced £2 (including p+p).

CHROME
3 Britannia Road
London SW6 2HJ
Tel/Fax 0171 736 3511

BRAME (BLUE RIBBONS FOR THE AWARENESS OF ME)

BRAME was set up by young ME sufferer Tanya Harrison and her mother, so that anyone who wants to show their support for people suffering from ME can wear a blue ribbon, which will increase awareness about the illness. The Blue Ribbon Awareness campaign is now known internationally. For further information, write to:

BRAME
30 Winmere Avenue
Winterton-on-Sea
Great Yarmouth
Norfolk NR29 4BA

PERSISENT VIRUS DISEASE FOUNDATION

A registered charity which supports research into diseases that may be caused by persistent viral infection, including ME. For further information, write to:

PVDF
4 One Tree Lane
Beaconsfield
Bucks HP9 2BU

World-wide ME/CFS Organizations

Countries and representatives of the European ME Alliance (as of June 1997):

England
Melanie Hume
Chair, ME Association UK
4 Corringham Road
Stanford le Hope
Essex SS17 OAH

Scotland
Ann Campbell
12 Vatisker
Isle of Lewis HS2 0JS

Northern Ireland
Derek Peters
ME Association
28 Bedford Street
Belfast BT2 7FE

Belgium
Alice Vertommen
Belgium ME Association
Dorp 73
3221 NEIUWRODE

Denmark
Anna-Louise Midsem
Danish ME/CFS Association
Magelhof 86
DK-3520 Farum

France
Carolyn Mckay
4 le Park des Tulipiers
316 Route de la Fontaine
01280 Prevessin

Germany
Herr u Frau Helmut Uhlisch
Forderverein fur CFS/ME
Erkante
'Fatigatio e V'
Postfach 410261
D-53024 Bonn

The Netherlands
Dutch ME Society
PO Box 57436
1040 BH Amsterdam

Dr MPL Jansen
Zwartezeestraat 74
8226 CB Leystad

Norway
Ellen Piro
Norges ME Forening
Eiksveien 96A
1345 Osteras

Switzerland
Christina Huber
Stapferstrasse 61
CH-8006 Zurich

Franzisca Moser
Casse 31
CH-2553 Safnern

Republic of Ireland
Donal Healy
92 Cypress Grove Road
Templeogue
Dublin 6W

AFFILIATED MEMBERS

Australia
ME/CFS Society of
Queensland
PO Box 398
Fortitude Valley
Queensland 4006

Canada
ME Canada
246 Queens Street
Suite 400
Ottawa
Ontario K1P 5E4

ME ORGANIZATIONS IN OTHER COUNTRIES

Australia
NSW ME/CFS Society
Royal South Sydney
Community Health Complex
Joynton Avenue
Zetland NSW 2017

New Zealand
ANZMES (NZ) Inc.,
(Produces the newsletter
'Meeting Place')
PO Box 35-429
Browns Bay,
Auckland 10

Sweden
Stodgruppen
Klinisk Ekologi
Gothenburg

South Africa
ME Association of South
Africa
PO Box 1802
Umhlanga Rocks
4320 Natal

United States
The CFIDS Association of
America Inc
PO Box 220398
Charlotte, NC 28222–0398
(CFIDS = Chronic Fatigue
and Immune Dysfunction
Syndrome)

Other Useful Resources

NUTRITION AND ALLERGIES

Action Against Allergy
24–26 High Street
Hampton Hill
Middlesex TW12 1PD
(please send SAE)

Biolab
The Stone House
9 Weymouth Street
London W1N 3FF
Tel 0171 636 5959/5905
For an assessment of nutritional status, doctor's referral needed

Breakspeare Hospital for Allergy and Environmental Medicine
High Street
Abbot's Langley
Hertfordshire

British Society of Allergy and Environmental Medicine
PO Box 28
Totton
Southampton SO40 2ZA
Tel 01703 812124

The British Society for Mercury Free Dentistry
1 Welbeck House
62 Welbeck Street
London W1M 7HB

**Lamberts Dietary
Products Ltd**
1 Lamberts Road
Tunbridge Wells
Kent TN2 3EQ
Tel 01892 552120

Biocare Health Products
Lakeside Centre
180 Lifford Lane
Kings Norton
Birmingham B31 3NT
Tel 0121 433 3727
*Many dietary supplements are
available in chemists and health
food shops: the best are gluten,
sugar, milk and additive free —
look at labels.*

**Henry Doubleday
Research Organisation**
Convent Lane
Braintree
Essex
*Advises on all aspects of organic
gardening, and has a list of organ-
ic produce suppliers.*

The Soil Associaton
86 Colston Street
Bristol BS1
Tel 0117 929 0661
*Information and help about various
conditions*

PREGNANCY AND CHILDBIRTH

**The National Childbirth
Trust**
c/o O'Farrell
6 Forest Road
Crowthorne
Berkshire RG11 7EH

**Foresight (Association
for preconceptual care)**
The Old Vicarage
Church Lane
Witley
Surrey GU8 5PN

SUPPORT AND INFORMATION

Samaritans
National Linkline number
0345 90 90 90 – Calls at local
rates
*24-hour telephone befriending
for the despairing or suicidal*

MIND (National Association for Mental Health)
Granta House
15–19 The Broadway
Stratford
London E15 4BQ
Tel 0181 519 2122
Gives legal advice on rights of mentally ill patients

Depressives Associated
PO Box 1022
London SE1 7QB
Send SAE for self-help information

Migraine Action Association
178a High Road
Byfleet
West Byfleet Surrey
KT14 7ED
Tel 01932 352468

Multiple Sclerosis Society
25 Effie Road
London SW6 1EE
Tel 0171 736 6267

Osteoporosis Society
PO Box 10
Radstock
Somerset BA3 3YB

Tel: 01761 471771

National Association for Premenstrual Syndrome (NAPS)
PO Box 72
Sevenoaks
Kent TN13 1XQ
Tel 01732 741709

Endometriosis Society
35 Belgrave Square
London SW1 8PQ

Pesticide Exposure Group Support (PEGS)
Enfys Chapman
4 Lloyds House
Regent Terrace
Cambridge CB2 1AA
Tel 01223 364707

Information on OrganoPhosphates
Endon Bank
Church Lane
Endon
Stoke on Trent ST9 9HF
Tel 01782 503615

ALTERNATIVE AND COMPLEMENTARY THERAPIES

NATIONAL FEDERATION OF SPIRITUAL HEALERS
Old Manor Farm Studio
Church Street
Sunbury-on-Thames
Middlesex TW16 6RG
Tel 01932 783164

Seka Nikolic (Bioenergy Healing)
Hale Clinic
Park Crescent
London W1N 3HE
Tel 0171 637 3377

British Homeopathic Association
27a Devonshire Street
London W1N 1RJ
Doctors trained in homeopathy

The National Institute of Medical Herbalists
56 Longbrook Street
Exeter EX4 6AH
Tel 01392 426022

British Acupuncture Council
Park House
206–208 Latimer Road
London W10 6RE
Tel 0181 964 0222
For register of acupuncturists

Yoga for Health Foundation
Ickwell Bury
Biggleswade
Bedfordshire SG18 9EF

The Osteopathic Information Service
PO Box 2074
Reading
Berkshire RG1 4YR
Tel 01734 512051

DISABILITY RESOURCES

Disability Law Service
Room 241
2nd Floor
49-51 Bedford Row
London WC1R 4LR
Tel 0171 831 8031
Free legal advice, assistance and information for disabled people and their families

Philips of Axminster
Philips House
West Street
Axminster
Devon EX13 5NX
Tel 01297 32701
Supplier of stool-sticks and other
useful equipment

The Computability Centre
PO Box 94
Warwick
Warwickshire CV34 5WS
Tel 01926 312847
Gives excellent free advice about
using computers, for all kinds of
disabilities

Disabled Living
Foundation
380–384 Harrow Road
London W9
Tel 0181 299 6111

Gardening for Disabled
Trust
Hayes Farmhouse
Hayes Lane
Peasmarsh
E Sussex TN1 6XR

British Telecom
Action for Disabled
Customers
FREEPOST
BS6295
Bristol BS1 2BR

The Disablement Income
Group (DIG)
Unit 5
Archway Business Centre
19–23 Wedmore Street
London N19 4RZ
Tel 0171 263 3981
Advice, advocacy, and publicity
for financial welfare of disabled
people

Door to Door – A Guide
to Transport for Disabled
People
Book, available from:
Department of Transport –
Door to Door Guide
Freepost
Victoria Road
South Ruislip
Middlesex HA4 ON2
Tel 0171 212 5022

Dial U.K. (Disability Information and Advice Line)
Park Lodge
St Catherine's Hospital
Tickhill Road
Balby
Doncaster DN4 8QN
Tel 01302 310123
Can give information on local DIAL centres, all over the UK

Royal Association for Disability and Rehabilitation (RADAR)
12 City Forum
250 City Road
London EC1V 8AF
Tel 0171 250 3222

Mobility Centre
Banstead
Damson Way
Orchard Hill
Queen Mary's Avenue
Carshalton
Surrey SM5 4NR
Tel 0181 770 1151
Information service, and assessment of disabled and elderly people for driving; training courses, driving tuition and research. Has list

of other accredited regional Mobility Centres in the UK.
Booklet available: 'Orange Badge Scheme, all you need to know' (£2)

Access Committee for England
38 Albion Street
Crewe CW2 8NH

Tripscope
Helplines: Tel 0181 994 9294
or 0117 941 4094
Advice on a range of travel needs for the disabled

SPOD (Sexual Problems Of Disabled people)
286 Camden Road
London N7 0BJ
Tel 0171 607 8851

EDUCATIONAL RESOURCES

ACE Advisory Centre for Education
18 Victoria Park Square
London E2 9PB
Tel 0171 354 8321

National Bureau for Students with Disabilities (SKILL)
336 Brixton Road
London SW9 7AA
Tel 0171 274 0565

Advice on entitlement to benefits, and local support networks for carers

Open University
Office for Students with Disabilites
Walton Hall
Milton Keynes MK7 6AA
Tel 01908 653745

SUPPORT FOR CARERS

Carers National Association
20/25 Glasshouse Yard
London, EC1A 4JS
Tel (office) 0171 490 8818
Tel (carers helpline)
0345 573369

Crossroads – Caring for Carers
Attendant Schemes Ltd
10 Regent Place
Rugby
Warwickshire CV21 2PN
Tel 01788 573653
Caring for Carers helpline:
0800 100 100

Appendix B

Information for Doctors: Diagnoses and Investigations

Differential Diagnosis of ME/CFS – Other Conditions to Be Excluded

(The following may be confused with ME/CFS. The list is not exhaustive.)

MUSCULOSKELETAL DISORDERS
Rheumatoid arthritis
Polymyalgia, fibromyalgia

NEUROLOGICAL DISORDERS
Motor neuron disease
Multiple sclerosis
Parkinsons Disease
Atypical siezures

PSYCHIATRIC DISORDERS
Melancholic depression
Pre-senile dementias
Withdrawal syndrome, phobias
Somatization (hysteric conversion disorders)

AUTO-IMMUNE DISORDERS
Systemic lupus erythematosis
Thyroiditis
Sjogren's syndrome
Myesthenia gravis
Crohn's disease
Chronic active hepatitis

ENDOCRINE DISORDERS
Diabetes
Thyroid diseases
Addison's disease

NUTRITIONAL DISORDERS
Iron-deficiency anaemia
B_{12} or folate deficiency

INFECTIONS
For example:
AIDS
Tuberculosis
Lyme disease

Brucellosis
Toxoplasmosis
Cytomegalovirus
Chronic parasitic infestations such as ameobic dysentery, guiardia, malaria, Q fever, etc.

OTHER CONDITIONS TO EXCLUDE

Malignancies and leukaemias
Heart conditions such as coronary artery disease, myocarditis, valvular disease, Syndrome X
Bornholm disease and pleurisy, if severe chest pains
Coeliac disease
Chronic pancreatitis
Drug abuse and alcoholism

Suggested Investigations

GENERAL INVESTIGATIONS

General investigations should be selected to exclude conditions such as those listed above, but unnecessary over-investigation should be avoided, especially with a typical acute post-viral onset:

Serial weight and growth (especially in children)
Serial a.m. and p.m. temperature measurements
Full blood count and ESR (PV), and differential WBC
Urea, electrolytes and liver function tests
Blood glucose, creatinine, calcium, phosphate
Thyroid tests – TSH, T3, T4
Autoantibodies profile
Urine analysis and microscopy

Serology

Viral titres (in early stages)

ELISA IgM to Coxsackie B virus

Immunoglubulins

EB virus – antibodies, viral capsid antigen, EB virus nuclear antigen

AIDS serology

Cytomegalovirus, toxoplasma, possibly for Lyme disease, yersinia

Hepatitis A, B, and C

Possibly chest X-ray, abdominal U/S, ECG, EEG – as symptoms indicate.

MORE SPECIALIZED TESTS – NOT DONE ROUTINELY

T-lymphocyte subsets, NK cell activity

Tensilon test (myesthenia gravis), muscle enzymes

Muscle biopsy, electromyogram

MRI, SPECT, PET scans of brain

Psychiatric assessment

Psychological/cognitive function tests

References

CHAPTER 1

1. Bell, D, The Disease of a Thousand Names (Lyndonville, NY: Pollard Publications, 1991).

2. Komaroff, A L, Address to the ME Association, London, November 18th, 1995

3. Behan, P O, 'Chronic fatigue syndrome as a delayed reaction to low dose organophosphate exposure', *Journal of Nutritional and Environmental Medicine* 6 (1997): 341–50

4. Beard, G M, 'Neurasthenia or nervous exhaustion', *Boston Med Surg Journal* 3 (1869): 217–20

5. Ramsay, A M, *Postviral Fatigue Syndrome: The Saga of Royal Free Disease* (Gower Medical Publishing, 1988): 12

6. *Ibid*

7. Komaroff, A L and Buchwald, D, 'Symptoms and Signs of Chronic Fatigue Syndrome', *Reviews of Infectious Diseases* 13, suppl 1 (1991): S8–11

8. Holmes, G P *et al.* 'Chronic fatigue syndrome: a working case definition', *Annals of Internal Medicine* 108 (1988): 387–9

9. Sharpe, M C *et al.*, 'A report – chronic fatigue syndrome: guidelines for research', *Journal of the Royal Society of Medicine* 84 (1991): 118–21

10. Fukuda, K, Strauss, S, Hickie I *et al.*, 'The chronic fatigue syndrome: a comprehensive approach to its definition and study', *Annals of Internal Medicine* 121 (1994): 953–9

11. Lloyd, A R, Hickie, I *et al.*, 'Prevalence of chronic fatigue syndrome in an Australian population', *Medical Journal of Australia* 153 (1990): 522–8

12. Ho-Yen, D O and McNamara, I, 'General Practioners' experience of the chronic fatigue syndrome', *British Journal of General Practice* 41 (1991): 324–6

13. Steele, L, Dobbins, J G, Fukuda, K *et al.*, US Centres for Disease Control and Prevention, 'Prevalence and characteristics of chronic fatigue in a diverse urban population', in Proc. American Association for CFS research conference, San Francisco, October 13th 1996

14. Wesseley, S, Chalder, T, Hirsch, S *et al.*, 'The Prevalence and Morbidity of Chronic Fatigue and Chronic Fatigue Syndrome: a prospective Primary Care Study', *American Journal of Public Health* 87.9 (1997): 1455

15. McEvedy, C P and Beard, A W, 'Concept of benign myalgic encephalomyelitis', *British Medical Journal* 1 (1967): 11–15

17. Komaroff, 1991 op cit

CHAPTER 2

1. Behan, P O, Behan, W M H, Bell, E J, 'The postviral fatigue syndrome – an analysis of the findings in 50 cases', *Journal of Infection* 10 (1985): 211–22

2. Dowsett, E G, Ramsay, A M, McCartney, R,A and Bell, E J, 'Myalgic Encephalomyelitis – a persistent enteroviral infection?', *Postgraduate Medical Journal* 66 (1990): 526–30

3. Goldstein, J A, 'Presumed pathogenesis and treatment of the chronic fatigue syndrome/fibromyalgia complex', Conference on chronic fatigue syndrome and fibromyalgia, Los Angeles February 1990. Abstract, p. 8

4. Steele, L, Dobbins, J G, Fukuda, K *et al.*, US Centres for Disease Control and Prevention, 'Prevalence and characteristics of chronic fatigue in a diverse urban population', in Proc. American Association for CFS research conference, San Francisco, October 13th 1996

5. Wesseley, S, Chalder, T, Hirsch, S *et al.*, 'The Prevalence and Morbidity of Chronic Fatigue and Chronic Fatigue Syndrome: a prospective Primary Care Study', *American Journal of Public Health* 87.9 (1997): 1455

6. Dowsett, E G and Colby, J, 'Long-term sickness absence due to ME/CFS in UK schools: an epidemiological study with medical and educational implications', *Journal of Chronic Fatigue Syndrome* 3.2 (1997): 29–42

7. Komaroff, A, Fagioloi, L, Doolittle, T *et al.*, 'Health status in patients with chronic fatigue syndrome and in general population and disease comparison groups', *American Journal of Medicine* 101.3 (1996): 281–90

8. Wesseley, S, Chalder, T, Hirsch, S *et al.*, 'Post infectious fatigue: a prospective study in primary care', *Lancet* 345 (1995): 1333–8

9. Calder, B D, Warnock, P J, McCartney, R A, Bell, E J, 'Coxsackie B viruses and the post-viral syndrome: a prospective study in general practice', *Journal of the Royal College of General Practitioners* 37 (1987): 11–14

10. Durndell, A, '2nd report to health and safety committee on postviral fatigue syndrome or myalgic encephalomyelitis' Glasgow College, 1989

11. Mowbray, J F, Yousef, G E, Bell, E J *et al.*, 'Chronic enterovirus infection in patients with postviral fatigue syndrome', *Lancet* 1 (1988): 146–9

12. Hyde, B, and Bergman, S, 'Chronic aspects of Akureyri disease', in *Post-viral Fatigue Syndrome* (Wiley, 1988): chapter 12

13. Gow, J W, Behan, W M H, *et al.* 'Studies on enterovirus in patients with chronic fatigue syndrome', *Clinical Infectious Diseases* 18, suppl 1 (1994): S126–9

14. McGarry, F, Gow, J and Behan, P O, 'Enterovirus in the chronic fatigue syndrome', *Annals of Internal Medicine* 120.11 (1994): 972–3

15. Clements, G B, Mcgarry, F, Nairn, C and Galbraith, D N, 'Detection of enterovirus specific RNA in serum: the relationship to chronic fatigue', *Journal of Medical Virology* 45 (1995): 156–61

16. Gow, J, Behan, W M H, Cash, P *et al.*, 'Genomic and template RNA transcription in a model of persistent enteroviral infection', *Journal of Neurovirology* 1997

17. Bruno, R L, Frick, N M *et al.*, 'Polioencephalitis and the Brain generator Model of postviral fatigue syndromes', Conference report, *Journal of Chronic Fatigue Syndrome* 2 (1996): 2–3

18. Stone, R, 'Post-Polio Syndrome: Remembrance of Viruses Past', *Science* 264 (1994): 909

19. White, P, Thomas, J, Amess, J *et al.*, 'The existence of a fatigue syndrome after glandular fever', *Psychological Medicine* 25 (1995): 907–16

20 Paitnik, M, Komaroff, A L *et al.*, 'Prevalence of IgM antibodies to human herpes virus 6 early antigen in patients with chronic fatigue syndrome', *Journal of Infectious Diseases* 172 (1995): 1364–7

21. Martin, W J and Anderson, D, 'Stealth virus epidemic in the Mojave valley', *Pathobiology* 65 (1997): 51–56

22. Inoue, Y K *et al.*, 'Virus associated with S.M.O.N. in Japan', *Lancet* 1 (1971): 853–4

23. Oldstone, M B A, 'Viral alteration of cell function', *Scientific American* (August 1989): 34–40

24. Komaroff, A L and Buchwald, D, 'Symptoms and Signs of Chronic Fatigue Syndrome', *Reviews of Infectious Diseases* 13, suppl 1 (1991): S8–11

25. Ayres, J G, Smith, E F and Flint, N, 'Protracted fatigue and debility after acute Q fever', *Lancet* 347 (1996): 378–9

26. Lerner, A M, Zervos, M, Dworkin, H J, Chang, C H *et al.*, 'New cardio-myopathy: pilot study of intravenous gangiclovir in a subset of the chronic fatigue syndrome', *Infectious Diseases in Clinical Practice* 6.2 (1997): 110–17

27. Nicolson, G L and Rosenberg-Nicolson, N L, 'Doxycycline treatment and Desert Storm', *Journal of the American Medical Association* 273.8 (1995): 618–19

28. Holmes, B, 'Life unlimited', *New Scientist* (10 February 1997)

29. Suhadolnik, R, Peterson, D *et al.*, 'Biochemical evidence for a novel low molecular weight 2-5A-dependent RNase L in chronic fatigue syndrome', *Journal of Interferon and Cytokine Research* 17 (1997): 377–85

30. Galland, L, Lee, M *et al.*, 'Giardia lamblia infection as a cause of chronic fatigue', *Journal of Nutritional Medicine* 2 (1990): 27–32

31. Buchwald, D and Komaroff, A L, 'Review of laboratory findings for patients with chronic fatigue syndrome', *Reviews of Infectious Diseases* 13, suppl 1 (1991): S12

32. Hilgers, A and Frank, J, 'Chronic fatigue syndrome: evaluation of 30-criteria-score and correlation with immune activation', *Journal of Chronic Fatigue Syndrome* 2.4 (1996): 35–47

33. Buchwald, D, Wener, M H *et al.*, 'Markers of inflammation and immune activation in chronic fatigue syndrome', *Journal of Rheumatology* 24.2 (1997): 372–6

34. Von Mikecz, A, Konstantinov, K *et al.*, 'High frequency of autoantibodies to insoluble cellular antigens in patients with chronic fatigue syndrome', *Arthritis and Rheumatism* 40.2 (1997): 295–305

35. Gompels, M M and Spickett, G P, 'Chronic fatigue, arthralgia, and malaise', *Annals of the Rheumatic Diseases* 55 (1996): 502–3

36. Nishikai, M, Akiya, K *et al.*, 'Seronegative Sjogren's syndrome manifested as a subset of chronic fatigue syndrome', *British Journal of Rheumatology* 35 (1996): 471–4

37. Gow, J, at the AGM of the Melvin Ramsay Society, Glasgow, November 14th 1997

38. Lane, R J M, Burgess, A P, Archard, L *et al.*, 'Exercise responses and psychiatric disorder in chronic fatigue syndrome', *British Medical Journal* 311 (1995): 544–5

39. Montague, T, Marrie, T J, Klassen, G A, *et al.*, 'Cardiac function at rest and with exercise in the chronic fatigue syndrome', *Chest* 95 (1989): 779–84

40. Riley, M S, O'Brien, C J, McCluskey, D R *et al.*, 'Aerobic work capacity in patients with chronic fatigue syndrome', *British Medical Journal* 301 (1990): 953–6

41. McCully, K, Natelson, B, Iotti, S *et al.*, 'Reduced oxidative muscle metabolism in chronic fatigue syndrome', *Muscle and Nerve* 19.5 (1996): 621–5

42. Doyle, D, 'Muscle biopsies in postviral fatigue syndrome', Symposium on myalgic encephalomyelitis, Cambridge, April 1990. Abstract, p. 9

43. Dr W M H Behan, the Ramsay Lecture, at the AGM of the Melvin Ramsay Society, Glasgow, November 14th 1997

44. *Ibid*

45. Arnold, D L, Bore, P, Radda, G K *et al.*, 'Enhanced intramuscular acidosis during exercise by patients with post viral exhaustion/fatigue syndrome', *Neurology* (Cleveland) 35, suppl 1 (1985): 165

46. Jamal, G A and Hansen, S, 'Post-viral fatigue syndrome: Evidence for underlying organic disturbance in the muscle fibre', *European Neurology* 29 (1989): 273–6

47. Majeed, T, De Simone, C *et al.*, 'Abnormalities of carnitine metabolism in chronic fatigue syndrome', *European Journal of Neurology* 2 (1995): 425–8

48. Plioplys, A V and Plioplys, S, 'Serum levels of carnitine in chronic fatigue syndrome: clinical correlates', *Neuropsychobiology* 32 (1995): 132–8

49. Peters, T J and Preedy, P R, 'Pathological changes in skeletal muscle', in *Postviral Fatigue Syndrome* (Wiley, 1991): chapter 7

50. Watson, W S, McCreath, G T, Chauduri, A and Behan, P O, 'Possible cell membrane transport defect in chronic fatigue syndrome?' *Journal of Chronic Fatigue Syndrome* 3.3 (1997): 1–13

51. Waldenstrom, A, Ronquist, G and Lagerquist, B, 'Angina pectoris patients with normal coronary angiograms but abnormal thallium perfusion exhibit low myocardial and skeletal muscle energy charge', *Journal of Internal Medicine* 231 (1992): 327–31

52. Burnet, R G, Yeap, B B *et al.*, 'Chronic fatigue syndrome: is total body potassium important?', *Medical Journal of Australia* 164.6 (1996): 384

53. Waldenstrom, A, Folehman, J *et al.*, 'Coxsackie B3 myocarditis induces a decrease in energy charge and accumulation of hyaluronan in the mouse heart', *European Journal of Clinicla Investigation* 23 (1993): 277–82

54. Pearn, J, 'Chronic ciguatera: one organic cause of the chronic fatigue syndrome', Conference Report, *Journal of Chronic Fatigue Syndrome* 2 (1996): 29–34

55. Friedman, A, Kaufer, D, Shemer, J *et al.*, 'Pyridostigmine brain penetration under stress enhances neuronal excitability and induces early immediate transcriptional response', *Nature Medicine* 2.12 (1996): 1382–5

56. Jamal, G A and Hansen, S, 'Electrophysilogical stuides in the post-viral fatigue syndrome', *Journal of Neurology, Neurosurgery and Psychiatry* 48 (1985): 691–4

57. Jamal and Hansen, 1989, op cit

58. Jamal, G A, Hansen, S *et al.*, 'The "Gulf-War Syndrome": Is there evidence of dysfunction in the nervous system?', *Journal of Neurology, Neurosurgery and Psychiatry* 60 (1996): 449–51

59. Boda, W L, Natelson, B H *et al.*, 'Gait abnormalities in chronic fatigue syndrome', *Journal of the Neurological Sciences* (1995), 156–61

60. Wysenbeek, A J, Shapira, Y and Leibovic, L, 'Primary fibromyalgia and the chronic fatigue syndrome', *Rheumatology International* 10 (1991): 227–30

61. Wigers, S H, Stiles, T C and Bogel, P A, 'Effects of aerobic exercises versus stress management treatment in fibromyalgia: a 4.5-year prospective study', *Scandinavian Journal of Rheumatology* 25 (1997): 77–86

62. McGregor, N R, Dunstan, R H *et al.*, 'Preliminary determination of a molecular basis to CFS', *Biochemical and Molecular Medicine* 57 (1996): 73–80

63. Natelson, B H, Cohen, J M *et al.*, 'A controlled study of brain magnetic resonance imaging in patients with the chronic fatigue syndrome', *Journal of Neurological Sciences* 120.2 (1993): 213–7

64. Schwartz, R B, Carada, B M *et al.*, 'Detection of intracranial abnormalities in patients with chronic fatigue syndrome: comparison of MR imaging in SPECT', *American Journal of Roentgenology* 162.4 (1994): 935–41

65. Buchwald, D, Cheney, P R, Peterson, D l *et al.*, 'A chronic illness characterised by fatigue, neurologic and immunologic disorders and active human herpes type 6 infection', *Annals of Internal Medicine* 116.2 (1992): 103–13

66. Cheney, P R, at a press conference, San Francisco, September 1990: 'Clinical findings in CFIDS –neurology', *CFIDS Chronicle* (September 1990): 8

67. Costa, D C, Tannock, C and Brostoff, J, 'Brainstem perfusion is impaired in patients with chronic fatigue syndrome', *Quarterly Journal of Medicine* 88 (1995): 767–73

68. Schwartz, Carada *et al,*, 1994, op cit

69. Schwartz, R B, Komaroff, A L *et al.*, 'SPECT imaging of the brain: comparison of findings in patients with chronic fatigue syndrome, AIDS dementia complex and major unipolar depression', *American Journal of Roentgenology* 162.4 (1994): 943–51

70. Goldberg, M, Mena, I and Darcourt, J, 'NeuroSPECT findings in children with chronic fatigue syndrome', *Journal of Chronic Fatigue Syndrome* 3.1 (1997): 61–7

71. Tavio, M, Chierichetti, F *et al.*, 'Brain Positron Emission Tomography (PET) in chronic fatigue syndrome: a useful tool for differential diagnosis', Abstract: Proceedings of Research Conference, AACFS, San Francisco, October 14 1996

72. Dinan, T, Majeed, T, Berti, C, Behan, P O *et al.* 'Blunted serotonin mediated activation of the hypothalamic-pituitary-adrenal axis in chronic fatigue syndrome', *Psychoneuroendocrinology* 22.4 (1997): 261–7

73. Majeed, T, Dinan, T G *et al.*, 'Defective dexamethasone induced growth hormone release in chronic fatigue syndrome: evidence for glucocorticoid receptor resistance and lack of plasticity?', *Journal of the Irish Colleges of Physicians and Surgeons* 24.1 (1997): 20–4

74. Bakheit, A M O, Behan, P O *et al.*, 'Abnormal arginine-vasopressin secretion and water metabolism in patients with postviral fatigue syndrome', *Acta Neurologica Scandinavica* 87 (1993): 234–8

75. Demitrack, M, Dale, J, Strauss, S et al., 'Evidence for impaired activation of the hypothalamic-pituitary-adrenal axis in patients with chronic fatigue syndrome', *Journal of Clinical Endocrinology and Metabolism* 73 (1991): 1224–34

76. Strauss, S, 'Perspectives on chronic fatigue syndrome and its treatment', Plenary address at Research Conference, AACFS, San Francisco, October 13 1996

77. Bou-Holaighah, I, Rowe, P C, Kan, J and Calkins, H, 'The relationship between neurally mediated hypotension and the chronic fatigue syndrome', *Journal of American Medical Association* 274.12 (1995): 961–7

78. Freeman, R and Komaroff, A, 'Does the chronic fatigue syndrome involve the autonomic nervous system?', *American Journal of Medicine* 102.4 (1997): 357–64

79. Chauduri, A, Majeed, T et al. 'Chronic fatigue syndrome: a disorder of central cholinergic transmission?' *Journal of Chronic Fatigue Syndrome* 3.1 (1997): 3–16

80. Behan, P O, 'Chronic fatigue syndrome as a delayed reaction to low-dose organophosphate exposure', *Journal of Nutritional and Environmental Medicine* 6 (1997): 341–50

81. Snorrason, E, Geirsson, A and Stefansson, K, 'Trial of a selective acetylcholinesterase inhibitor, galanthamine hydrobromide, in the treatment of chronic fatigue syndrome', Conference Report, *Journal of Chronic Fatigue Syndrome* 2 (1996): 35–54

82. Ash-Bernal, R, Wall, C, Komaroff, A L et al. 'Vestibular function test anomalies in patients with chronic fatigue syndrome', *Acta Otolarygology* (Stockholm) 115 (1995): 9–17

83. Poser, C M, 'The Differential Diagnosis between Multiple Sclerosis and Chronic Fatigue Postviral Syndrome', in Hyde, B M et al., *The Clinical and Scientific Basis of ME/Chronic Fatigue Syndrome* (Ottawa: Nightingale Research Foundation, 1992): chapter 42

84. Cavanaugh, S A 'Depression in the medically ill', in Judd, S K, Burrows, G D, Lipsett, D R, *Handbook of Studies on General Hospital Psychiatry* (Amsterdam: Elsevier, 1991)

85. Hickie I, Lloyd A, et al. 'The psychiatric status of patients with the chronic fatigue syndrome', *British Journal of Psychiatry* 156 (1990): 534–40

86. Stenager, E, Knudson, L and Jenson, K, 'Psychiatric and cognitive aspects of multiple sclerosis' *Seminars in Neurology* 10 (1990): 254–61

87. Deluca, J, Johnson, S K and Natelson, B H, 'Information processing efficiency in chronic fatigue syndrome and multiple sclerosis', *Archives of Neurology* 50.3 (1993): 301–4

88. Prasher, D, Smith, A and Findlay, L 'Sensory and cognitive event-related potentials in myalgic encephalomyelitis', *Journal of Neurology, Neurosurgery and Psychiatry* 53 (1990): 247–53

89. Smith, A P, Behan, P O *et al.*, 'Behavioural problems associated with the chronic fatigue syndrome', *British Journal of Psychology* 84 (1993): 411–23

90. Daugherty, S A, Henry, B E, Peterson, D L *et al.*, 'Chronic fatigue syndrome in Northern Nevada', *Reviews of Infectious Diseases* 13, suppl 1 (1991): S39–44

91. Deluca J, Johnson, S, Ellis, S and Natelson, B, 'Cognitive functioning is impaired in patients with chronic fatigue syndrome devoid of psychiatric disease', *Journal of Neurology, Neurosurgery, and Psychiatry* 62 (1997): 151–5

92. Jamal, G A, 'Neurophysiological findings in the post-viral fatigue syndrome (ME)', in Jenkins and Mowbray (eds), *Post-Viral Fatigue Syndrome* (Wiley, 1992): 169

CHAPTER 3

1. Beard, G M, 'Neurasthenia or nervous exhaustion', *Boston Med Surg Journal* 3 (1869): 217–20

2. Ramsay, A M and O'Sullivan, E, 'Encephalomyelitis simulating poliomyelitis', *Lancet* 1 (1956): 761–6

3. Holmes, G P *et al.*, 'Chronic fatigue syndrome: a working case definition', *Annals of Internal Medicine* 108 (1988): 387–9

4. Sharpe, M C *et al.*, 'A report – chronic fatigue syndrome: guidelines for research', *Journal of the Royal Society of Medicine* 84 (1991): 118–21

5. Fukuda, K, Strauss S, Hickie, I, *et al.*, 'The chronic fatigue syndrome: a comprehensive approach to its definition and study', *Annals of Internal Medicine* 121 (1994): 953–9

6. David, A S, Wesseley, S and Pelosi, A J, 'Postviral fatigue syndrome – time for a new approach', *British Medical Journal* 296 (1988): 696–8

7. Royal Colleges of Physicians, Psychiatrists and General Practitioners, 'Report of a Joint Working Group: Chronic fatigue syndrome' (London: Cathedral Print Services, 1996): chapter 7, p. 15

8. Taylor, R and Jason, L A, 'The effects of psychiatric instrumentation and scoring on psychiatric diagnoses for individuals with CFS', *Psychology and Health and International Journal* (in press)

CHAPTER 5

1. Aylward, M, 'Government's expert group has reached consensus on prognosis of chronic fatigue syndrome', *British Medical Journal* 313 (1996): 885

2. Franklin, A, 'Children with ME: Guidelines for School Doctors and General Practitioners' (booklet published by the UK ME Association, 1994): 7

CHAPTER 7

1. Lane, R J M, Burgess, A P, Archard L, *et al.*, 'Exercise responses and psychiatric disorder in chronic fatigue syndrome', *British Medical Journal* 311 (1995): 544–5

2. Fulcher, K Y and White, P D, 'A randomised controlled trial of graded exercise in patients with chronic fatigue syndrome', *British Medical Journal* 314 (1997): 1647–52

3. Butler, S, Chalder T, Ron, M and Wesseley, S, 'Cognitive behaviour therapy in chronic fatigue syndrome', *Journal of Neurology Neurosurgery and Psychiatry* 54 (1991): 153–8

4. Sharpe, M, Hawton, K *et al.*, 'Cognitive behaviour therapy for the chronic fatigue syndrome: a randomised controlled trial', *British Medical Journal* 312 (1996): 22–6

5. Ho-Yen, D, 'Patient management of postviral fatigue syndrome', *British Journal of General Practice* (January 1990): 37–9

6. Montague, T, Marrie, T J, Klassen, G A *et al.*, 'Cardiac function at rest and with exercise in the chronic fatigue syndrome', *Chest* 95 (1989): 779–84

7. Riley, M S, O'Brien, C J, McCluskey, D R *et al.*, 'Aerobic work capacity in patients with chronic fatigue syndrome', *British Medical Journal* 301 (1990) 953–6

8. McCully, K, Natelson, B, Iotti, S *et al.*, 'Reduced oxidative muscle metabolism in chronic fatigue syndrome', *Muscle and Nerve* 19.5 (1996): 621–5

9. Lapp, C and Cheney, P, *CFIDS Journal* (February 1991)

CHAPTER 8

1. Report from the National Task Force on Chronic Fatigue Syndrome (CFS), PVFS and ME, (Westcare, Bristol, 1994): chapter 6, p. 18

CHAPTER 9

1. McGarry, F, Gow, J and Behan, P O, 'Enterovirus in the chronic fatigue syndrome', *Annals of Internal Medicine* 120.11 (1994): 972–3

2. Vercoulen, J H M M, Swanink, C M A *et al.*, 'Randomised double-blind, placebo-controlled study of fluoxetine in chronic fatigue syndrome', *Lancet* 347 (1996): 858–61

CHAPTER 10

1. Strauss, S, 'Perspectives on chronic fatigue syndrome and its treatment', Plenary

address at Research Conference, AACFS, San Francisco, October 13th 1996

2. Vercoulen, J H M M, Swanink, C M A *et al.*, 'Randomised double-blind, placebo-controlled study of fluoxetine in chronic fatigue syndrome', *Lancet* 347 (1996): 858–61

3. Behan, P O, Behan W M H and Horrobin, D, 'Effect of high doses of essential fatty acids on the postviral syndrome', *Acta Neurologica Scandinavica* 82 (1990): 209–16

4. Lloyd A, Hickie I, Wakefield D, *et al.* 'A double-blind, placebo-controlled trial of intravenous immunoglobulin therapy in patients with chronic fatigue syndrome', *American Journal of Medicine* 89 (1990): 561–8

5. Peterson, P K, Shepard, J, Macres, M *et al.*, 'A controlled trial of intravenous immunoglobulin G in chronic fatigue syndrome', *American Journal of Medicine* 89 (1990): 554–60

6. Strayer, D R, Carter, W *et al.* 'Long-term improvements in patients with chronic fatigue syndrome treated with Ampligen', *Journal of Chronic Fatigue Syndrome* 1.1 (1995): 35–53

7. Snorrason, E, Geirsson, A and Stefansson, K, 'Trial of a selective acetylcholinesterase inhibitor, galanthamine hydrobromide, in the treatment of chronic fatigue syndrome', Conference Report, *Journal of Chronic Fatigue Syndrome* 2 (1996): 35–54

CHAPTER 11

1. Behan, P O, Behan, W M H and Horrobin, D, 'Effect of high doses of essential fatty acids on the postviral syndrome', *Acta Neurologica Scandinavica* 82 (1990): 209–16

2. Pauling, L *How to Live Longer and Feel Better* (W H Freeman and Co, 1986)

3. Cheney, P R, CFIDS Chronicle Physician's Forum, *CFIDS Chronicle* 1.1 (1991): 4

4. Cox, I M, Campbell, M J and Dowson, D, 'Red blood cell magnesium levels and the chronic fatigue syndrome (ME): a case-controlled study and randomised controlled trial', *Lancet* 337 (1991): 757–60

CHAPTER 12

1. Awdry, R, 'Homeopathy and chronic fatigue – the search for proof', *International Journal of Alternative and Complementary Medicine* (February 1996): 19–22

2. Perrin, R, 'Research into Osteopathic treatment of M.E', *InterAction* 23 (Spring 1997): 21–2

3. Perrins, D J D, 'The diagnosis of postviral syndrome', *Journal of the Royal Society of Medicine* 83 (1990): 413

4. Lapp, C W, 'Management of chronic fatigue syndrome in children: a practising clinician's approach', *Journal of Chronic Fatigue Syndrome* 3.2 (1997): 59–76

CHAPTER 13

1. Jessop, C, 'Food and environmental factors in disease', *InterAction* (Winter 1990): 6

   2. *Ibid.*

CHAPTER 14

1. Hunter, J O, 'Food allergy – or enterometabolic disorder?', *Lancet* 338 (1991): 495–6

CHAPTER 15

1. Bell, D S, in Hyde, B M (ed), *The Clinical and Scientific Basis of ME/CFS* (Ottawa: Nightingale Research Foundation, 1992): 209–18

   2. Dowsett, E and Colby, J, 'Long term sickness absence due to ME/CFS in UK schools: An epidemiological study with medical and educational implications', *Journal of Chronic Fatigue Syndrome* 3.2 (1997): 29–42

CHAPTER 16

1. Harlow, B L, Signorello, L B, Daily, C and Komaroff, A, 'The influence of gynaecological factors on the risk of CFS: a case control study', in Proc. AACFS Research Conference, San Francisco, October 14th 1996

   2. Studd, J and Panay, N, 'Chronic Fatigue Syndrome' letter to *Lancet* 348 (1996): 971

   3. Hoskin, L, Clifton-Bligh, P *et al.*, 'Bone mineral density in premenopausal nulliparous women with chronic fatigue syndrome compared with age-, weight-matched controls', *Journal of Bone and Mineral Research* 12 (1997): suppl.S. 228 – Meeting Abstract

CONCLUSION

1. Fennel, P A, 'CFS Sociocultural Influences and Trauma: Clinical Considerations', *Journal of Chronic Fatigue Syndrome* 1.3 (1995): 159–73

List of Abbreviations

5 HT	5 hydroxytriptamine
ACTH	adrenocorticotrophic hormone
ADH	anti-diuretic hormone
AIDS	acquired immune deficiency syndrome
ATP	adenosine triphosphate
BA	Benefits Agency
CAT	cognitive analytic therapy
CBT	cognitive behaviour therapy
CDC	Centres for Disease Control
CEBV	chronic Epstein Barr virus
CFIDS	chronic fatigue and immune dysfunction syndrome
CFS	chronic fatigue syndrome
CFSUM	chronic fatigue syndrome urinary marker
CRH	corticotrophin releasing hormone
DDA	Disability Discrimination Act
DIS	diagnostic interview schedule
DLA	Disability Living Allowance
DNA	deoxyribonucleic acid
DSS	Department of Social Security
DWA	Disability Working Allowance
EBV	Epstein Barr virus
ECG	electrocardiogram
EEG	electroencephalogram
EFAs	essential fatty acids
EMG	electromyography
EPA	ecosapentanoeinic acid
EPD	enzyme potentiated desensitization
EPO	evening primrose oil

FMS	fibromyalgia syndrome
FSH	follicle stimulating hormone
GH	growth hormone
GLA	gamma linolenic acid
GWS	Gulf War Syndrome
HBO	hyperbaric oxygen therapy
HHV–6	human herpes virus type 6
HLTV	human lymphotropic virus
HPA	hypothalamic-pituitary-adrenal axis
HRT	hormone replacement therapy
IB	Invalidity Benefit
ICA	Invalid Carers Allowance
IgA, IgG, IgM	immunoglobulins A, G, M
IMV	Innouie Melnik virus
IUs	international units
MAFF	Ministry of Agriculture, Fisheries and Food
ME	myalgic encephalomyelitis
MOAIs	monoamine oxidase inhibitors
MRI	magnetic resonance imaging
MS	multiple sclerosis
NHS	National Health Service
NI	National Insurance
NIH	National Institutes of Health
NK cells	natural killer cells
OPs	organophosphates
OT	occupational therapist
PCR	polymerase chain reaction
PET	positron emitted tomography
PGE1	prostaglandin E1
PMS	premenstrual syndrome
PPS	postpolio syndrome
PVFS	postviral fatigue syndrome
REE	resting energy expenditure
REM	rapid eye movement
RNA	ribonucleic acid
SCID	semistructured clinical interview
SDA	Severe Disablement Allowance
SLE	systemic lupus erythematosis
SMON	subacute myelo-optic neuropathy
SPECT	single proton emitted tomography
SSP	Statutory Sick Pay
VDUs	visual display units
VP1	virus protein 1

Index